LEARN TO WATERCOLOR

ADORABLE ANIMALS

20 Step-by-Step Beginner-Friendly Lessons on Watercolor Paper

LACEY WALKER

OF REBEL UNICORN CRAFTS

Walter Foster

CONTENTS

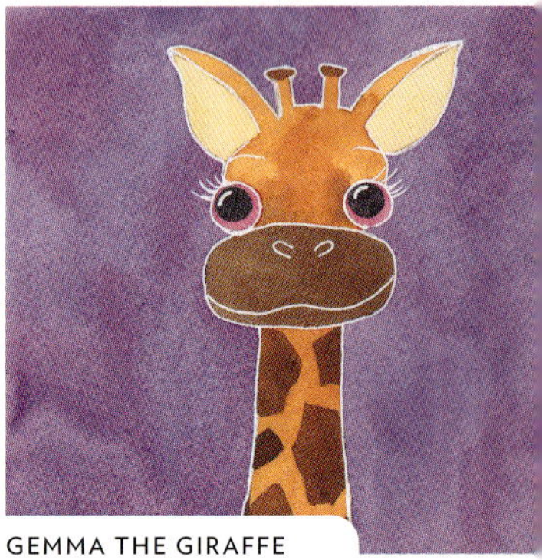

GEMMA THE GIRAFFE

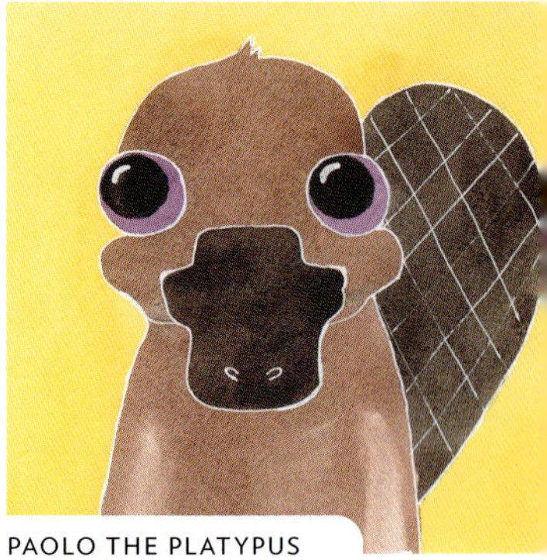

PAOLO THE PLATYPUS

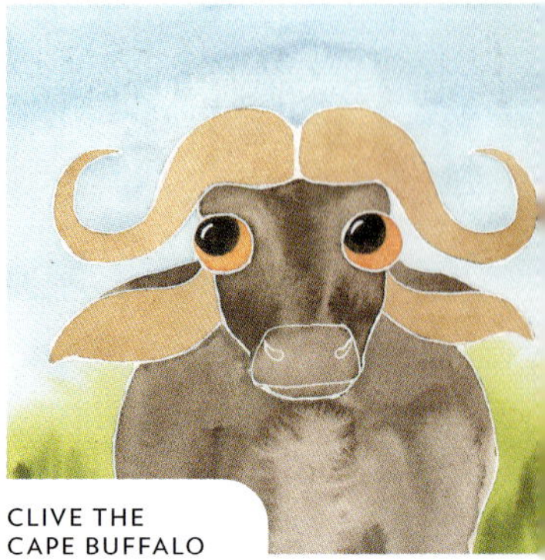

CLIVE THE CAPE BUFFALO

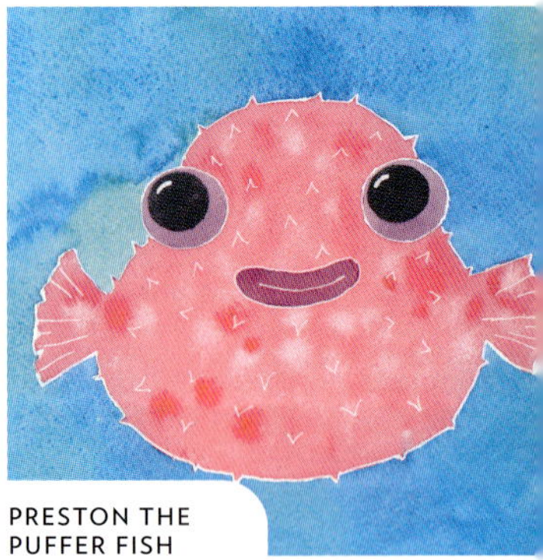

PRESTON THE PUFFER FISH

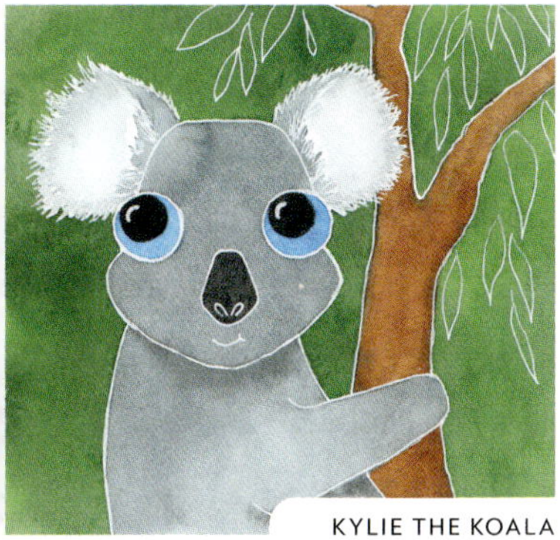
KYLIE THE KOALA

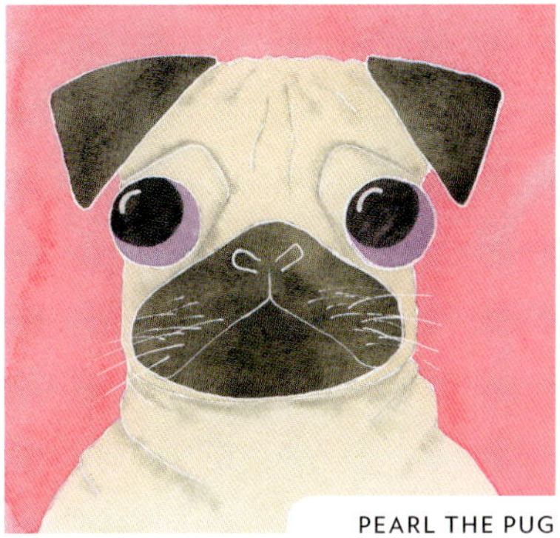
PEARL THE PUG

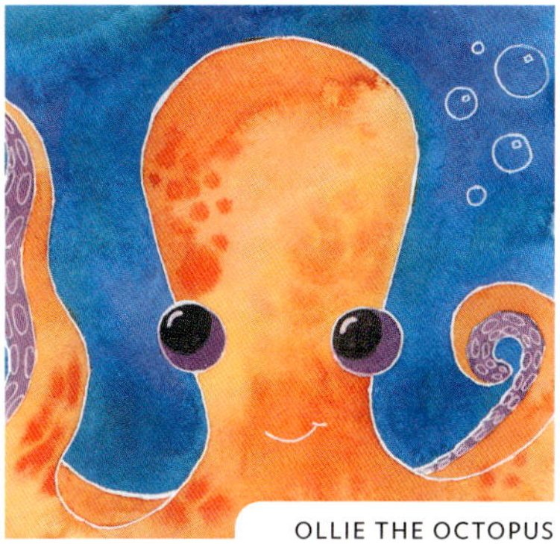
OLLIE THE OCTOPUS

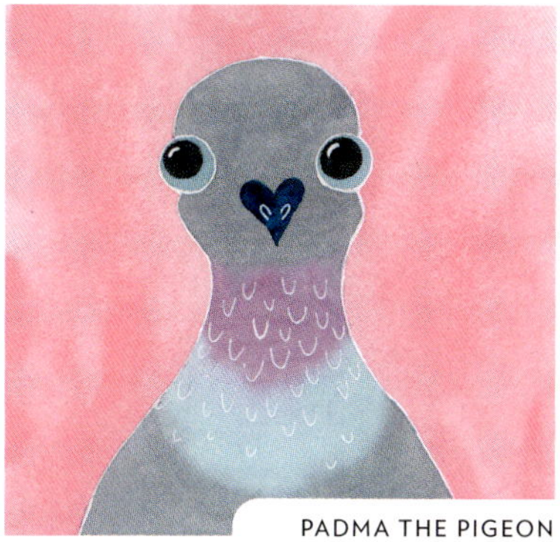
PADMA THE PIGEON

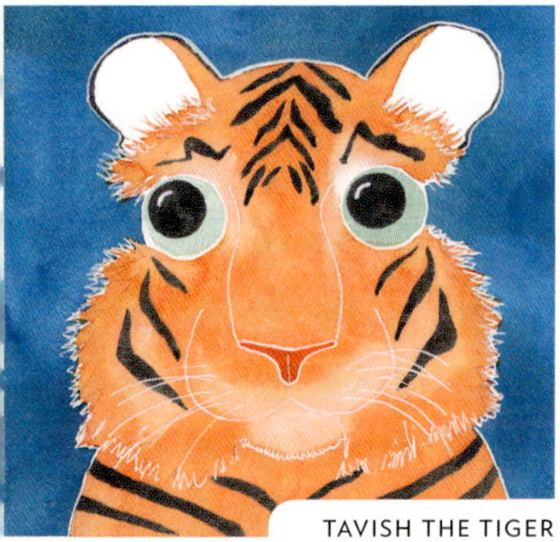
TAVISH THE TIGER

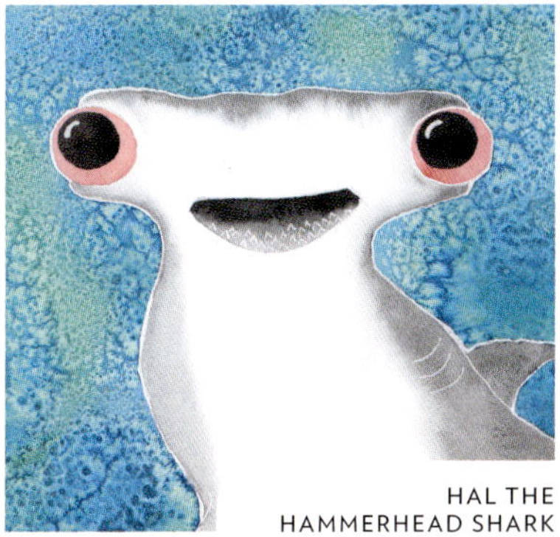
HAL THE
HAMMERHEAD SHARK

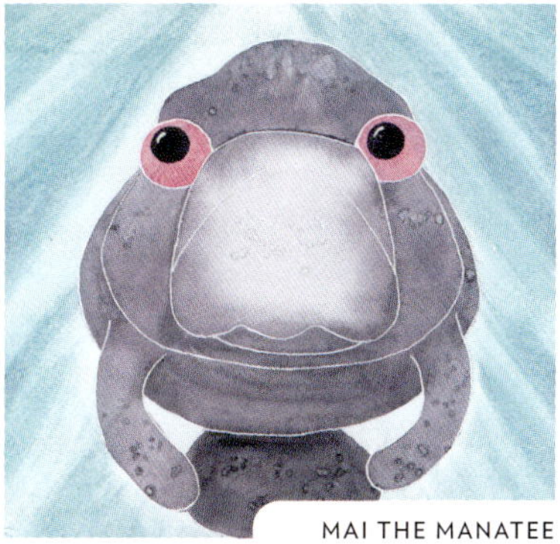
MAI THE MANATEE

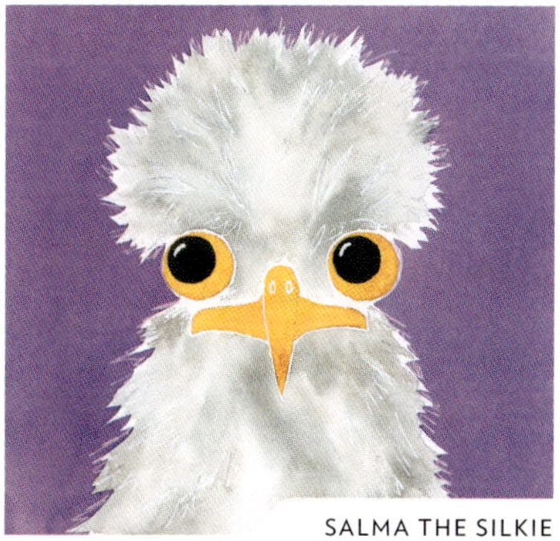
SALMA THE SILKIE

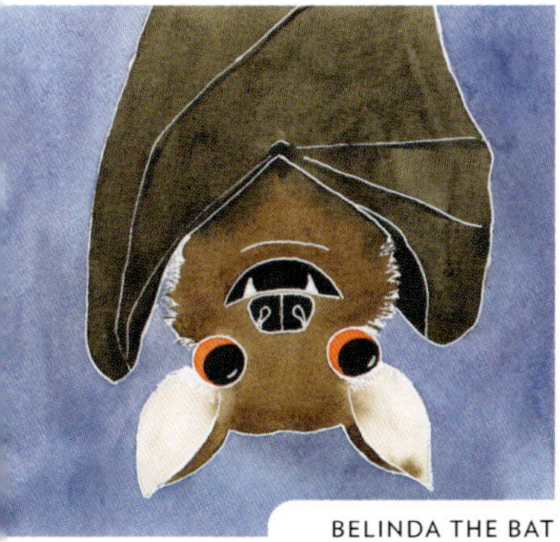
BELINDA THE BAT

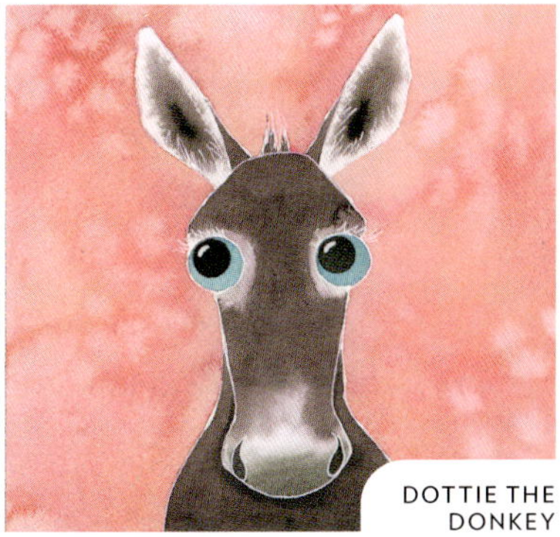
DOTTIE THE
DONKEY

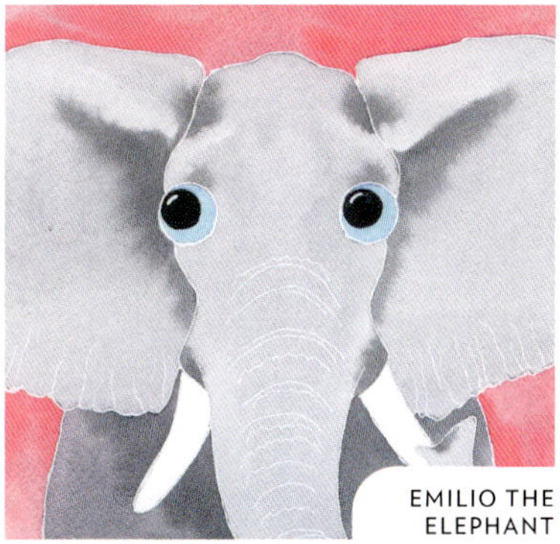
EMILIO THE
ELEPHANT

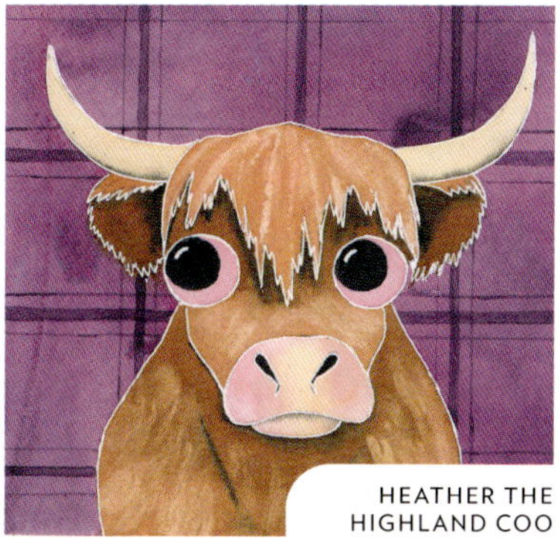
HEATHER THE
HIGHLAND COO

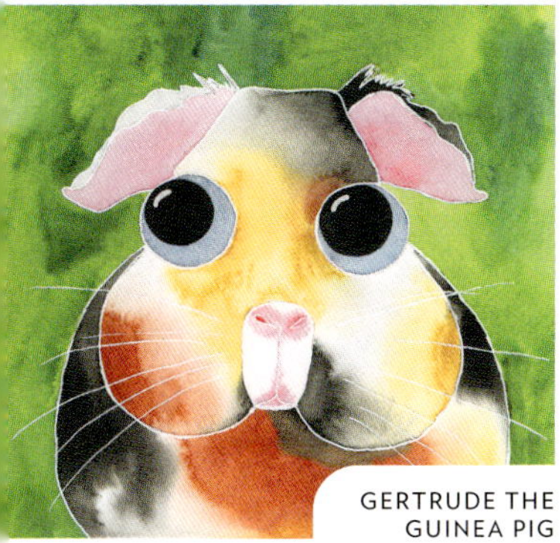
GERTRUDE THE
GUINEA PIG

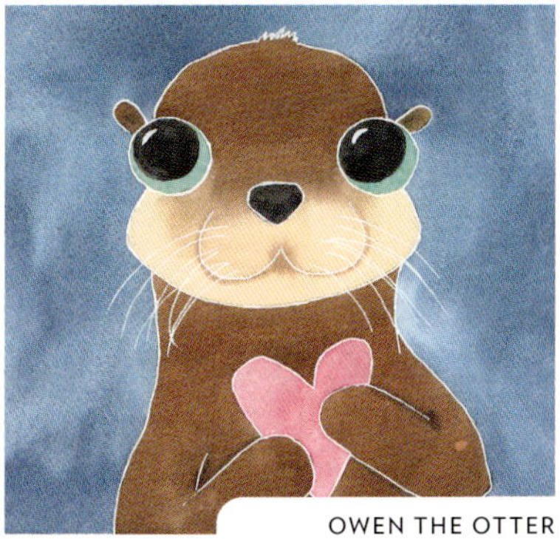
OWEN THE OTTER

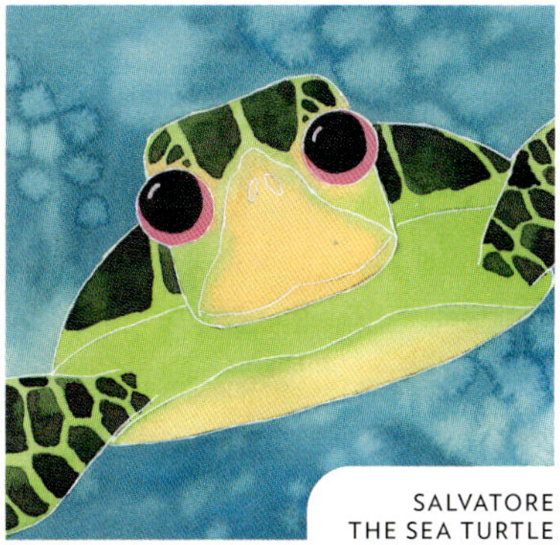
SALVATORE
THE SEA TURTLE

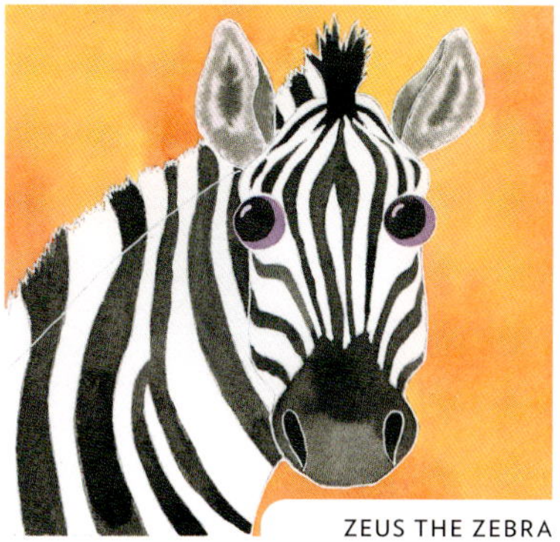
ZEUS THE ZEBRA

INTRODUCTION

HI! I'M LACEY WALKER and I love all things art. You might be familiar with my work through social media, where I go by @RebelUnicornCrafts. Or maybe you purchased my previous book, *Learn to Watercolor*. If so, thank you! On social media, I share painting tutorials, creative challenges, art explorations, and tips for painting with watercolor. I have an unstoppable curiosity for all things creative, and I absolutely love teaching people to paint and encouraging them in their creative endeavors.

This book grew out of a fun series of cute little paintings I do through my social media. I wanted to create this book to expand on this series in a way that would teach watercolor techniques in more depth. Also, the format of this book provides outlines so that if you struggle with proportions, placements, or just don't enjoy sketching, you could still have fun painting these animals all while learning watercolor.

I am a self-taught artist who has been creating most of my life. I have been a full-time, self-employed artist for eight years, and I feel incredibly fortunate that I get to do this every day and share my passion for art. Over the years, I have dabbled in charcoal drawing, acrylic painting, silversmithing, pottery, and of course, watercolor painting. I am always on the lookout for my next new art passion. Right now, my two main art loves are watercolor and pottery. When I am not painting in my studio, you can find me out in my pottery shed throwing mugs or watercolor accessories.

Watercolor is my absolute favorite thing to teach. My goal when teaching is to show you something fun to make and sneak in little lessons along the way. I think the "why" of something is just as important as the "how." So, as you work through this book, I hope you'll notice that we'll learn with intention, but my goal is to make it feel fun and less like work.

The most important thing I have found in my own art practice is embracing imperfections to allow yourself to grow, so as you work through this book, please remember to be kind to yourself and not expect perfection. If you find yourself feeling frustrated because you're not "good enough," I promise that you are and you are worth the time and effort it takes to learn a new skill.

How I recommend you use this book:

- **Allow yourself the room to make mistakes** and for things to turn out a little different. It's OK—you're learning!
- **The beginning of this book** is full of all the knowledge you're going to need to complete the paintings—and there are all sorts of tips and tricks—so try not to skip this section. Not only that, but there are also QR codes sprinkled throughout where you can get exclusive video content to add more context or show you things in real time.
- **Paint on the watercolor pad included for practice.** I recommend taking each page out as you tackle the painting so you can tape it to some cardboard. This makes painting the backgrounds easier because you can move the painting to get the right angle.

- **Paint your favorites again** or paint with friends or kiddos by downloading the included outlines and tracing them onto your favorite paper!
- **Hate QR codes?** Go to this website to find all the links in this book from the outlines to the video tutorials: www.quarto.com/files/LTWatercolorAATemplates
- **Use the supplies you already have.** This book isn't about perfect color matching—it's about exploring watercolor techniques while painting fun animals!
- **The book has been written in an order** that I think helps you progress through the techniques, but I know you might want to jump around, so each exercise lists the skills you'll need to be familiar with in order to complete it, and you can flip back to the beginning to learn more.
- **If you need a little extra courage to get started,** three of these animals include full-length painting videos—Gemma the Giraffe, Mai the Manatee, and Salma the Silkie. Watching the videos while creating these paintings can give you a little confidence boost.

Most importantly, have fun! Make bold color choices and discover the magic of watercolor.

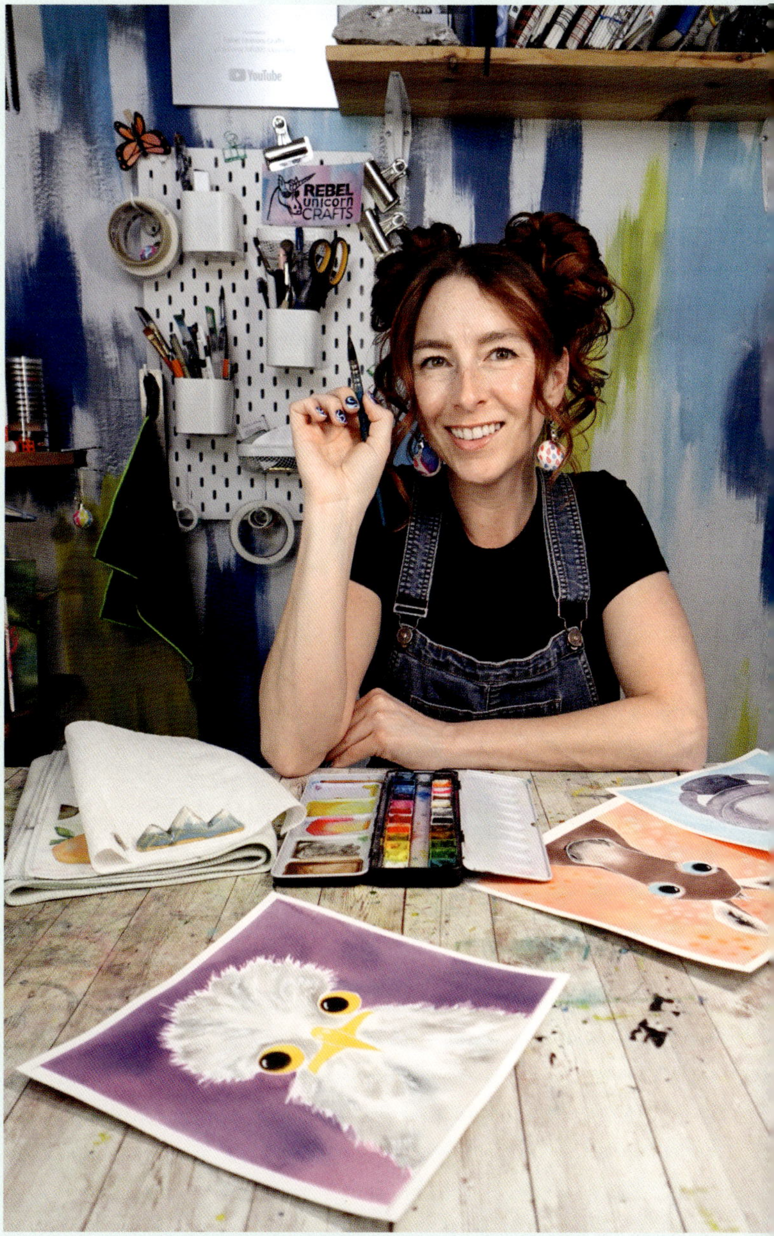

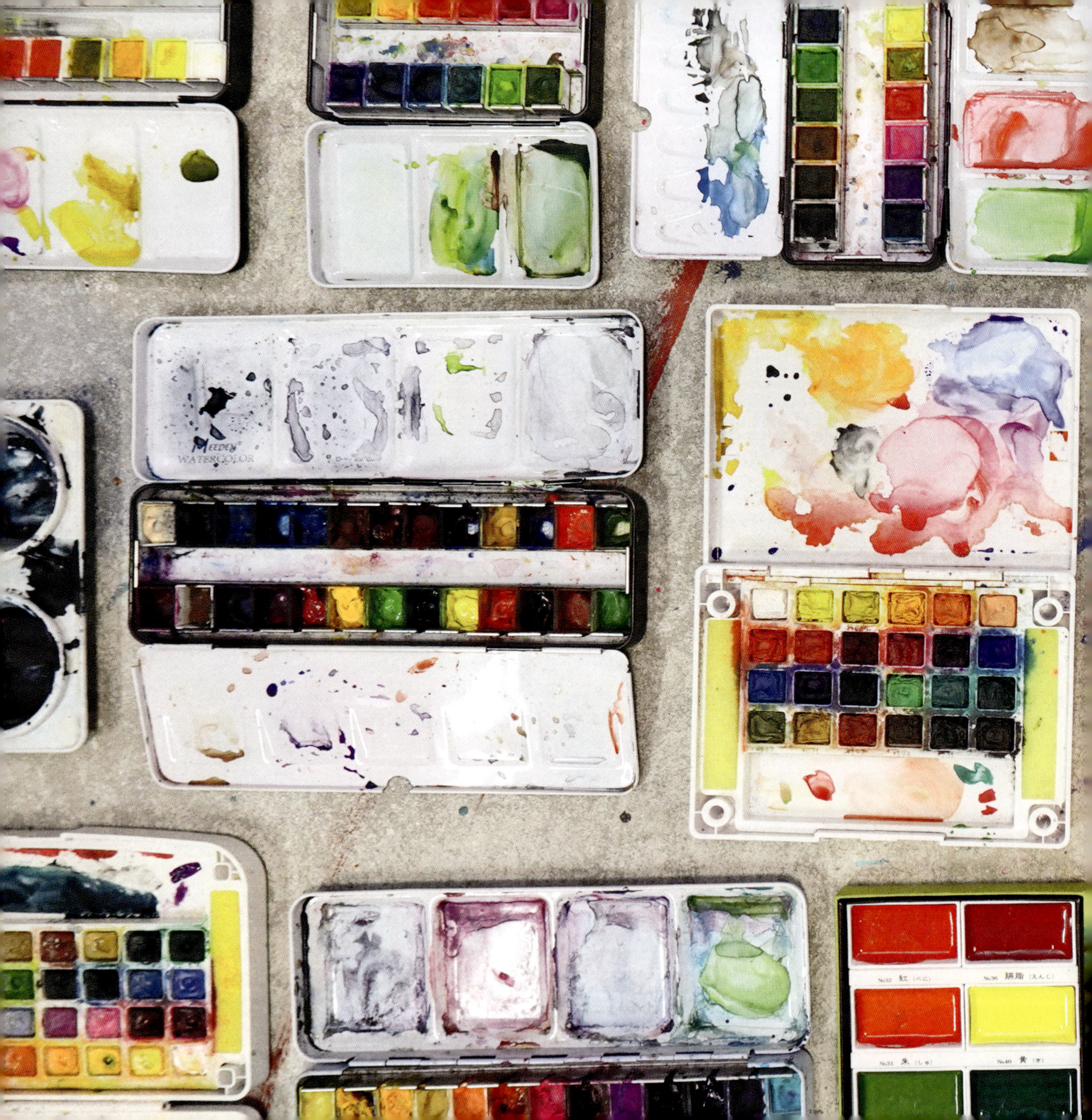
WATERCOLOR

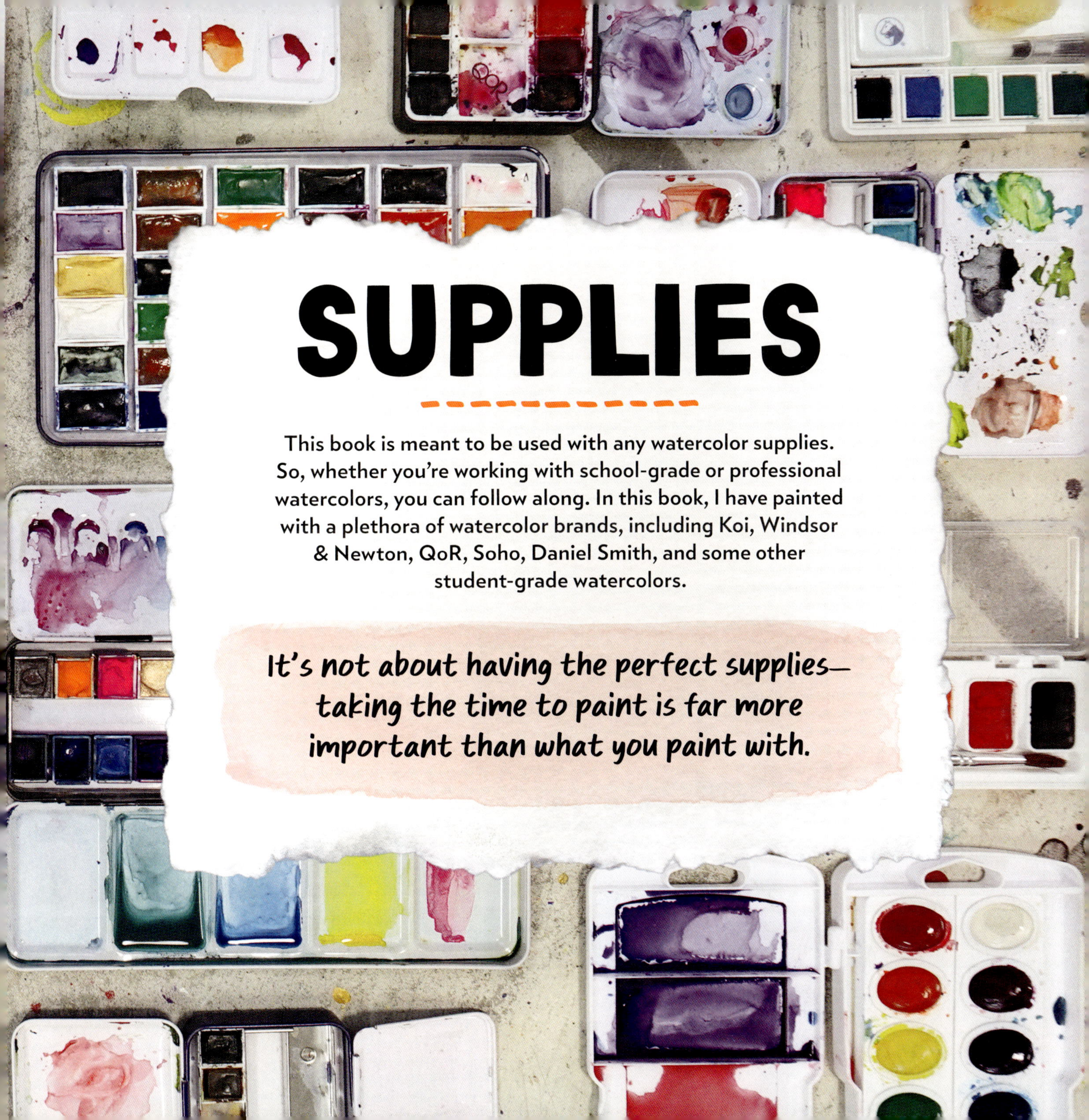

SUPPLIES

This book is meant to be used with any watercolor supplies. So, whether you're working with school-grade or professional watercolors, you can follow along. In this book, I have painted with a plethora of watercolor brands, including Koi, Windsor & Newton, QoR, Soho, Daniel Smith, and some other student-grade watercolors.

It's not about having the perfect supplies—taking the time to paint is far more important than what you paint with.

WHAT YOU'LL NEED

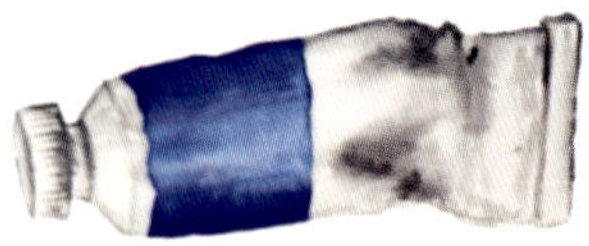

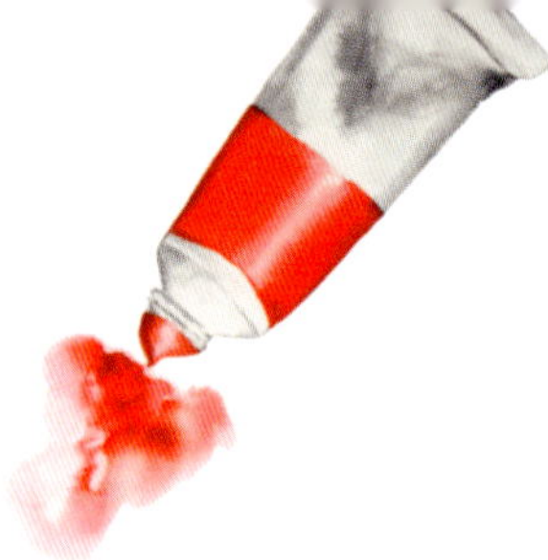

These are the must-have supplies you'll need to complete the paintings in this book. I've kept the list short so you can dive in with what you have on hand. No trip to stock up on supplies needed.

WATERCOLORS

If you don't already have a set of watercolors, I recommend picking up a set of pan watercolors like Koi. Even a set of Crayola watercolors will work great to get you started. There is not a specific set of colors required for this book—it's meant to be adaptable to your watercolors. One color to keep in mind, though, is pink. Many of my paintings feature a bright pink color, and most sets don't include a bright pink. So, you might want to grab a tube or pan of Opera Pink. I'll touch on pink again in the Mixing Colors section.

Don't overthink your watercolors. If you already have some, you don't need to buy anything new. As an example, see image 1.1. The donkey painting I created for this book was done using SoHo watercolors (on the left). I have recreated this painting (on the right) using paints you might see in an elementary classroom, Prang watercolors. The colors you can achieve will vary slightly, but even with a limited watercolor selection, you can create the paintings in this book, and they will turn out great!

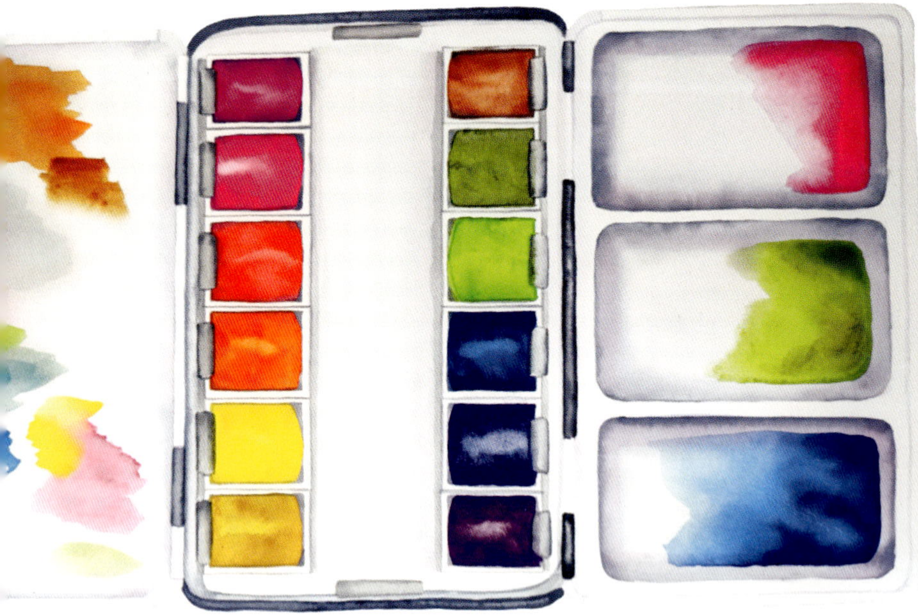

Tubes vs. pans?

If you're brand-new to watercolors, I recommend starting with dried pans of watercolor paint. They're the ones that come in a handy-dandy case or tin with mixing wells. For beginners, I find tubes can be confusing to use, and budget brands of tube paints are often disappointing in quality. But if you are accustomed to working with tubes of watercolor paint, they will of course work great for making these fun paintings!

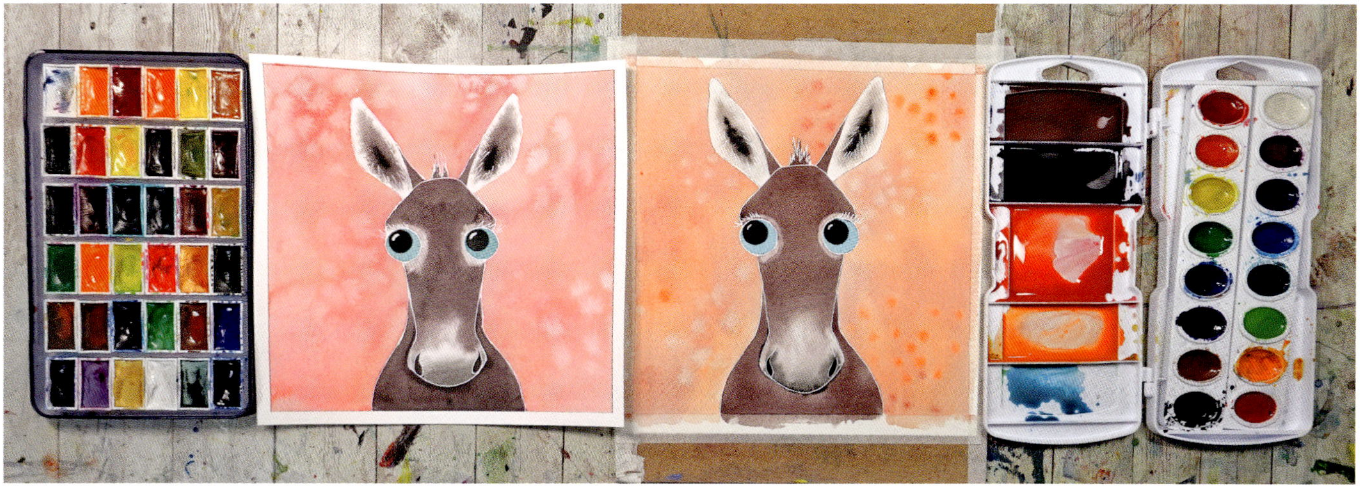

IMAGE 1.1

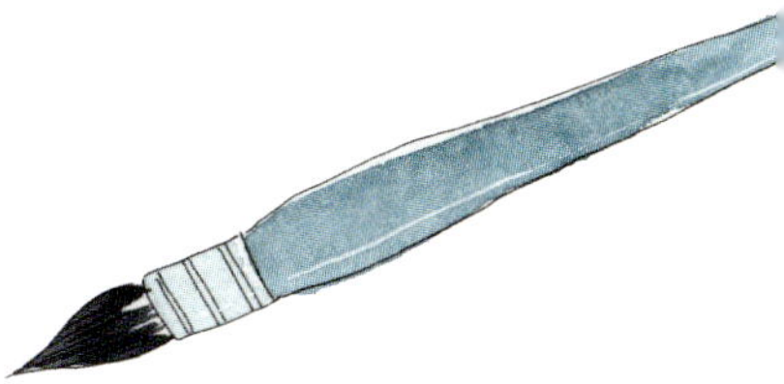

WATERCOLOR BRUSH

If you already have watercolor supplies, feel free to use your brushes. But if you're just starting out, everything in this book can be painted using just one brush—any of the following will work great!

Round brush, size 10 or 12, or a quill brush, size 3 or 4

WATERCOLOR PAPER

This book comes with a pad of paper with pre-sketched outlines built in so you can get right to painting! The paper included in this book is student-grade paper and great for practicing. The paper I used to paint the paintings is Stonehenge's 140-lb (300 gsm) cold-pressed cotton watercolor paper. If you want to recreate any of the paintings in the book, you can download the outlines using the QR code on page 5, and then print or trace them onto the paper of your choice!

When you're painting on the practice pad, you might notice some differences in how the paper behaves—all the techniques are possible in this book, but the pad is meant for practice. If you'd like to see some samples of my paintings on Stonehenge vs. the practice pad, you can scan this QR code to see examples.

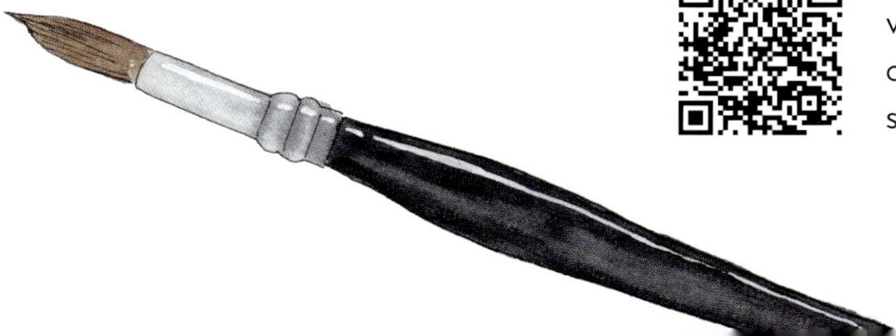

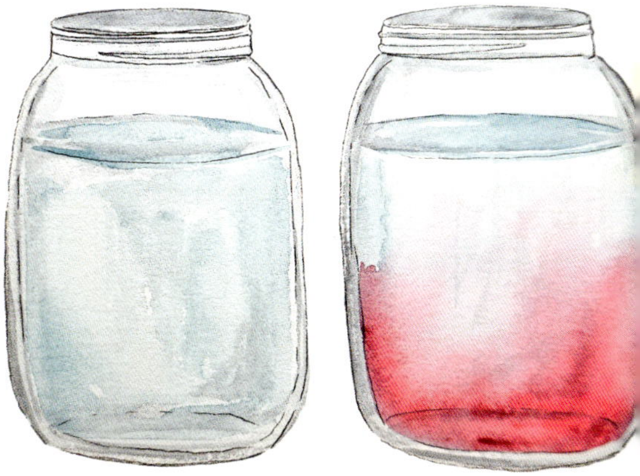

CUPS FOR WATER

Having two containers for your water is nice, so you can use one for washing your brush and keep one clean for mixing.

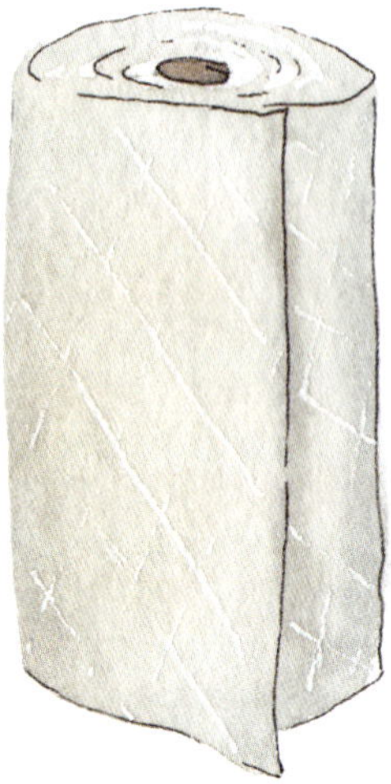

PAPER TOWEL OR RAG

You'll need a paper towel or rag to dry your brush off. I like to put a rag down first and then layer a couple paper towels on top. I find paper towels are better for controlling how much water is in my brush, but a rag makes them last longer and keeps my workspace dry.

WHITE PEN OR MARKER FOR FINISHING TOUCHES

You'll need a white pen or marker to add details to the projects after you've painted them. I prefer to use a white gel pen for this, but there are lots of other options you can use if you find white gel pens frustrating or can't find a good one.

In image 1.2, you can see how a crayon, gouache, colored pencil, acrylic marker, and white gel pen appear on a dark background. They are all good options!

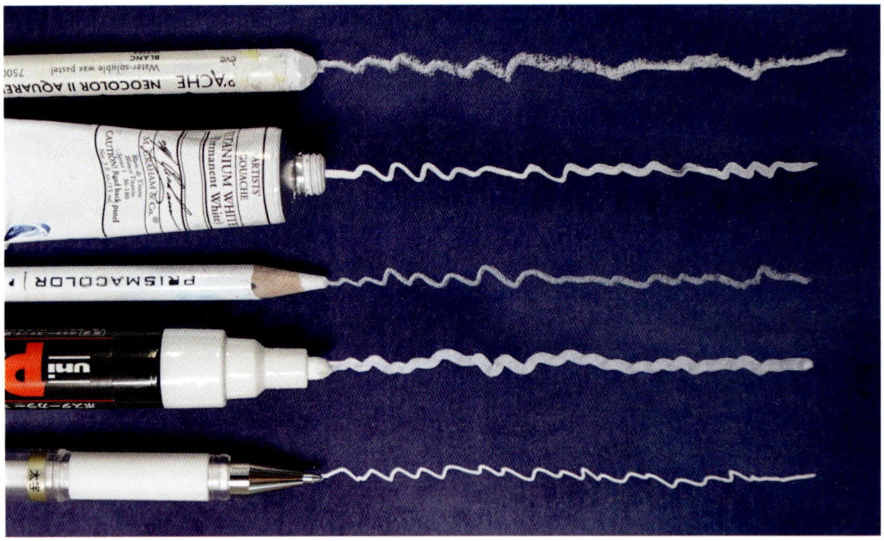

IMAGE 1.2 Options for white finishing touches

Tips for white gel pens

There's something about the white outlines on these little cartoon animals that really add a fun touch and bring them together. You could use a black outline pen, but I think the white is just more fun, plus it can be used to add the highlights to the eyes!

I prefer using a Uni-Ball Signo white gel pen and find it works great for me. White gel pens in general can be tricky, so here are some tricks to making your white gel pen work better:

1. **Pressure matters:** Don't push too hard or it will impede the flow of white ink or make it streaky.
2. **Scribble to start:** Sometimes white gel pens take a little time to warm up; the ink seems to dry on the ball. Scribbling them a bit on a scrap paper will get them warmed up and remove the dried ink so they are ready to go!
3. **Think about your angle:** I find holding the pen at about a 45-degree angle and dragging the pen to allow the ball to roll smoothly allows for the best application.

NICE TO HAVE

There are a few other supplies you might find handy in the painting process, but they are not essential.

SPRAY BOTTLE

If you notice that your colors aren't as saturated as mine, it probably doesn't mean your supplies are bad. Watercolors work best when activated. To activate your watercolors, just spray them with a little water or put a few drops on each pan and wait 15 to 30 seconds. I also use the spray bottle to add water to my mixing wells to make color mixtures. Check out images 1.3 and 1.4 to see what my paints look like before I activate them just using a wet brush (1.3) and after I activate them with the spray bottle (1.4).

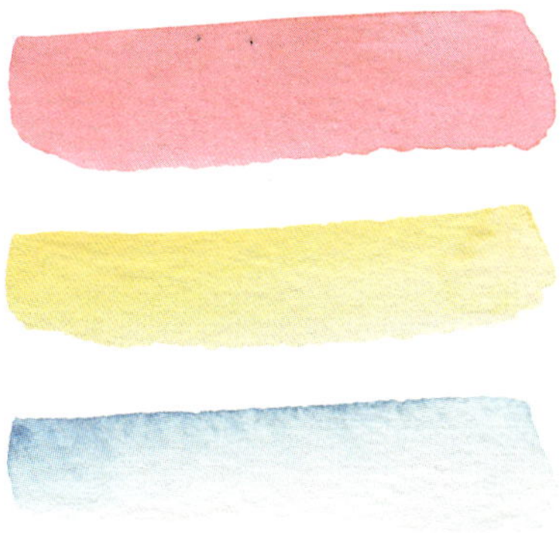

IMAGE 1.3 Without activation

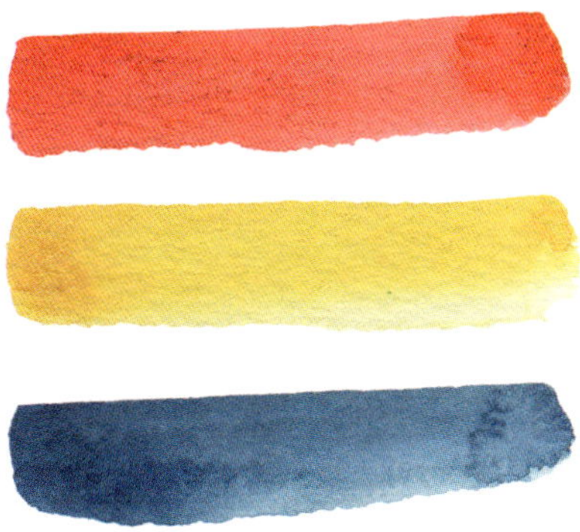

IMAGE 1.4 After activation

CRAFT HEAT GUN OR HAIR DRYER

If you're impatient like me, using a craft heat gun or hair dryer helps speed up the process between drying layers of paint. You can "make it dry" along with me!

TAPE

If you prefer to take the pages out of this book to work, I recommend taping them down to cardboard or a backing board. Masking tape, washi tape, or painter's tape work great for taping the edges.

MIXING WELLS

If you will be working with tube paints or your set of watercolor pans doesn't come with built-in mixing wells, you will need somewhere to mix the colors.

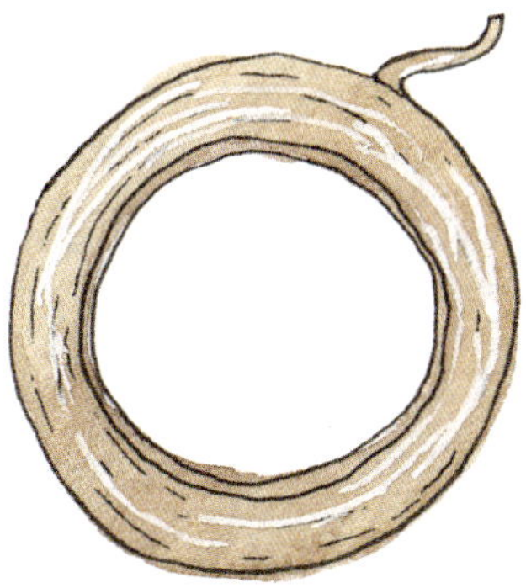

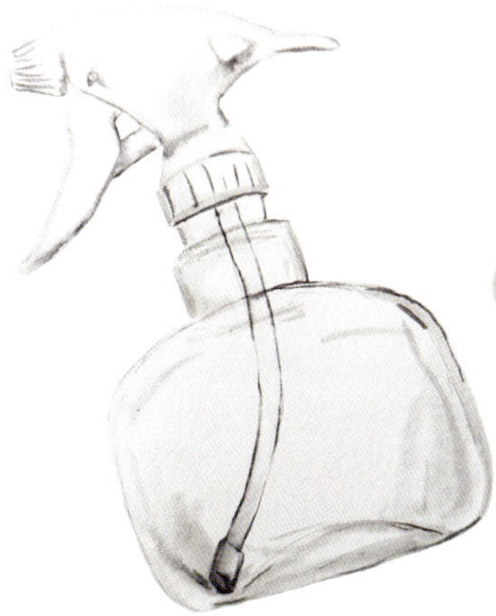

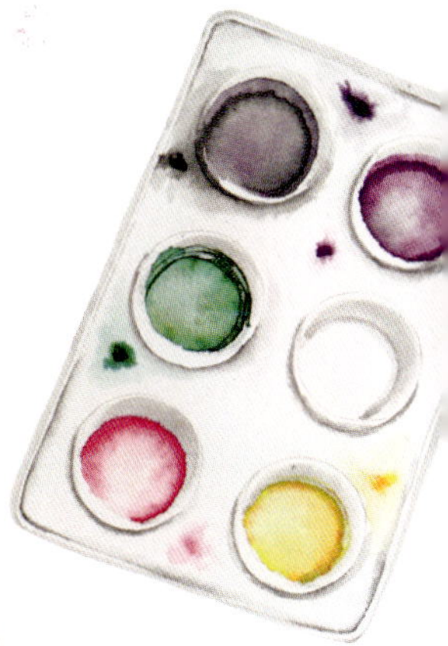

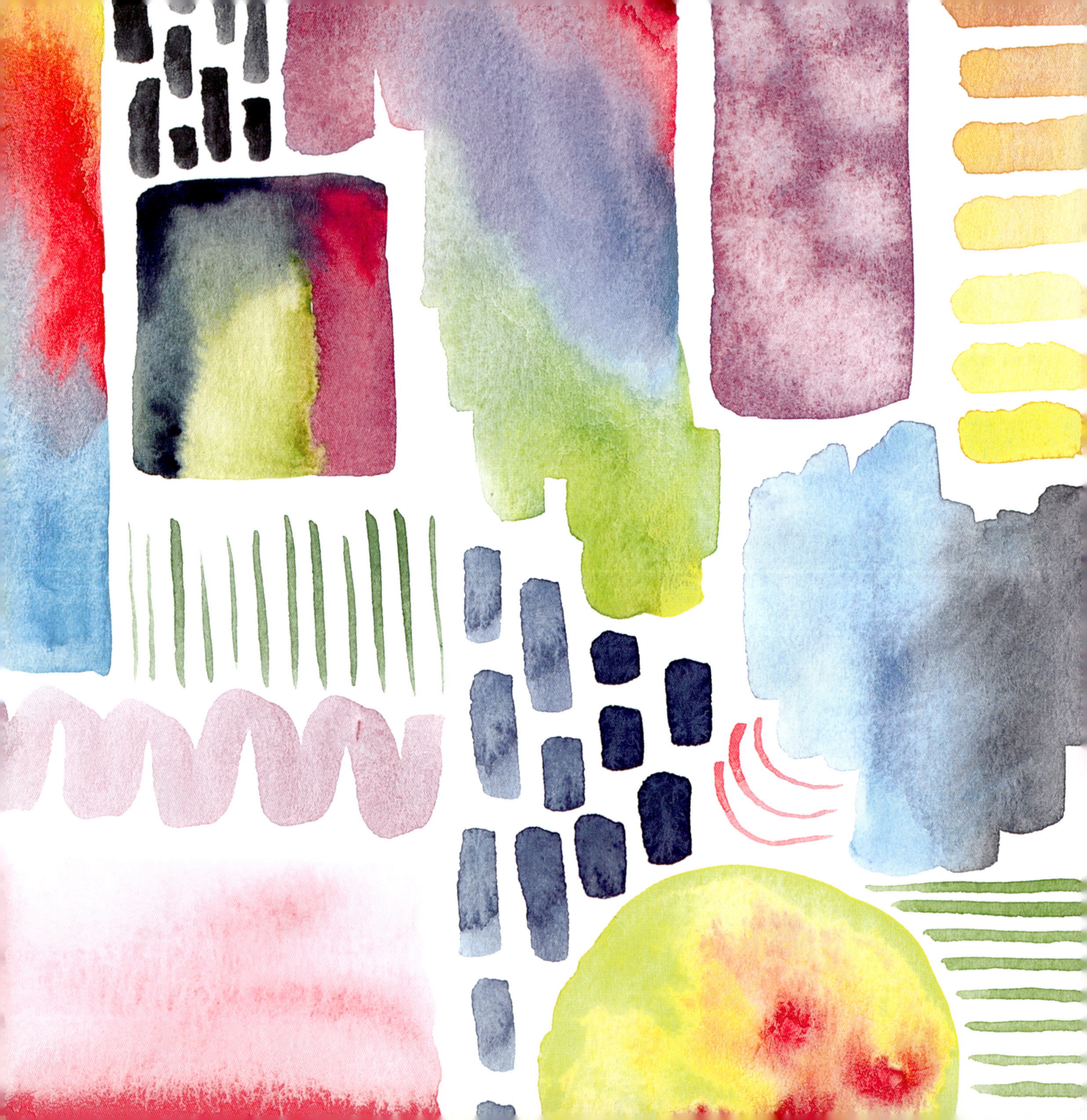

THE BASICS

If you're new to watercolor, getting started can feel a little daunting. There's a lot of new terminology and techniques, but don't worry—we'll tackle this together! Each animal painting helps teach techniques, but I want to acquaint you with the basic techniques and a few things you'll need to know before we get started. In this chapter, you'll learn why watercolor behaves the way it does, as well as how to work with it.

I know that it's tempting to jump right into the projects, and if that's your speed, go for it! Each animal has page references to the techniques you'll need to know, so you can always flip back to this chapter for reference.

WORKING WITH WATER

The beauty of watercolor is water's wonderfully flowy nature. The key, though, is understanding how much water to use and when to use it, so let's explore some of the terminology as well as water conditions.

Wet-on-Wet vs. Wet-on-Dry

One of the first sets of terms to learn in watercolor is "wet-on-wet" and "wet-on-dry." On the surface it's a simple clarification of the conditions of the paper before you start painting: Wet-on-wet means the paper was pre-wet before you began painting. Wet-on-dry means the paper was dry when you began painting.

I will always let you know if I have pre-wet the paper, and to what stage I pre-wet the paper, if you need to work wet-on-wet. If the instructions don't specify, assume my paper was dry when I started painting.

Wetness Stages

When you're told to wet an area or cover an entire area with a color, how wet you make your paper matters for what you want to achieve. The general rule of thumb is: The wetter your paper is, the less control you have over what happens, and the drier, the more control you have. When I am painting, I consider there to be five stages of wetness, and knowing them helps me understand how wet to make my paper to achieve different effects. I like to use the reflection of the water with a light to evaluate them. To better get to know these stages, let's explore the conditions and an analogy for each stage.

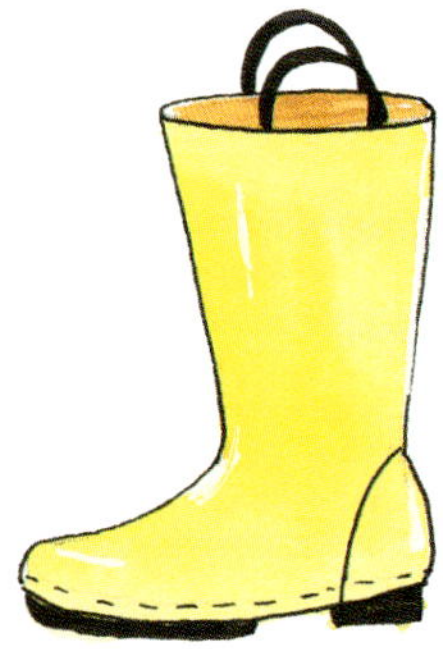

Stage 1: Flood

In the flood stage, the application of water on the page is uncontrolled; there are puddles of water that flow across the paper. If you were to shrink yourself down so that the paper was the ground you walk on, you'd need to wear rain boots.

The general rule of thumb is: The wetter your paper is, the less control you have over what happens, and the drier, the more control you have.

Wetness stages in action

Want to see the wetness stages in action? Scan the QR code to watch a short video demonstrating the five stages.

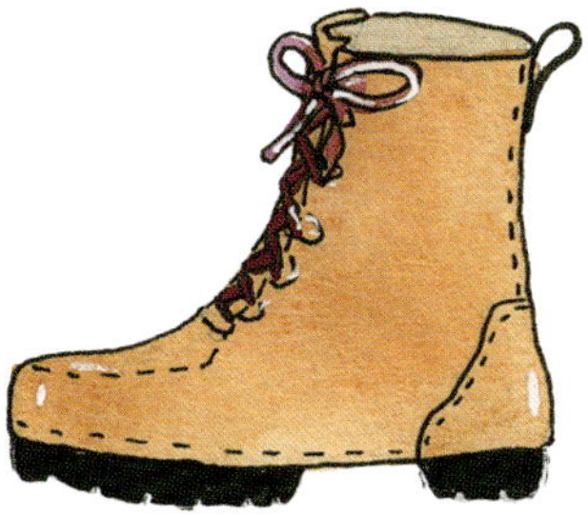

Stage 2: Gloss
In this stage, an even coat of water covers the page, obscuring the texture of the paper, creating a smooth and shiny appearance. If you were to shrink yourself down, you'd need something like hiking boots to navigate it.

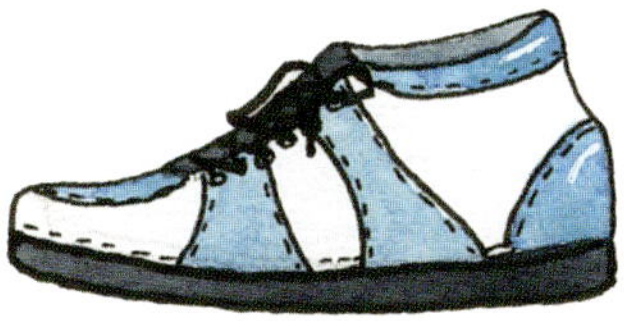

Stage 3: Satin
When observing the reflection of this stage, you're still going to see some shine, but you can start to see some of the texture on the paper within that reflection. If you were to shrink yourself down, you'd want something like tennis shoes.

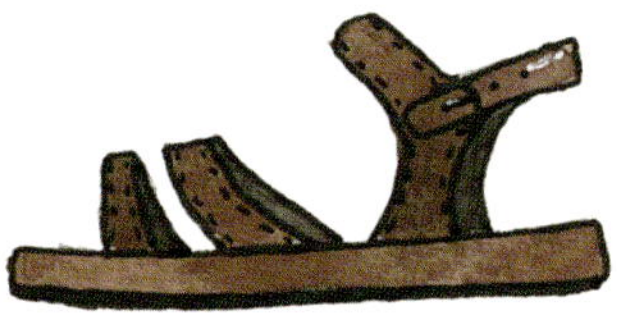

Stage 4: Damp
This stage is typically achieved by waiting for the water to soak in a bit. In the reflection, it will be hard to see the shine of the water, but you'll see it a little, and the texture of the paper will be obvious. If you were to shrink yourself down, you could start considering something like sandals, but anything with a heel would be dicey.

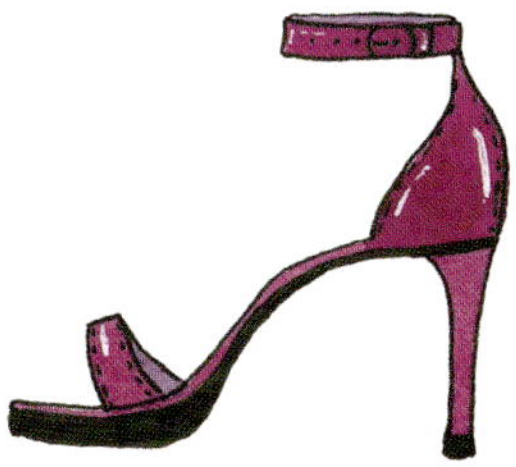

Stage 5: Dry
The paper is completely dry, and no reflection will be seen. If you were to shrink yourself down, you could wear any type of shoes—even stilettos!

If you want things to stay exactly where you put them, paint on dry layers. If you want fun, uncontrollable watercolor reactions, use the flood or gloss stages. If you want the colors to soften together a little but stay mostly where you put them, consider the satin or damp stages.

MIXING COLORS

Using and mixing colors can feel intimidating. This book is not about perfect color matching. In fact, I want you to make color decisions that feel right to you, grab colors straight from the pan, and just have fun. If you are interested in getting to know a bit about mixing colors, there are a few things that will help you get started.

COLOR WHEEL BASICS

In image 2.1, you will see a fun color wheel based off three primary colors: pink, yellow, and blue. This might differ slightly from what you are used to, as many color wheels use red, yellow, and blue. Neither is wrong; this is my personal preference. I chose pink instead of red because I like the color mixes it makes better, especially when it comes to purples.

In image 2.2, you can see the difference between a couple color mixtures using pink vs. using red. Whether or not you use red or pink, the three primary colors mix together to make all the other colors around the color wheel.

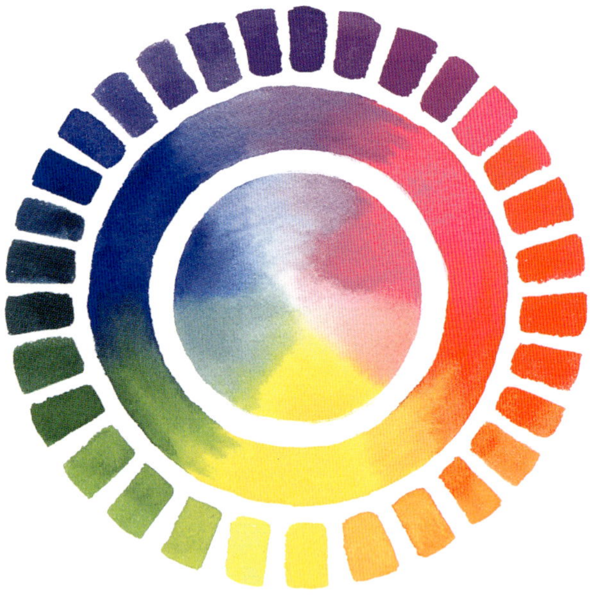

IMAGE 2.1

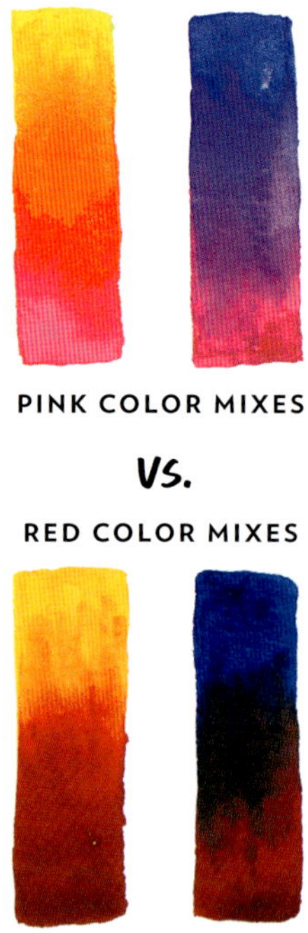

IMAGE 2.2

SATURATION AND LIGHTER COLORS

Watercolors at 100 percent saturation means they are being used directly from the pan or tube at their full color potential, just enough water to get them on the page and lots of that color. As you can see in image 2.3, the pink color is at its full saturation on the left side. I mixed more and more water into it until it was at 1 percent saturation all the way on the right side.

The beauty of watercolor is you don't have to mix white paint into your colors to get a lighter color—you just need to add more water.

MIXING CUSTOM COLORS

When you mix a custom color, you will take at least two colors and mix them together. You can see in image 2.4 I mixed pink and yellow. In the middle, they make a lovely orange color.

But what I want you to really notice is how many different colors can be made between the two colors. It just depends on how much of each color you mix in. In other words, mixing two colors together doesn't just make one additional color—there are lots that you can make!

IMAGE 2.3

IMAGE 2.4

Try it out: Experiment with saturation!

In image 2.3, you can see individual brushstrokes that decrease in saturation and make lighter colors. To try this out, start by wetting your brush, then fill it with as much of your color as you can and make a stroke. Then dip your brush into water and swirl your brush around in the mixing well to mix in the water and incorporate it with the color remaining in your brush. Then make another stroke on your paper. Repeat this over and over until there is barely any color left in your brush and mainly just water. This will help you get an idea of the different saturation possibilities in a single color.

Try it out: Practice mixing between colors!

Choose two colors. In your mixing well, place a little water and then mix in lots of one of your colors and make a stroke on the page. Then dip the tip of your brush into your second color and grab just a tiny amount. Mix it into the puddle you made of the first color, and make a second stroke. Repeat this as many times as you like so you can see how the color changes as more and more of the second color gets mixed in.

EXAMPLES OF COLOR MIXES

In image 2.5, you can see nine examples of color mixtures. The first column shows the primary colors mixed together to show you the possible secondary colors you can make. The second column shows how mixing primary colors with secondary colors makes tertiary colors. But you're not limited to just mixing those colors together; you can really mix any two colors together, so the third column shows what happens when you mix colors that don't fall along the lines of the traditional color wheel. Sometimes you can get fun and surprising color results, so I recommend playing with mixing different colors together just to see what happens!

MIXING GRAY

What about gray? You'll mix up some gray colors for a number of these animals, like Emilio the Elephant and Padma the Pigeon. To make a gray color, add water to your black paint to desaturate it (see image 2.6).

As you can see in image 2.7, you can also change the color of the gray. For example, to make a blue-gray, mix a little blue into it. To make a brown-gray, mix a little brown into it!

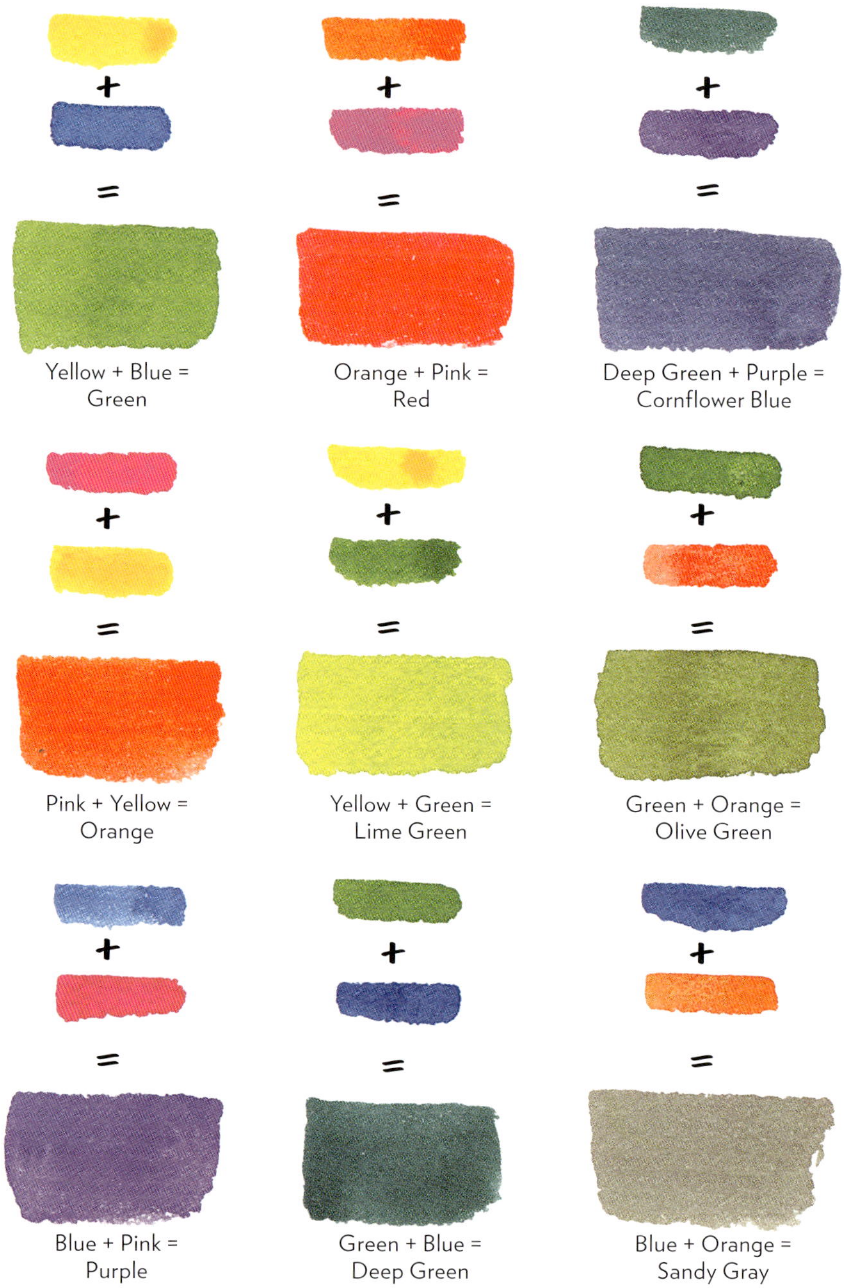

IMAGE 2.5

IMAGE 2.6

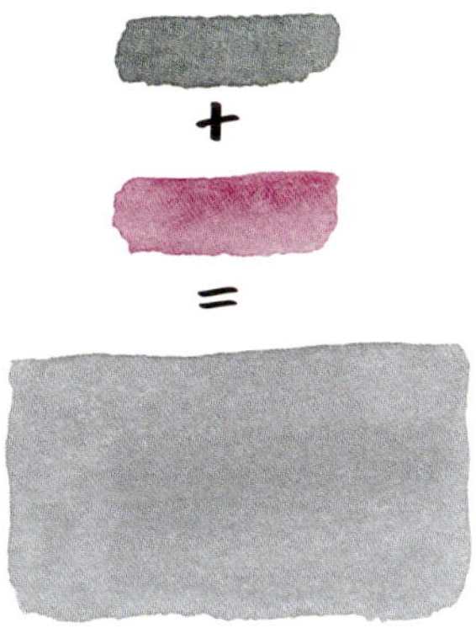

Payne's Gray + Magenta = Neutral Gray

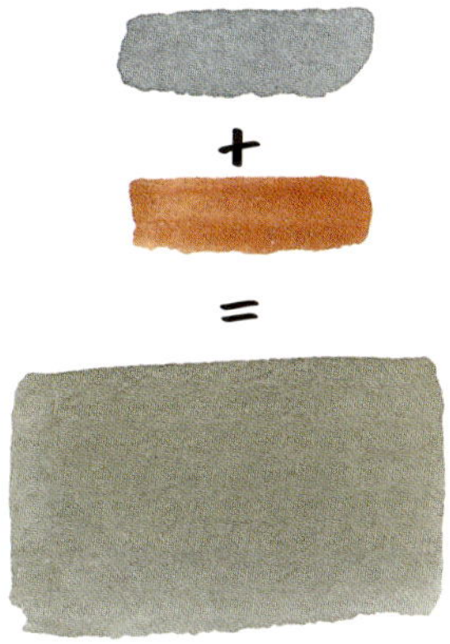

Payne's Gray + Orange = Sandy Gray

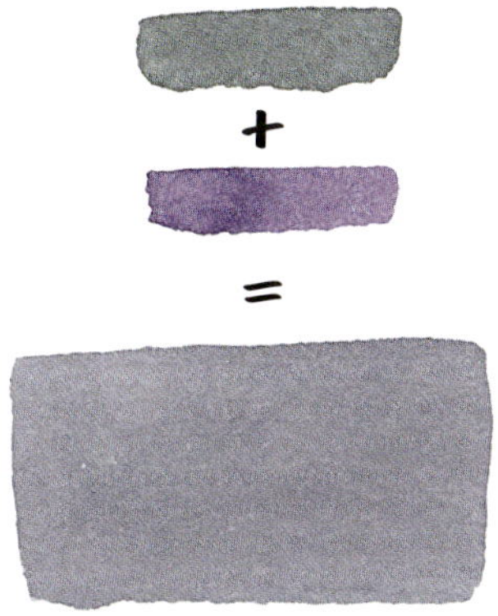

Payne's Gray + Purple = Purple Gray

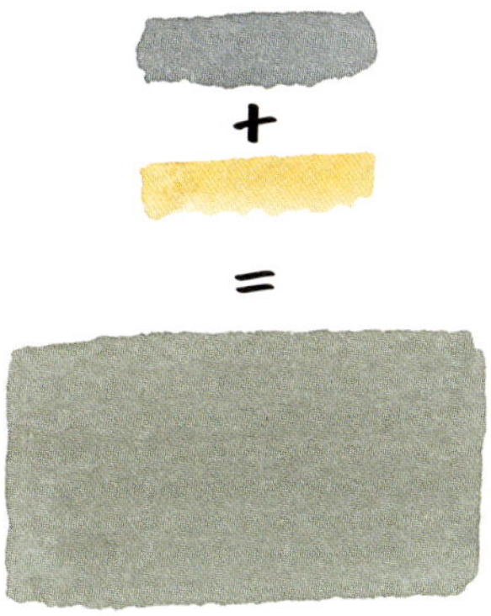

Payne's Gray + Yellow = Warm Green Gray

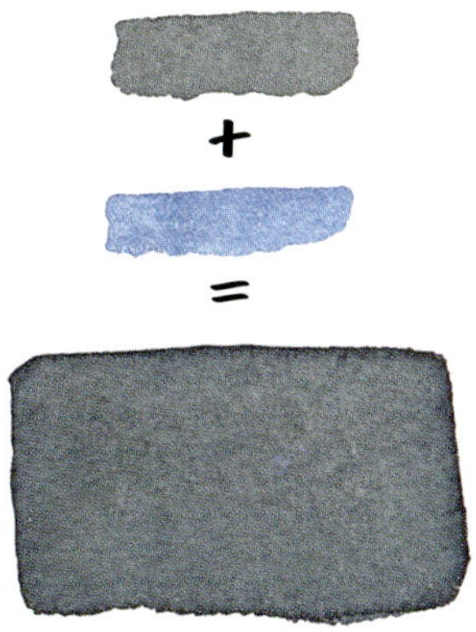

Payne's Gray + Blue = Steel Gray

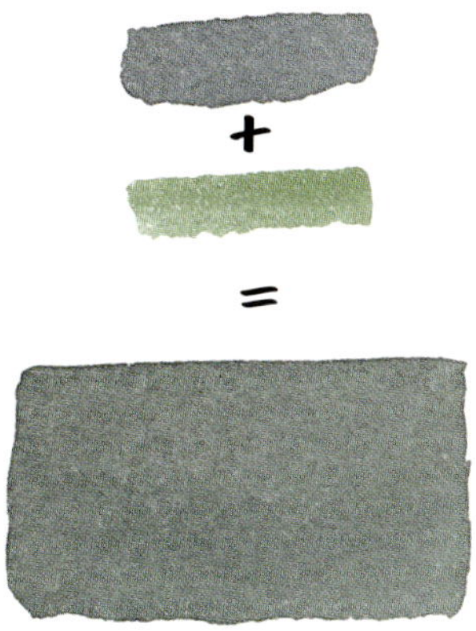

Payne's Gray + Green = Cool Green Gray

IMAGE 2.7

DARKENING COLORS

You may have noticed that in the color wheel I presented, as well as other color wheels you've seen, only bright, vibrant colors are included. But what about darker colors? There are two main ways to darken your colors.

1 **Mix black into your color.** As you can see in image 2.8, I mixed black paint into blue. The color turns more and more dark and gray the more you mix into your original color. This is a quick way to darken colors, but it's not my favorite method.

2 **Mix the complementary color into your color.** This is my favorite way to darken colors because I think you get far more interesting colors. As you can see in image 2.9, I mixed blue with its complementary color, orange. Complementary colors fall on opposite sides of the color wheel from one another (see image 2.10). In other words, they are the direct opposite colors. A complementary color can mute and darken its complement in ways that other colors don't. When I mix blue and orange together, it makes a lovely gray color, and on either side of the middle, it creates darkened versions of both the blue and the orange. For this method, you only want to add a little of the complement to darken.

IMAGE 2.8 Darkening with black

IMAGE 2.9 Darkening with complementary colors

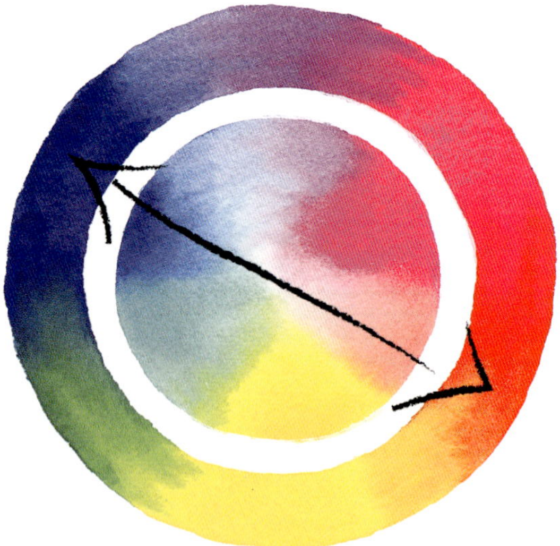

IMAGE 2.10 Complementary colors

How to use complementary colors

Complementary colors are also an easy way to select colors that work nicely together in your paintings. If you look at each complementary color pair, you may notice familiar combinations from sports teams and holidays—that's because color complements look good together! In this book I sometimes choose the complementary color of the animal's body to be the background. Check out Gemma the Giraffe to see this in practice. In image 2.11, Gemma's body is yellow, so I chose the complement, purple, for the background. If the animal is gray or brown, I sometimes use the animal's eye color to choose the complement. You can see this in the Paolo the Platypus painting.

But, you don't have to make all your color choices this way. Sometimes, color choices can just be fun. In image 2.12, I repainted Gemma the Giraffe using fun colors that I liked.

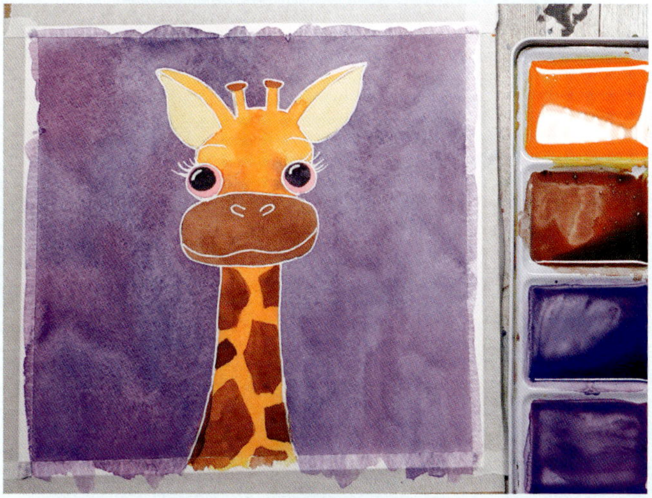

IMAGE 2.11

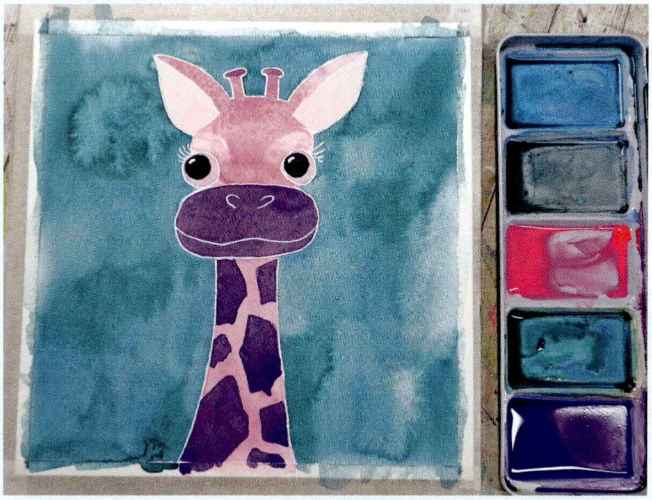

IMAGE 2.12

Getting More Saturated Colors

When you first start mixing colors, you might find them lacking in vibrancy, because getting super saturated or dark colors in watercolor can be tricky. In order to do this, you're going to need to consider a few things:

1. If you're using pan watercolors, make sure you activate them by dropping some water on the pans, or I like to use a spray bottle to activate them all before painting. This will get you access to so much more color. Without pre-wetting them, you only have access to a little of the pigment, but an activated pan will allow you to pick up so much more!

2. Patience is your friend. It can take a bit of time to actually mix up a larger amount of a saturated color. When I mix colors, I start with an amount of water based on how much paint I will ultimately need (a lot if I'm painting a large part of the page and just a little if I'm only painting a small detail). Then I grab some color with my paintbrush and mix it in, grab some color, mix it in, and repeat that over and over again while testing on a tester strip to make sure the color is as dark as I want (see image 2.13). So, if your color isn't as vibrant as you want, you're just not there yet—keep going!

Remember, any color you mix or darken can also be lightened by adding water!

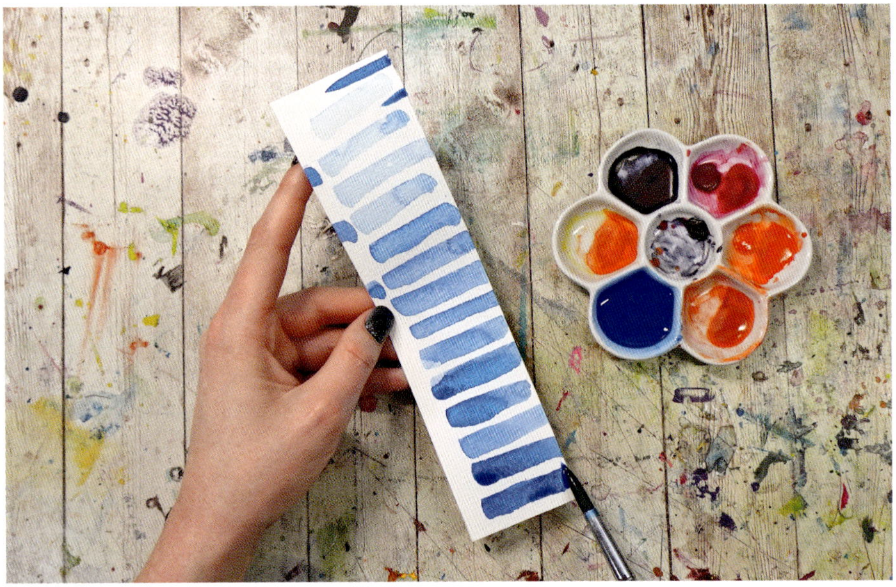

IMAGE 2.13

Mixing saturated colors

Patience is your friend when mixing saturated colors. See how long it takes in real time to get a saturated color!

How much color should I mix?

If you're wondering how much color you should mix, scan this QR code to watch a video where I demonstrate a few examples of how much you'll need to cover various area sizes.

DIPPING DIRECTLY INTO PANS VS. PRE-MIXING PUDDLES

When I'm painting, I sometimes dip my brush directly into pans and sometimes I pre-mix larger quantities of colors. I find that the use case for each varies depending on the goal.

Dipping into a pre-activated pan is the easiest way to grab a little bit of super-saturated color, so if you want to make one small area a very saturated color, this is very useful. However, if you want to be able to paint that color over a large area, this will be unreliable, because you'll have a hard time keeping enough water on the pan to repeatedly refill your brush with the same color. Take a look at image 2.14 as an example. On the top, I dipped my brush directly into the pan each time. You can see the resulting paint saturation varies quite a bit.

Pre-mixing larger quantities of colors is great for covering large areas with a consistent color. It ensures you can resubmerge your brush and grab the same color saturation level, as you can see in the paint strips on the bottom of image 2.14.

Pan dipping vs. pre-mixing

Scan the QR code to watch a video of examples of when I might dip directly into a pan vs. mixing up a color in a paint well.

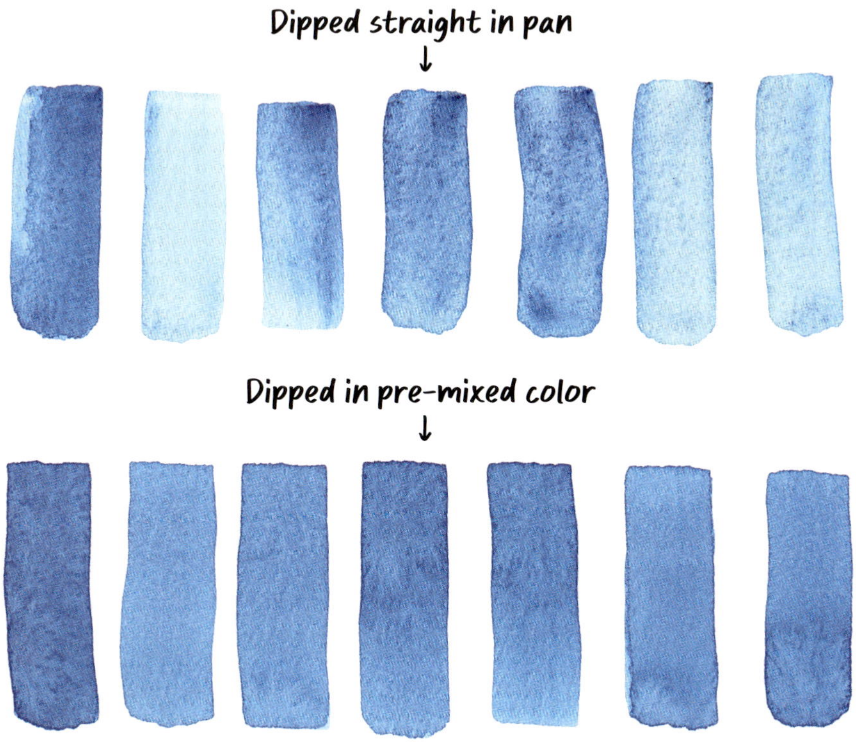

IMAGE 2.14

SOFTENING COLORS AND EDGES

This technique helps you achieve subtle gradients and avoid harsh lines. It's simple to do: Place your initial color down where you want it, and then, while it's still wet, wash your brush and leave some clean water in it. Then, using the tip of your brush, touch and drag along the edge of the initial color, allowing the water in the brush to deposit on the page and soften the dark color. We use this technique on the ears of the Kylie the Koala (see image 2.15) to get a subtle change from the darker gray on the outside of the ear to the lighter gray of the inner ear.

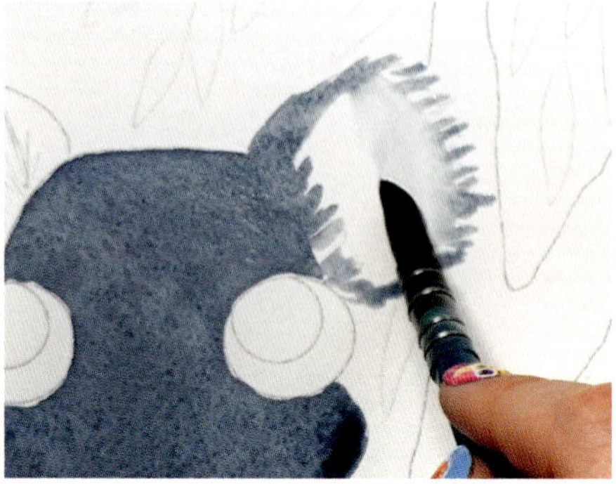

IMAGE 2.15

WATERCOLOR WASHES

In watercolor, a wash means applying an even layer of watercolor paint over a large area. Different washes are used to achieve different effects.

FLAT WASH

A flat wash is probably the most common wash, and it is made by covering an area with a single solid color. For example, we use a flat wash of yellow to paint in the face and ears of Gemma the Giraffe (see image 2.16).

This is done by pre-mixing enough of your color to dip into repeatedly, keeping the color consistent each time, and working in one direction stroke by stroke to evenly apply the color across the desired area.

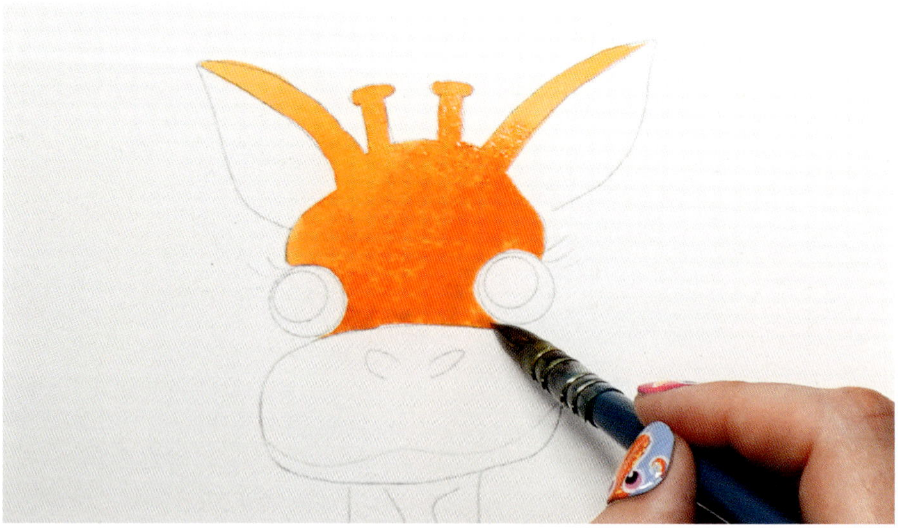

IMAGE 2.16

GRADIENT WASH

A gradient wash is a variation of the flat wash, but instead of working with just one color, you transition the color or saturation as you refill your brush.

To do this, start with a flat wash and leave a bead of water and color at the bottom where you want to transition the color. Then, dip into either water or a mixture of the color you want to transition to. If you want a long, smooth transition, only dip the tip of your brush each time. If you want a more rapid transition, wash your brush and then grab the new color. We use a gradient wash to transition to a less saturated color on Owen the Otter's face (image 2.17) and a gradient between multiple colors on Padma the Pigeon's neck (image 2.18).

VARIEGATED WASH (A.K.A. MESSY WASH)

A variegated wash is my favorite wash because it's the most forgiving. I like to call it a messy wash because it doesn't need to be perfect, and in this wash, you can dip into any number of colors as you move around the page, which creates some natural variation. It also builds in the little "mistakes" we often try to avoid in the other washes.

The key with this wash is to always leave each area with a little puddle of the previous color so you can pull it into the new one. Most of the backgrounds in this book use a variegated wash. Some have subtle variation and some have more obvious variation, like Gertrude the Guinea Pig's background (see image 2.19).

Washes in action

Want to see how each of these washes is achieved in real time? Scan the QR code to watch the video.

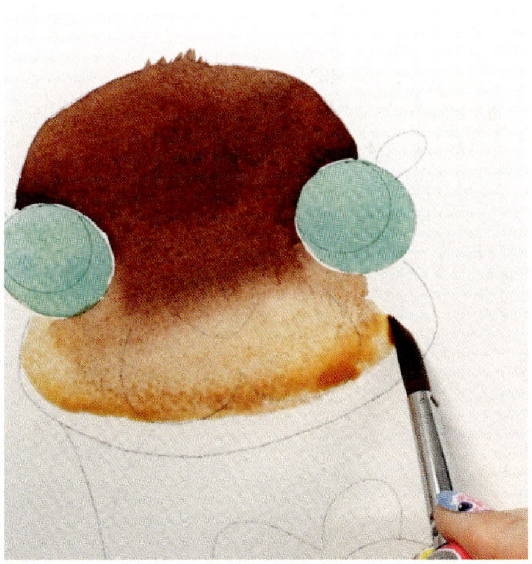

IMAGE 2.17

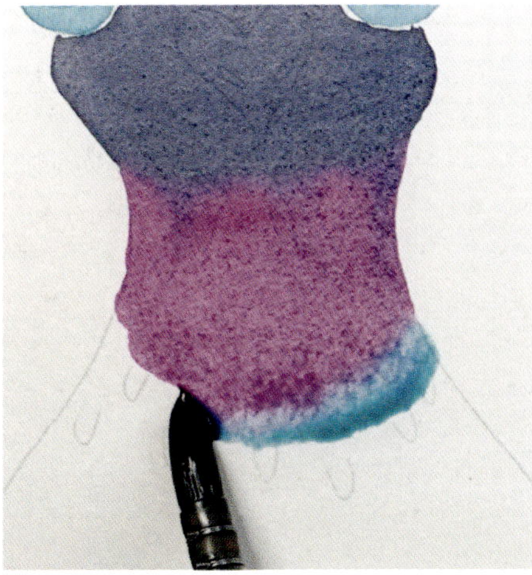

IMAGE 2.18

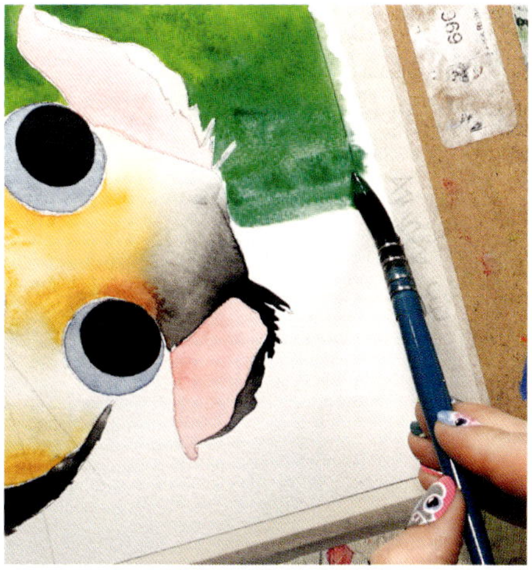

IMAGE 2.19

LIFTING

Lifting is one of my favorite watercolor techniques. It can be used to fix mistakes or accidental puddles of water as well as create texture and variation in saturation. There are just so many things you can do with lifting—I love its versatility!

Lifting in action

Watch this video for some tips and tricks about lifting. You can practice lifting with Mai the Manatee.

To lift watercolor means you remove some of the color you've previously placed on the page. You can lift watercolor when it's wet or dry using the following techniques:

- **To lift wet watercolor,** simply either dab the area with a paper towel or rag, or wash and dry your brush and then run it along the area where you want to remove color.
- **To lift dry watercolor,** you need to re-wet the area with a bit of water, and then you can use a brush or a paper towel to lift the pigment.

Image 2.20 shows how to lift out light rays for the background of Mai the Manatee's painting. Typically, not all of the color will be removed, but it will lighten. You might observe that some colors lift better than others.

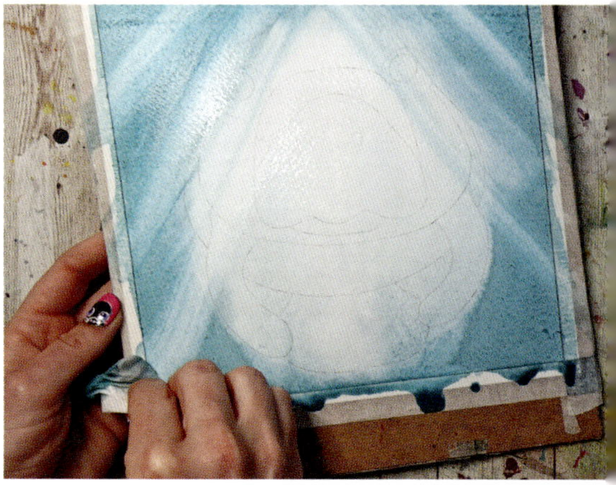

IMAGE 2.20

KEEPING WHITE SPACE

Making things white in watercolor is super easy because you simply don't have to paint them. For example, in the Belinda the Bat painting (see image 2.21), the teeth are created by painting around them and leaving them white. If you forget to keep the white space, you can always use your white gel pen to draw it back in!

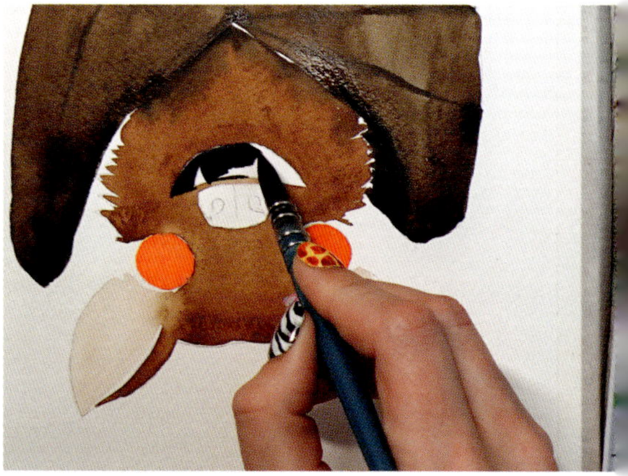

IMAGE 2.21

CHARGING

Charging means loading your brush with concentrated pigment and touching the brush on another color that's still wet on the page, dropping some of the new color into the wet paint. Charging has a couple of primary uses:

- **Adding colors and variation.** Using another color or another saturation of a color with the charging technique can add some fun texture and color. In this book, we do this in the Ollie the Octopus painting in order to give the skin some fun texture (see image 2.22).
- **Adding shadows.** Strategically charging in darker colors along an edge you want to push back creates shadow. We often do this to separate the body from the head in the paintings of this book. You can see this demonstrated on Kylie the Koala.

CHARGING TIP

You'll notice that the areas where you place your brush down and pick it up have bigger dots of color, because more of it is deposited at these points—so be strategic about where you begin and end your strokes!

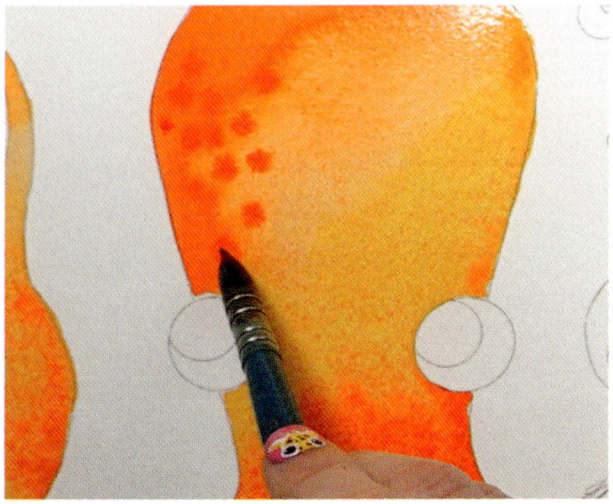

IMAGE 2.22

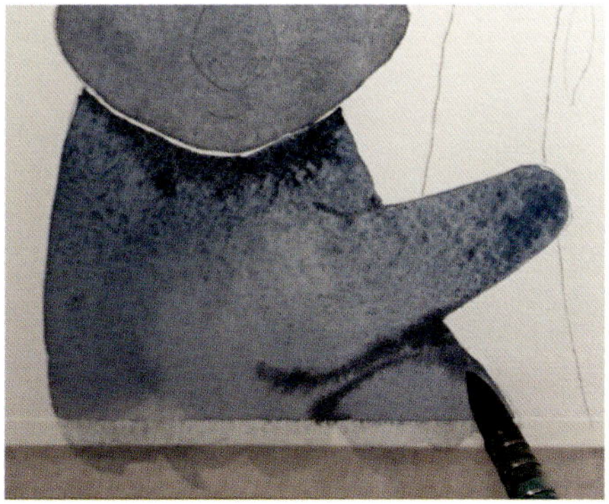

IMAGE 2.23

Charging in action

Do you tend to add too much color or water when charging? Watch this video for some tips on charging.

As you can see in image 2.23, I painted the body with a solid gray color and then, while it was still wet, dipped the tip of my brush into black and dragged it along the underside of the head, as well as the arm and leg shadows.

DROPPING IN

Charging is also often referred to as "dropping in." Dropping in usually means adding touches of color into an unpainted, wet area of the page, allowing the color to organically spread through the water-only wash. This technique is used in Gertrude the Guinea Pig to create the multi-colored fur. You can also drop in on a color wash, which you can see in Preston the Puffer Fish.

ADDING TEXTURE

Sometimes you want a nice smooth color and appearance, but sometimes you want to add a bit more texture to a background or area. I have two favorite ways to achieve this.

1 **Salt.** Sprinkling salt onto a wet area creates a really interesting texture. We use salt a couple times in this book, as you can see with the Hal the Hammerhead Shark example in image 2.24—the unique background texture is a result of salt. The water and pigment surround the salt particles and make interesting patterns as it dries. Here are a couple things to keep in mind with salt:

- The type of salt you use matters; you will get different effects depending on the grain of salt you choose. I typically like a flaky or course-ground sea salt. You can get some effects from table salt, but they are a lot more subtle.
- Add salt to really wet color. If you don't have enough water and color, the salt won't do much, so make sure you sprinkle it on while your paint is nice and wet. Let this dry on its own to get the most impact.

2 **Blooms.** Blooms happen when clean water pushes wet pigment away and creates fun dots with interesting patterns. The way you create a bloom is to wash your brush and fill it with water and then lightly dot the water onto the colored area while it is still wet, ideally around the satin stage. We use blooms to create a fun background texture on the Dottie the Donkey painting (see image 2.25).

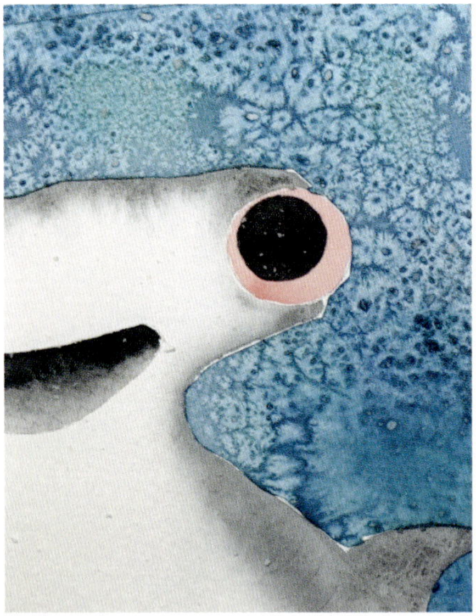

IMAGE 2.24

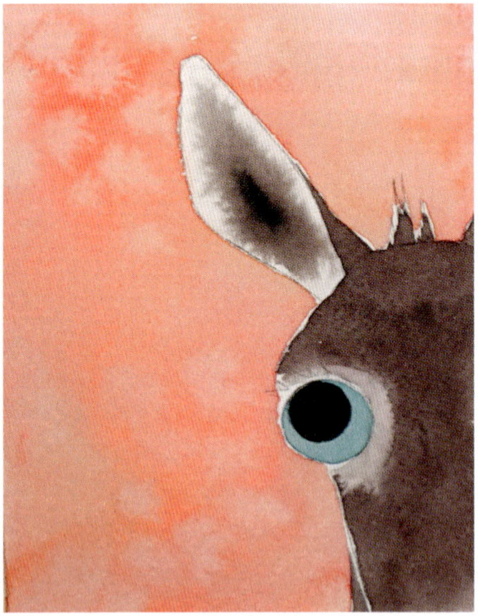

IMAGE 2.25

Blooms in action

Blooms grow more than expected, so don't add too many. Scan the QR code to see blooms develop!

LAYERING

Layering is a powerful watercolor technique that allows you to add contrast between different shapes. To layer watercolor, the previous layer must be completely dry, otherwise the colors will just run together. You'll use this technique in each painting in this book to add the pupils to the eyes, like in Paolo the Platypus (see image 2.26). In order to do this, you'll paint the full circle with the eye color, dry it, and then paint in the black pupil on top.

Dry layers can be achieved through patience and simply waiting for them to dry. Or you can use a hair dryer or heat gun to speed up this process. If you choose to use a tool to help speed drying time, make sure your desk is free of things that might blow away, and keep the tool moving around the page at all times so it doesn't sit too long on any one spot and burn your paper. I am an impatient painter, so unless the effect I want to achieve requires me to wait, I always choose to make it dry!

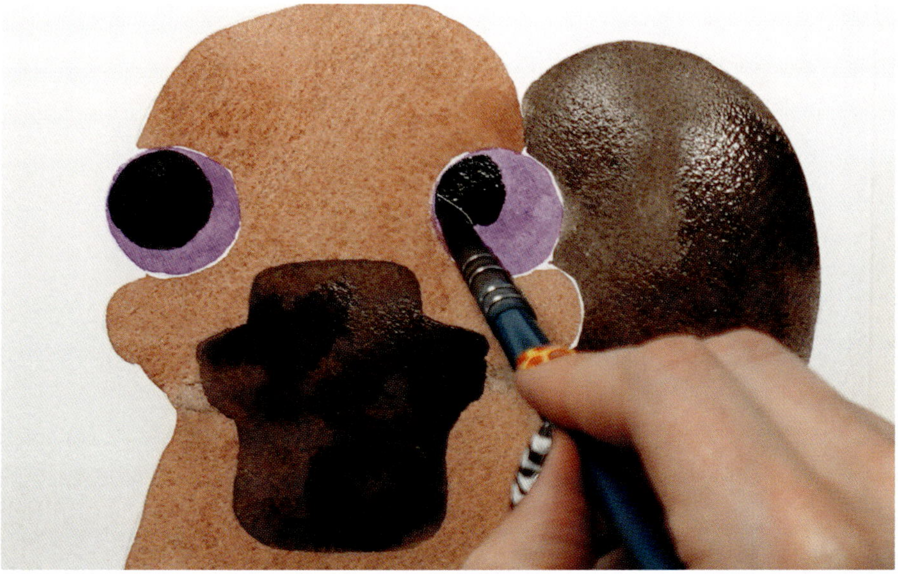

IMAGE 2.26

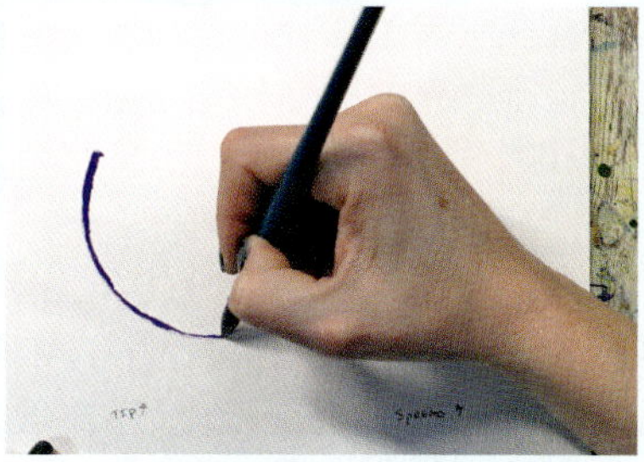

IMAGE 2.27

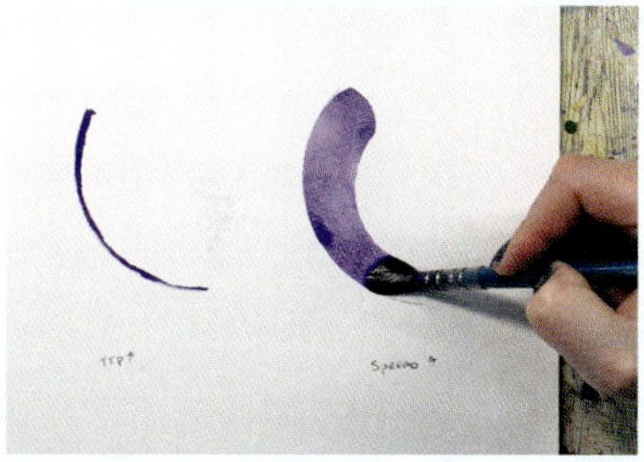

IMAGE 2.28

Brush control tip

The tip of your brush is key to getting into tight spaces, but it can be tricky to make smooth lines. In image 2.27, I am trying to follow the curve of a line I drew, and by using the tip of my brush I can get close, but it's a little shaky. One of the best things you can do to get smooth lines is spread your brush. Using the full range of the bristles to spread and then drag them along the curve will help you get a smoother appearance, as you can see in image 2.28.

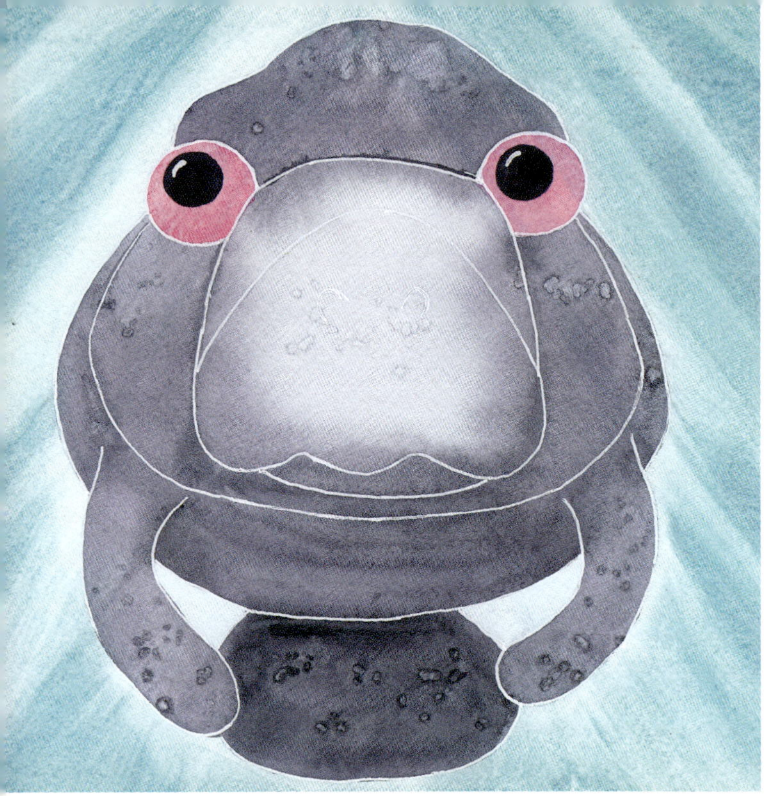
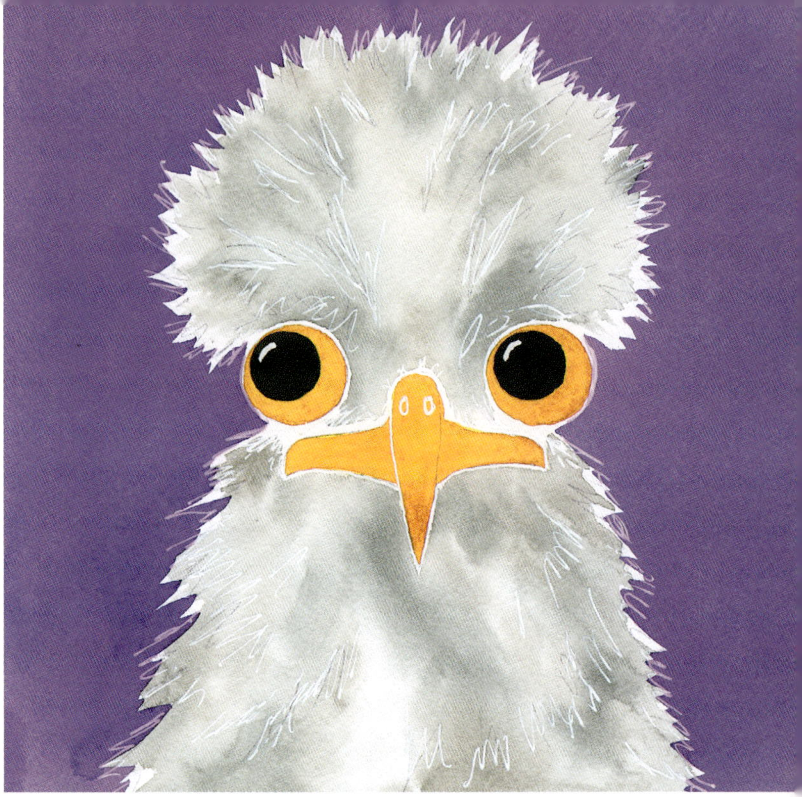
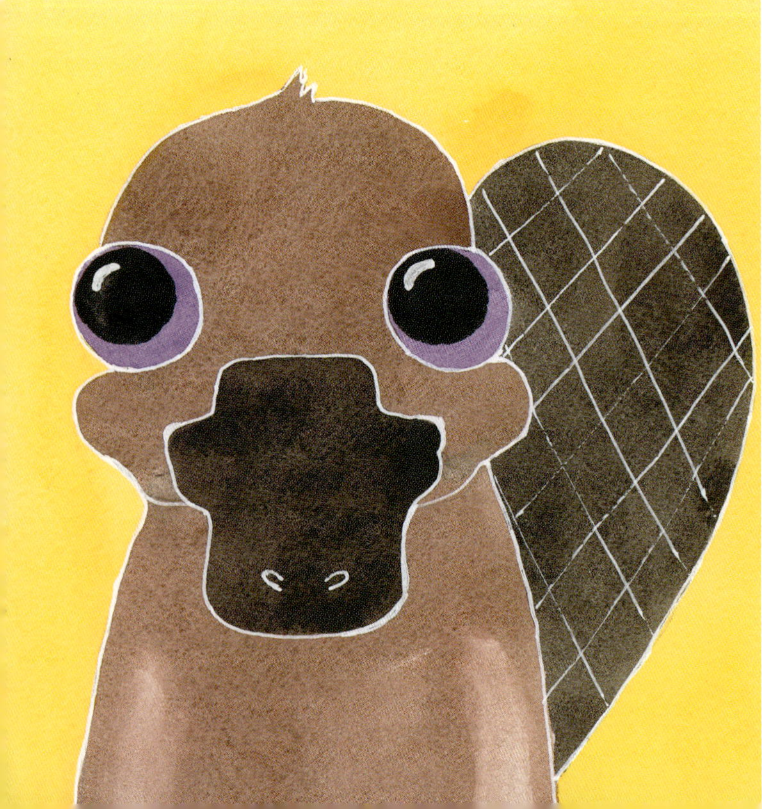
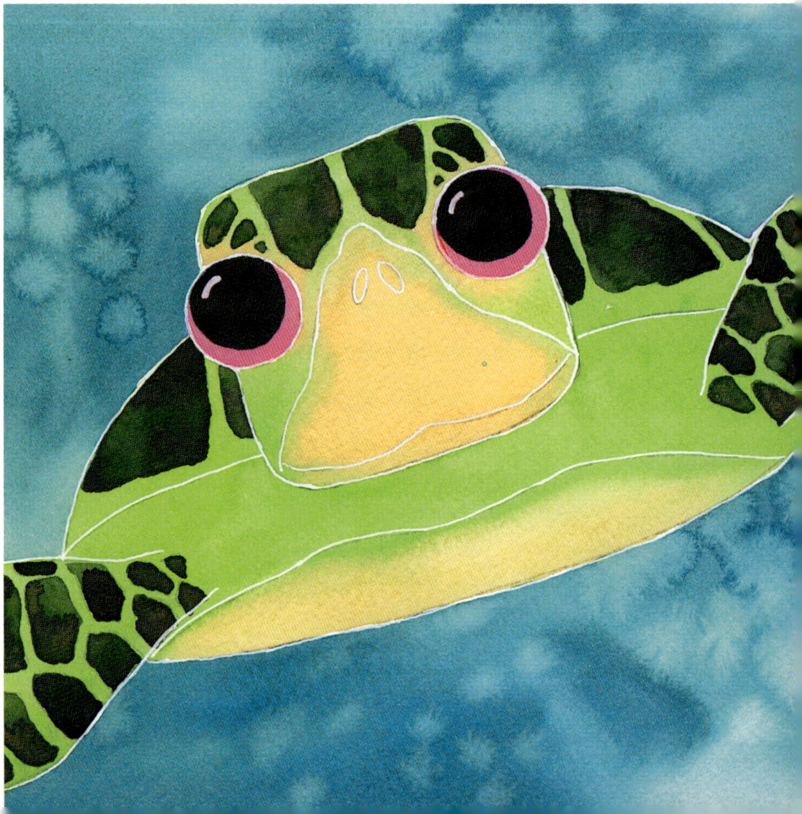

PAINTINGS

Color Palette

Orangey Yellow
Light Beige
Dark Brown
Pink
Black
Purples

Techniques

Layering, page 29
Lifting, page 26
Watercolor Washes, page 24
Wet-on-Wet, page 14

Paint along with me Scan the QR code to watch a video where I paint Gemma the Giraffe.

GEMMA THE GIRAFFE

Did you know that the pattern of spots on every giraffe is unique, just like our fingerprints? So, if you paint outside of the lines a bit or add an extra spot, it will make your giraffe unique, just like they are in real life. You may think I've exaggerated the eyelashes on our friend, Gemma, but giraffes actually do have huge eyelashes, so don't forget those!

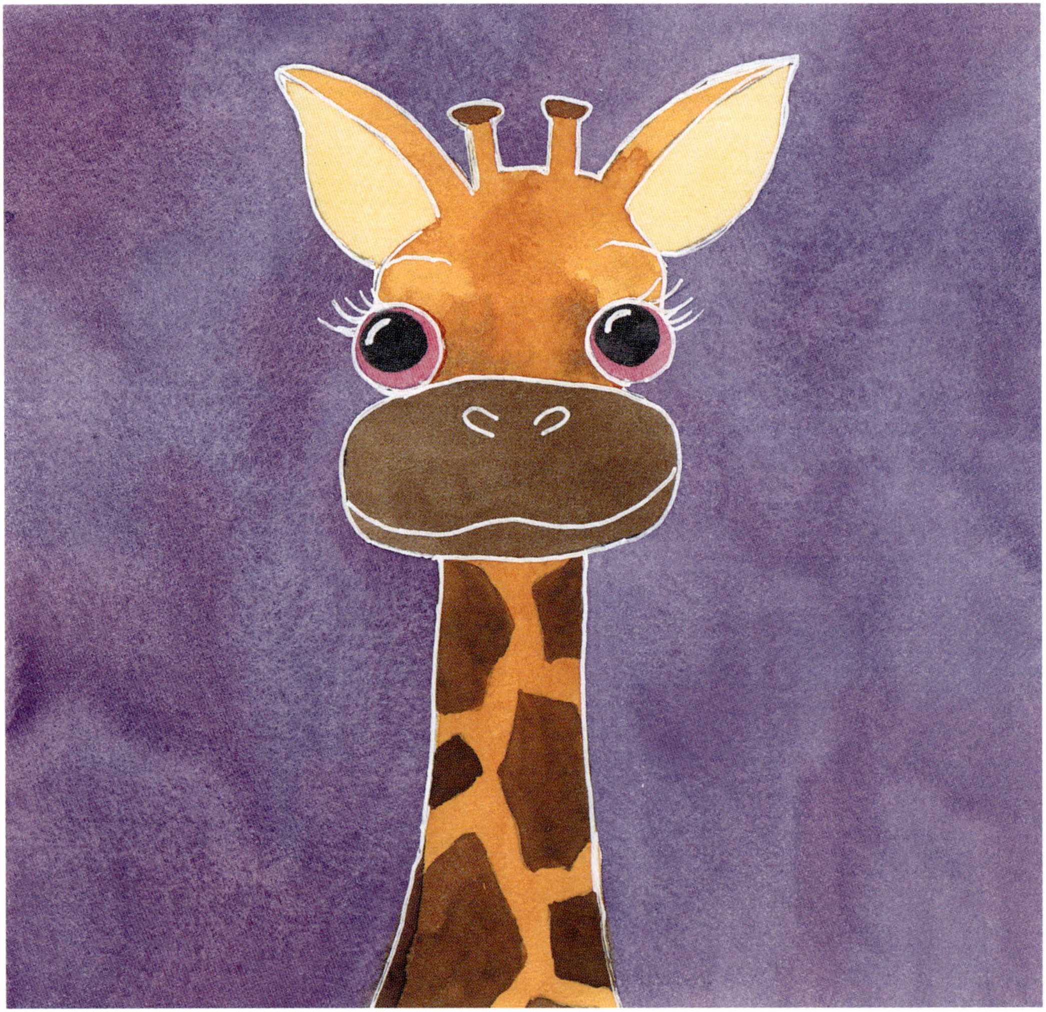

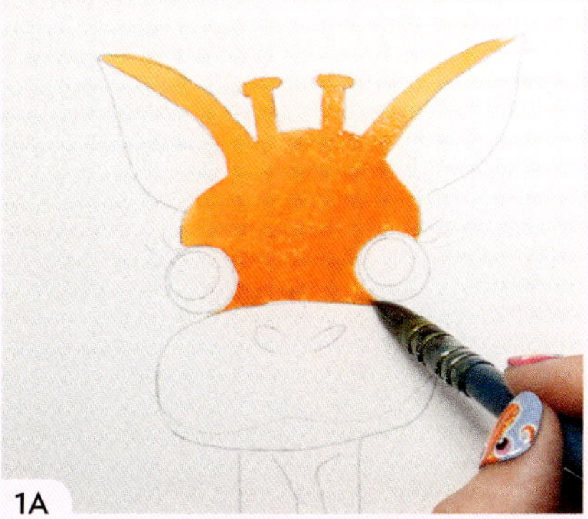

1A

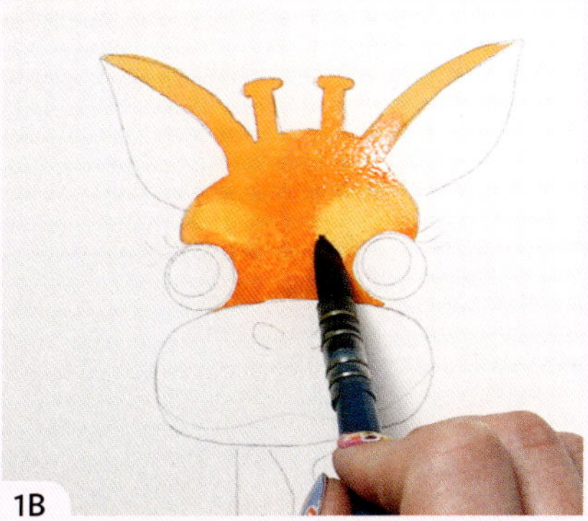

1B

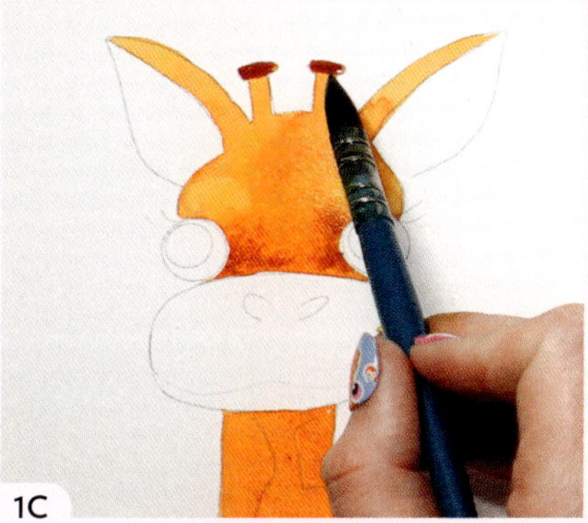

1C

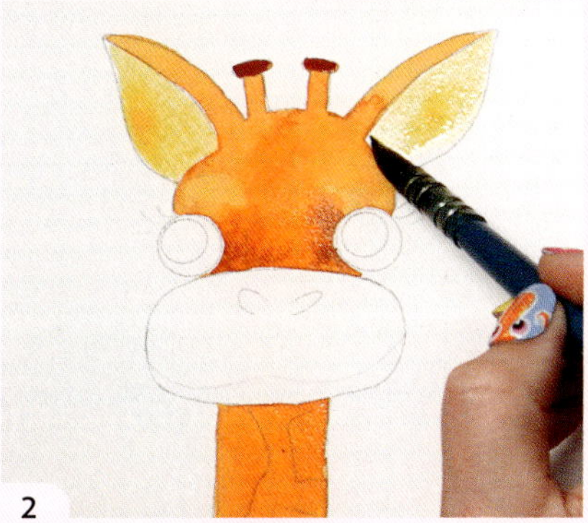

2

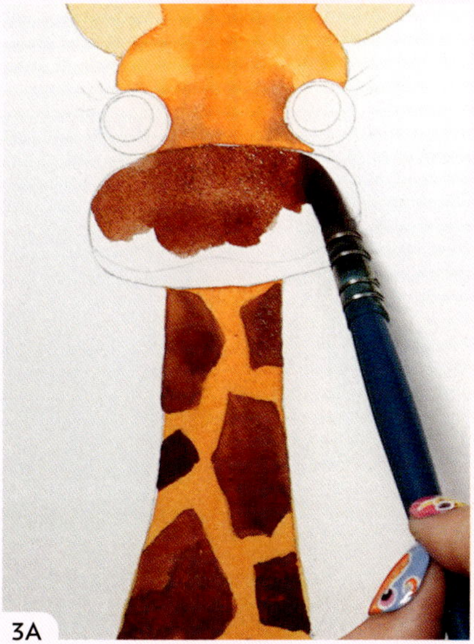

3A

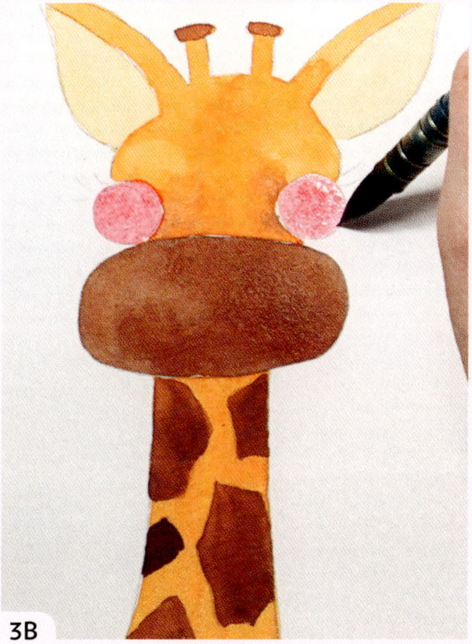

3B

Step 1

Put some water in a mixing well and add in yellows and oranges until you have a nice bright color. Avoiding the giraffe's eyes, apply this color to the head, tops of the ears, and ossicones (the two points on the top of a giraffe's head) (1A).

Giraffes have pronounced brow bones above their eyes, so we're going to gently lift a little color to bring those forward. To do this, wash and dry your brush off and gently swipe your brush on the still-wet color (1B).

Then continue this color onto her long neck. While the head is still wet, wash and dry your brush and dip straight into a pan of brown paint. Drop that color around the eyes and tops of the ossicones (1C).

Step 2

Put some clean water in one of your mixing wells and then fill your brush with the color you used for the giraffe's head and neck. Mix this into the clean water to create a more desaturated color for inside the ears. Apply this within the ears. Let this layer dry or make it dry!

Step 3

Prepare by mixing a dark brown color and a little of a light pink color. Paint the dark brown color in each of the spots and on the snout (3A).

Paint the insides of the eyes with the light pink color or a color of your choice (3B). Let this dry or make it dry!

Step 4

Make sure your black watercolor is activated so you can grab the concentrated color straight from the pan. Also, place some water in two mixing wells, and then mix up lots of purple or pinky colors for the background. I chose purple because it's the complement to the yellow in the body. Fill your brush with concentrated black and add the pupils of the eyes (4A).

Using a messy wash for the background, switch between your purply colors and adding water with your brush to completely cover the background (4B). Remember, we'll be cleaning things up with white outlines, so if some areas don't touch or some areas slightly overlap previous layers, that's completely fine. Let this dry or make it dry!

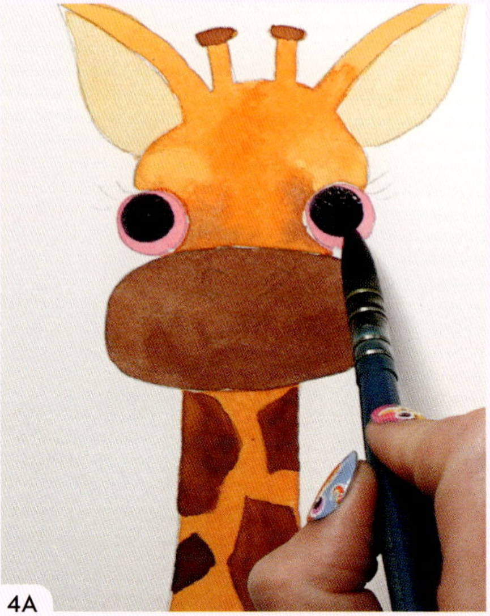

4A

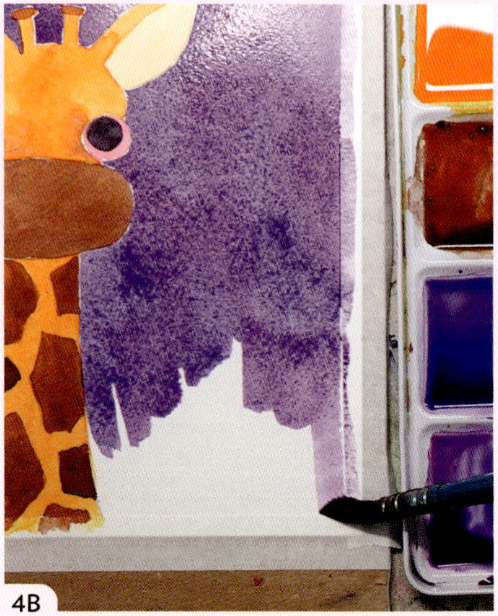

4B

Step 5

Once the painting is dry, the white outlines will really bring it to life. Outline the neck, head, and all the individual shapes, and then add in details like the mouth, nostrils, eyelashes, and highlights in the eyes!

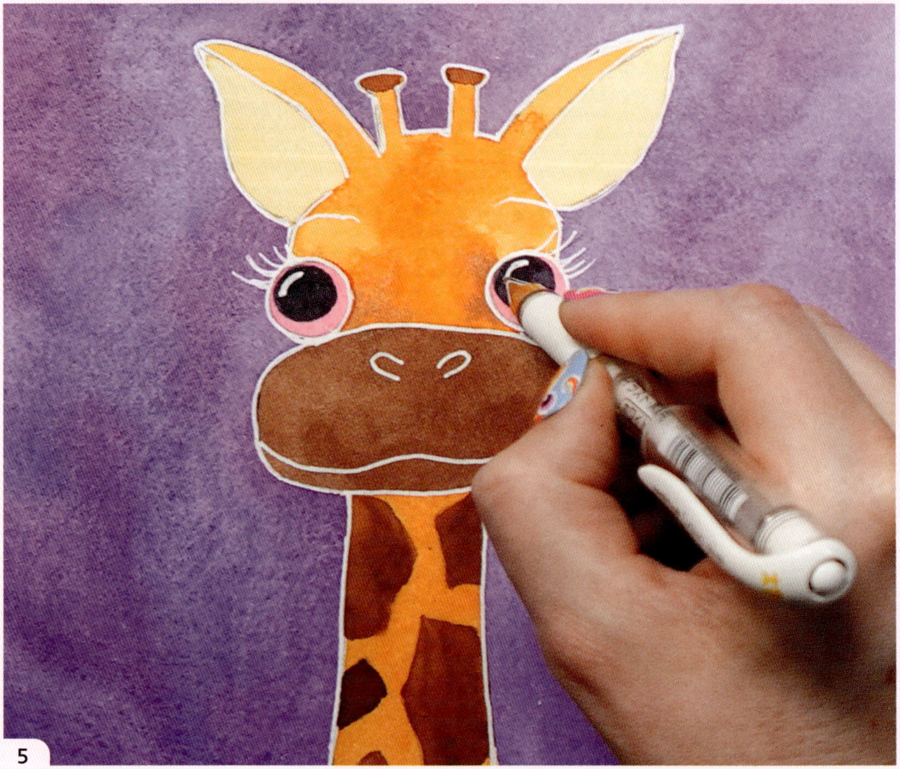

5

KYLIE THE KOALA

Fun fact: Koala bears aren't bears at all. In fact, they are marsupials, which means they are more closely related to kangaroos than bears! In this cute koala painting, a green background and a few simple outlines of leaves help create the feeling of being in a forested area.

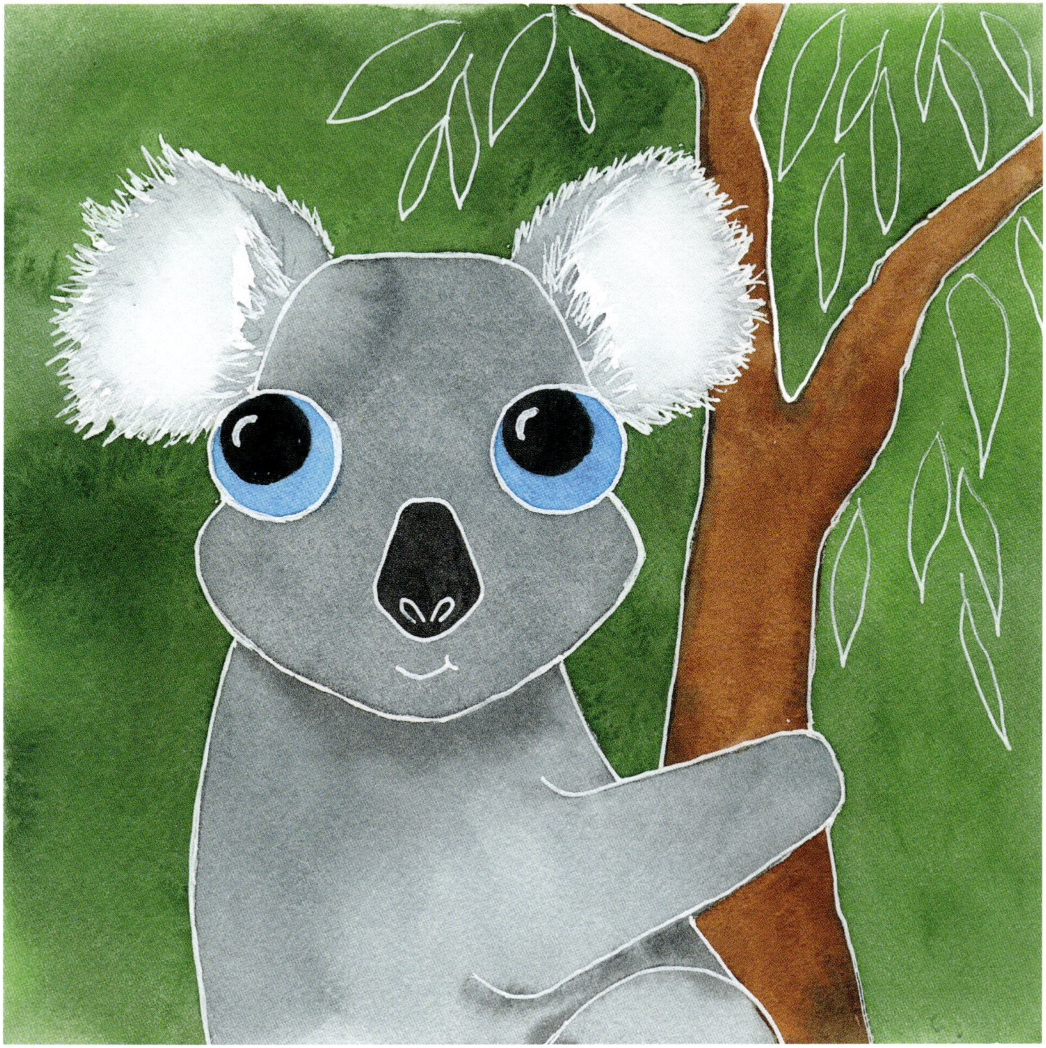

Color Palette

Gray
Light Blue
Brown
Black
Greens

Techniques

Charging, page 27
Layering, page 29
Softening Colors and Edges, page 24
Watercolor Washes, page 24

Step 1

Start by spraying some water into a mixing well and then mixing up a gray color. You'll want to have a good amount of this color to paint the koala's head and body. Start by painting the head, avoiding the eyes (1A). Once the entire head, including over the nose, has been painted, bring the color up onto the tops of the ears, and then flick your brush around the edges to give a furry appearance (1B).

Quickly wash your brush and fill it with clean water. Then touch the tip of your brush to the part of the ear you just painted and bring it toward the inner ears (1C). This will soften the color from the outside fur to the inside of the ear. Leaving a little white space is fine here. Repeat this on the other ear.

Use the same gray color as the head to fill the body and arm of the koala. I like to leave a little gap between the head and the body so they don't touch (1D).

To add a little shadow to the body, you can dip your brush directly into your black watercolor and then drop that color lightly along the top of the body, under the arm, and on top of the leg (1E). Let this dry or make it dry!

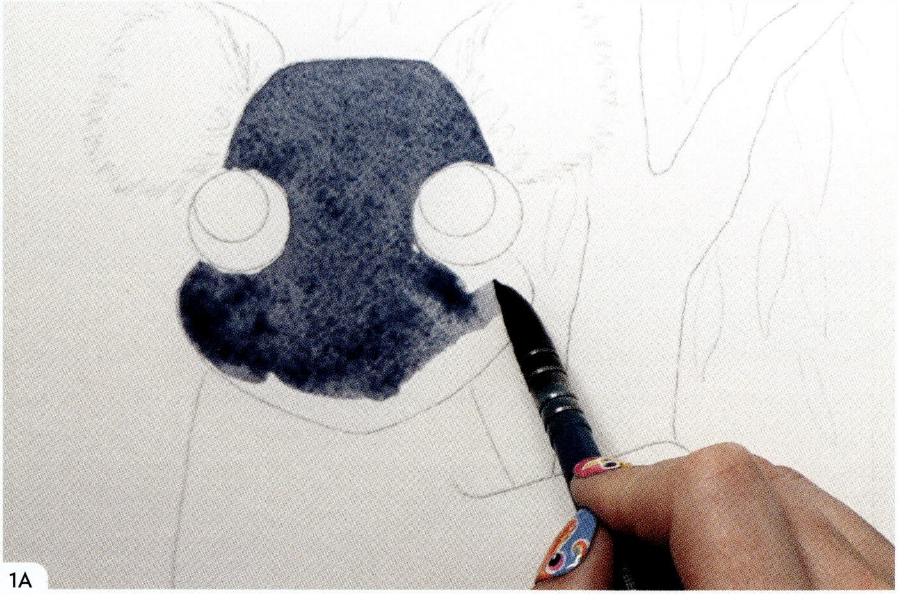

1A

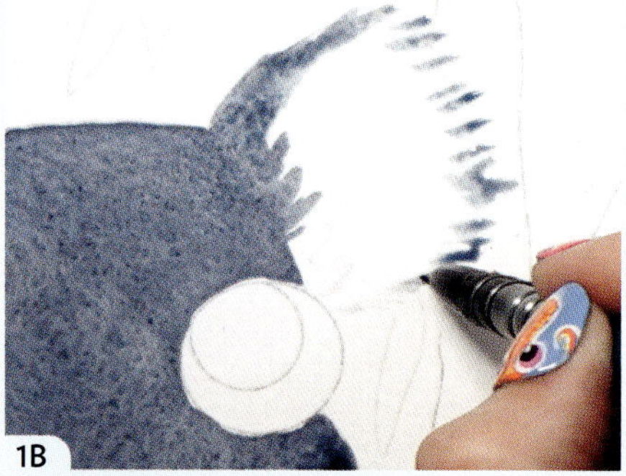

1B

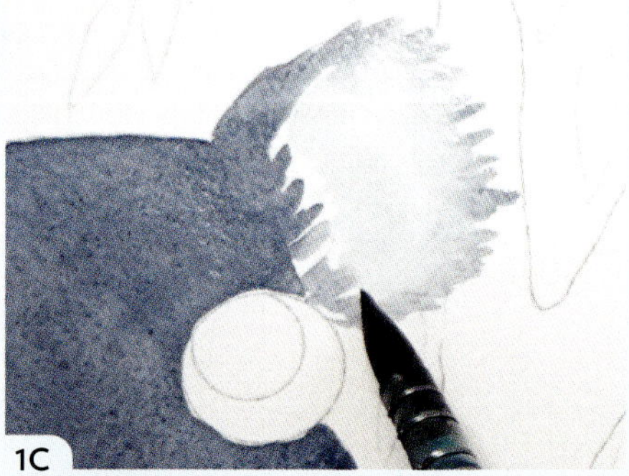

1C

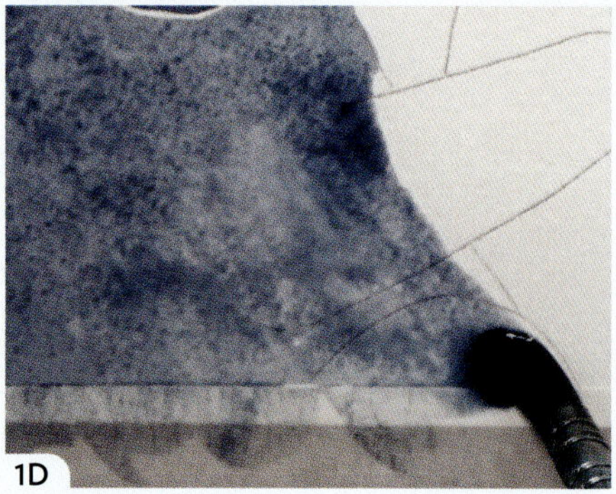

1D

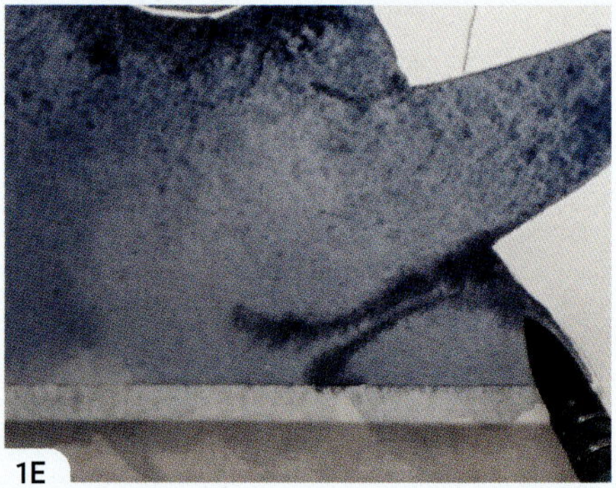

1E

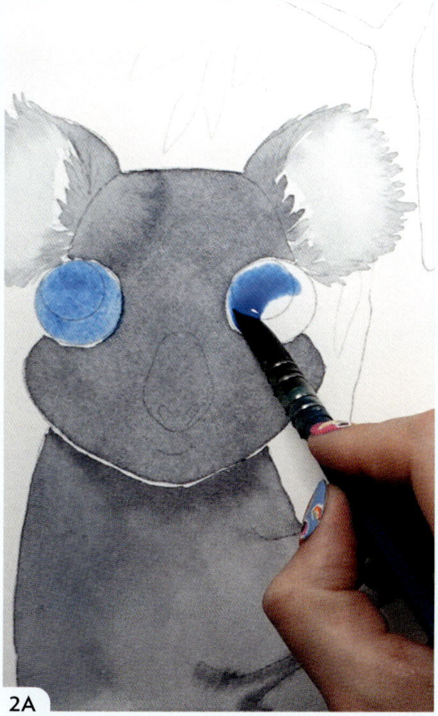
2A

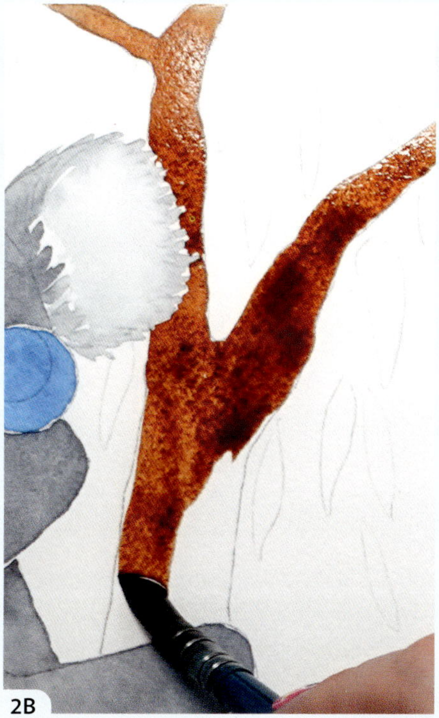
2B

Step 2

Before beginning this step, mix up some light blue and brown. I chose to go with a reddish-brown to complement the green background we'll be using. Paint the eyes with the light blue color (2A).

Fill the trunk of the tree with the brown color (2B). After you've filled in the trunk, you can dip straight into your black watercolor, fill your brush with a concentrated amount, and then drop it along the edges of the tree to add a little variation (2C). Let this dry or make it dry!

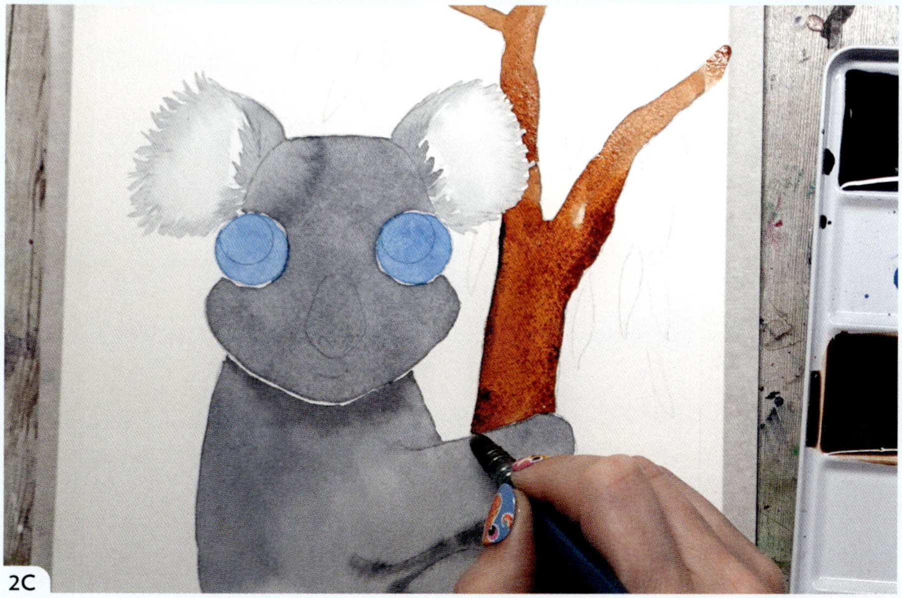
2C

Step 3

Start by making a small puddle of a concentrated black color and mixing up larger quantities of a couple green colors, enough to allow you to cover the background. Using the concentrated black color, fill the pupils of the eyes and the nose (3A).

Use a messy wash of greens to fill the entire background (3B). Remember, we'll be cleaning things up with white outlines, so if some areas don't touch or some areas slightly overlap previous layers, that's completely fine. Let this dry or make it dry!

Step 4

Grab your white gel pen and outline all the parts of the painting. Add in details like extra scribbles on the ears for fur, the nostrils, the little smirk, the leaves in the background, and, of course, the highlights in the eyes!

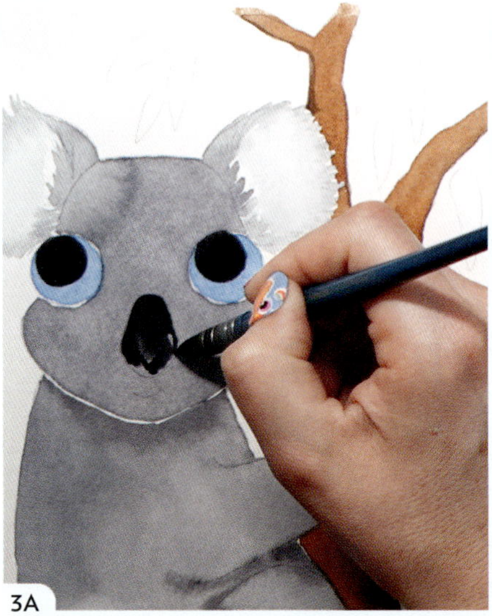
3A

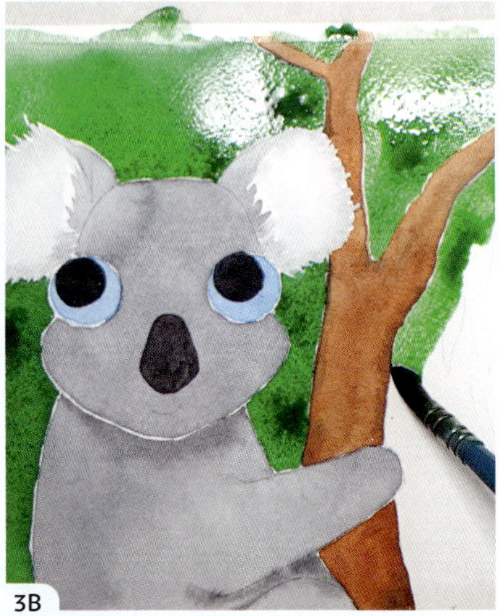
3B

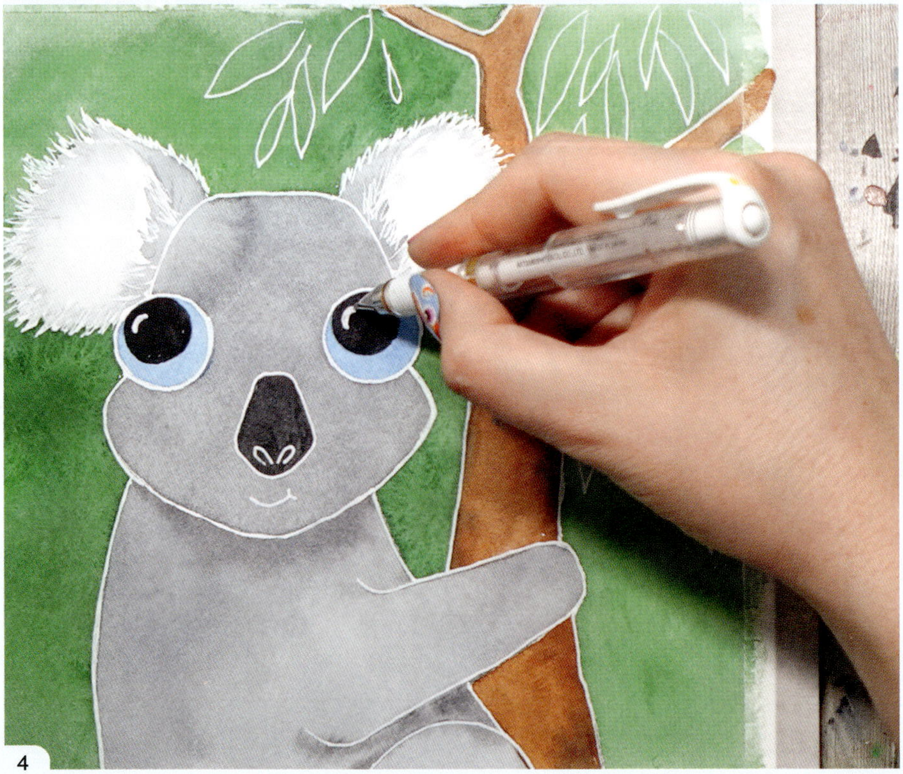
4

PEARL THE PUG

Did you know that pugs are one of the oldest breeds of dogs? They can be traced back to 400 BCE and were originally bred as devoted companions in China. Painting pugs in this style is perfect, because their natural eye position is quite complementary to this cartoon look!

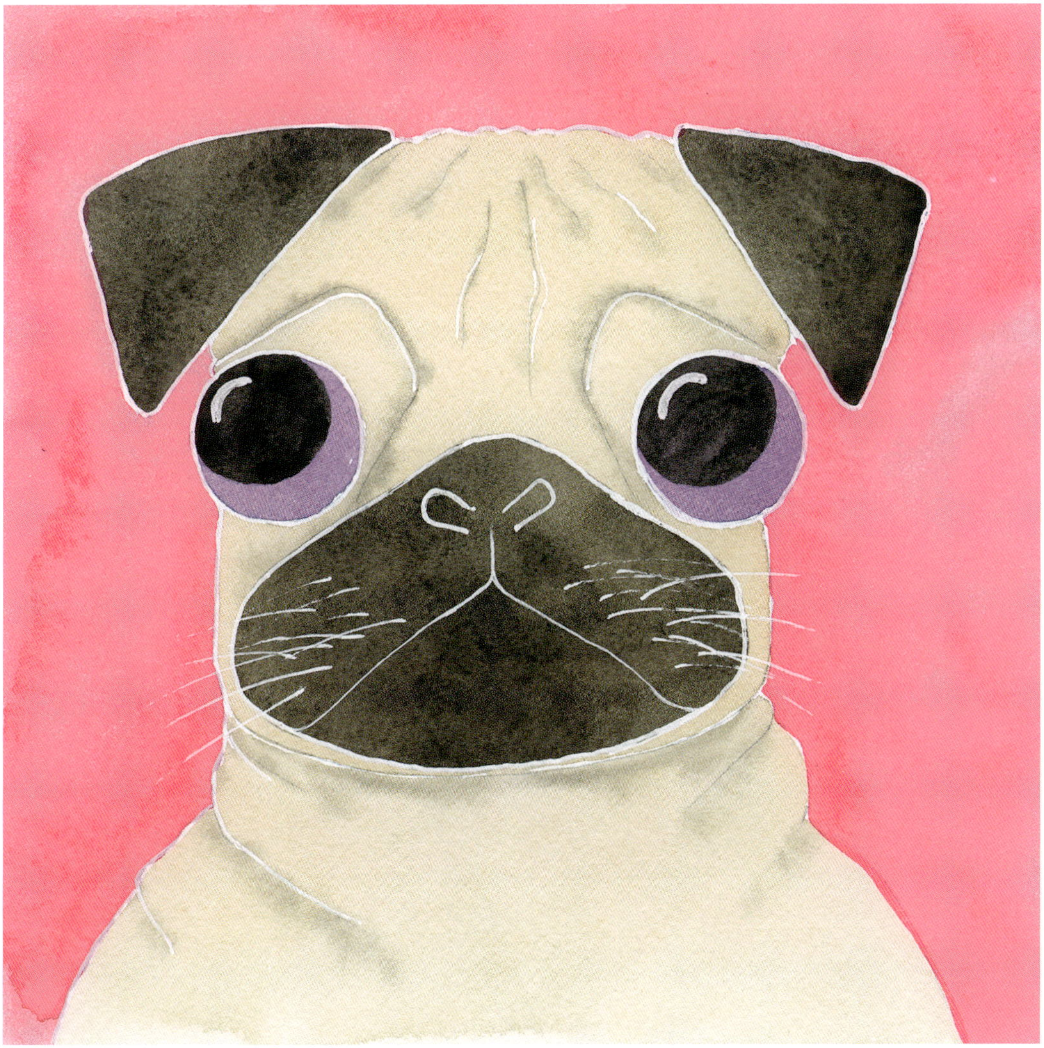

Color Palette

Light Beige
Dark Brown
Black
Purple
Pinks

Techniques

Layering, page 29
Lifting, page 26
Watercolor Washes, page 24
Wet-on-Wet, page 14

Step 1

Spray some water into a well and mix up a light beige color, or any color you want, for the pug's fur. Make sure there's enough to easily cover the head and body. Paint the face, avoiding the eyes (1A).

While the paint is still wet, dip the tip of your brush into a dark brown or black color, and lightly add some of that color along the indicated fold lines in the face (1B).

Repeat on the body, dropping a little of the dark color along the top edge where the body meets the chin and indicated folds while the beige color is still wet (1C). Dropping this in while it's wet means it will soften into the body instead of making harsh lines. Let this dry or make it dry!

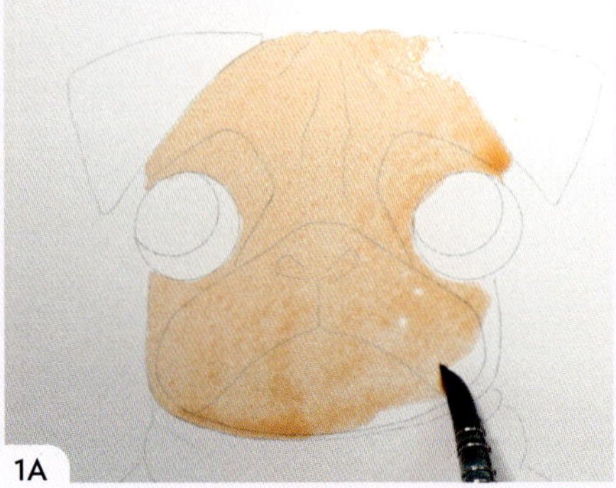

1A

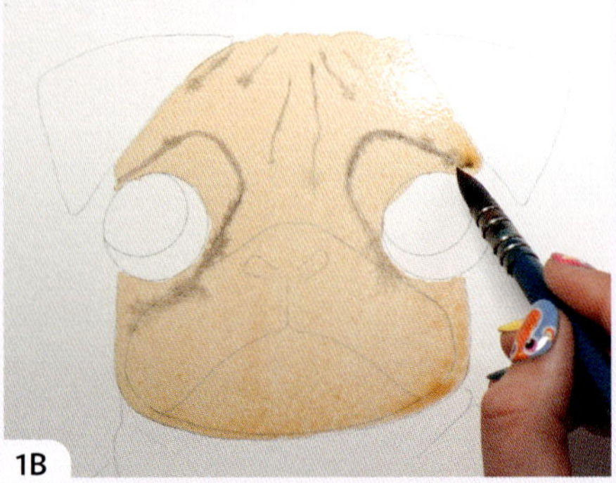

1B

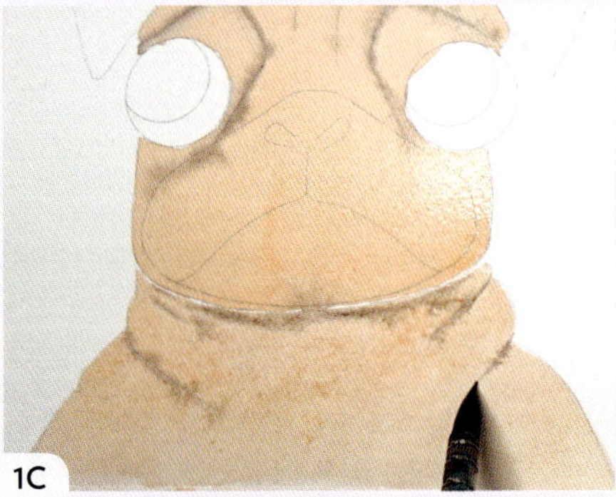

1C

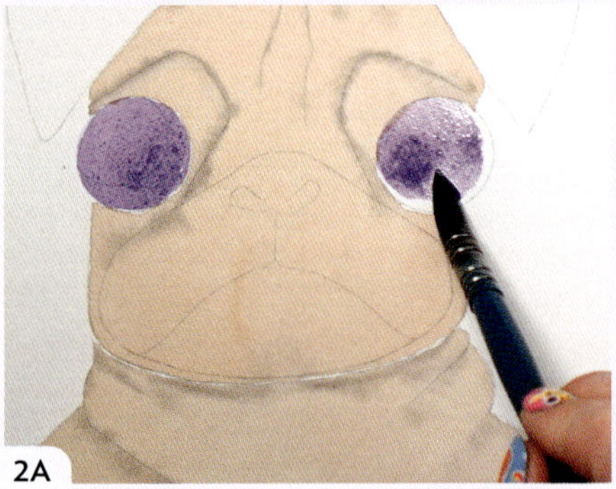

2A

Step 2

Mix up a little puddle of a light purple and a larger puddle of dark brown. Fill the eyes with the purple color (2A).

Using the dark brown color, paint the ears and the snout (2B). Let this dry or make it dry!

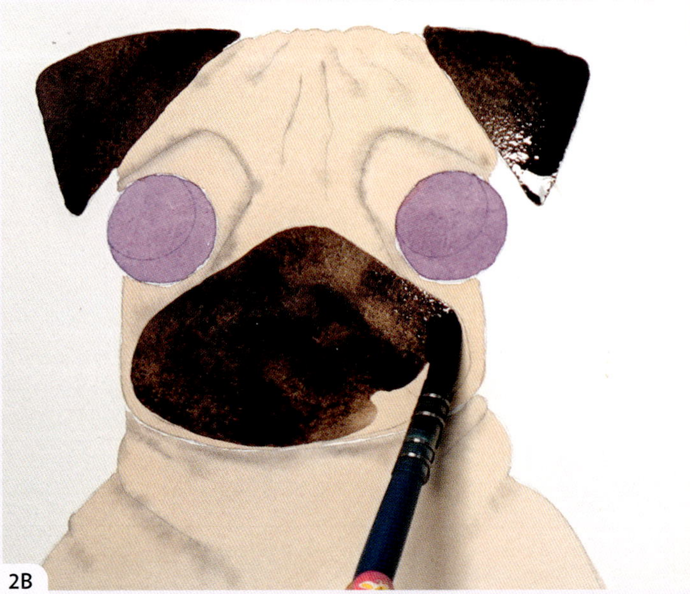

2B

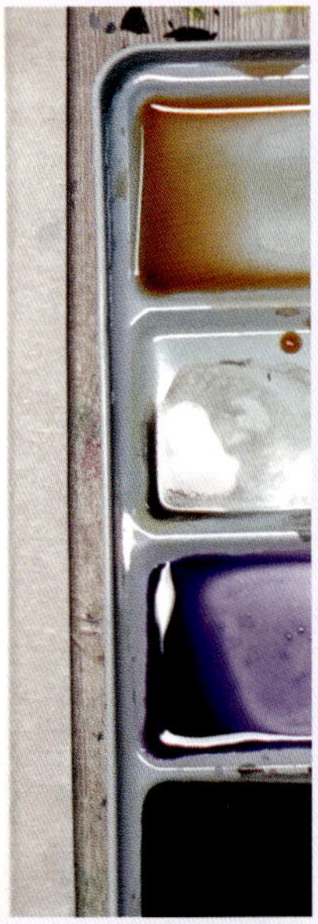

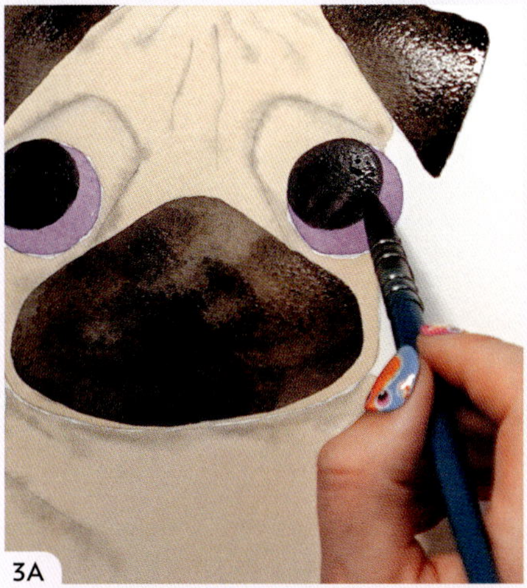

3A

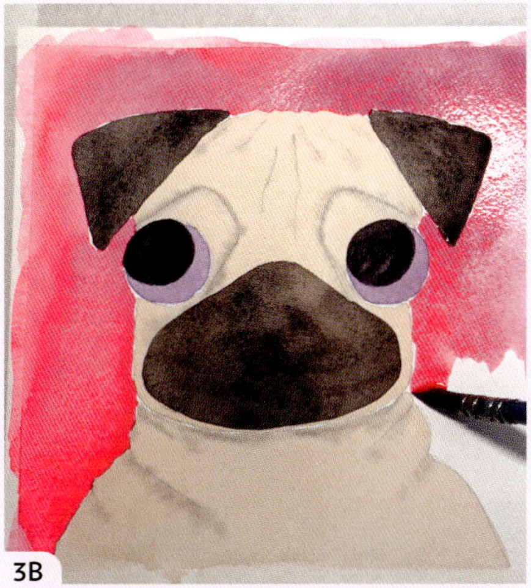

3B

Step 3

Spray some water into two wells and mix up larger quantities of a couple of pink colors, enough to cover the background. Activate your black watercolor so you have easy access to concentrated black. Dip your brush into your black watercolor, grab a concentrated amount, and paint the pupils of the eyes (3A).

Paint a messy wash of pinks on the background (3B). Remember, we'll be cleaning things up with white outlines, so your background doesn't have to exactly touch the outlines. It's okay if a little white pops out or you slightly overlap with the outline. Let this dry or make it dry!

Step 4

Grab your white gel pen and outline all the shapes, add in the nose and mouth details, and don't forget the whiskers and highlights in the eyes!

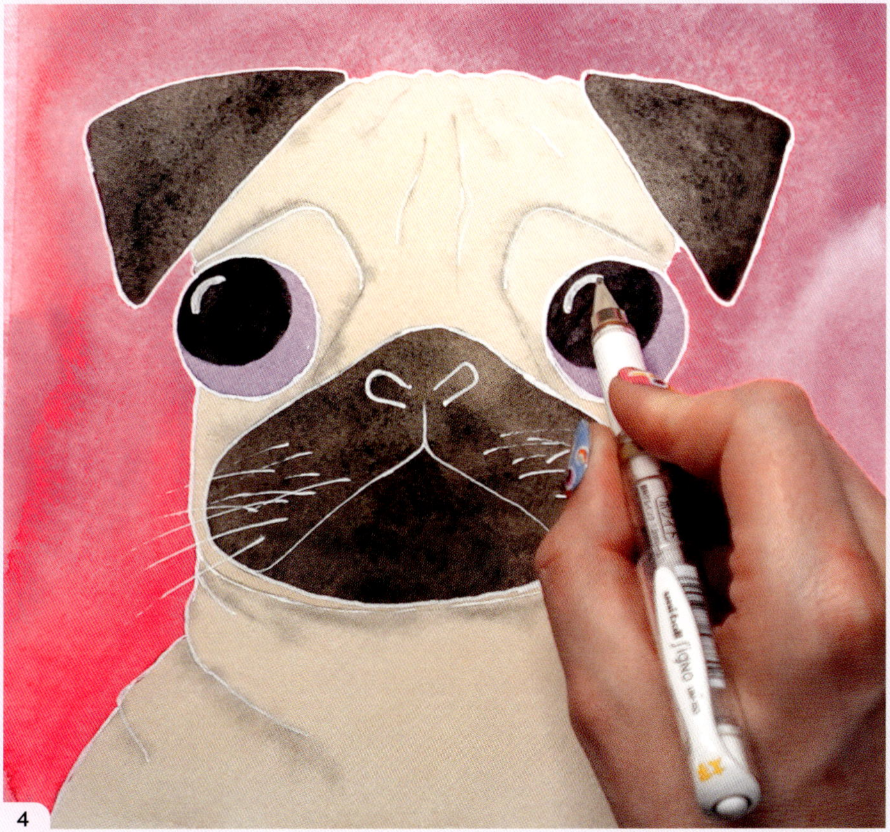

4

Color Palette

Orange

Yellow

Purple

Blue

Teal

Black

Techniques

Charging, page 27

Layering, page 29

Watercolor Washes, page 24

OLLIE THE OCTOPUS

Octopi are smart and curious creatures—they're capable of solving puzzles and mazes! This octopus is super fun to paint because it allows the opportunity to drop lots of fun colors onto his body and really take advantage of the magic of watercolor.

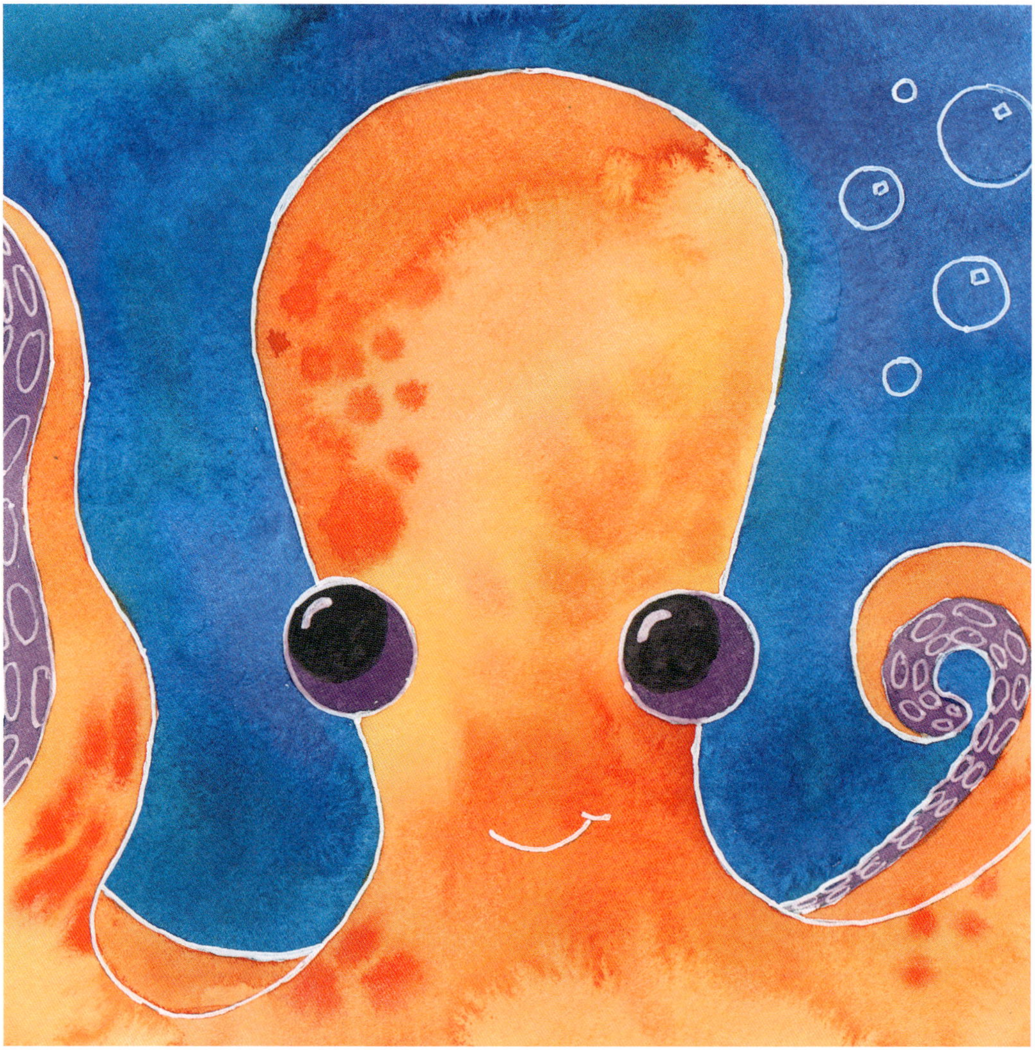

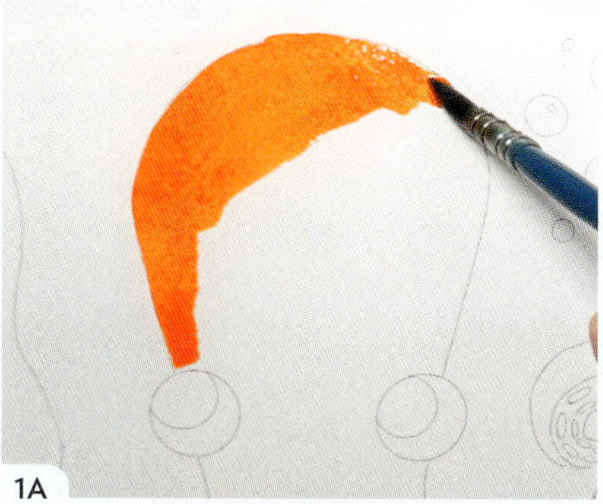

1A

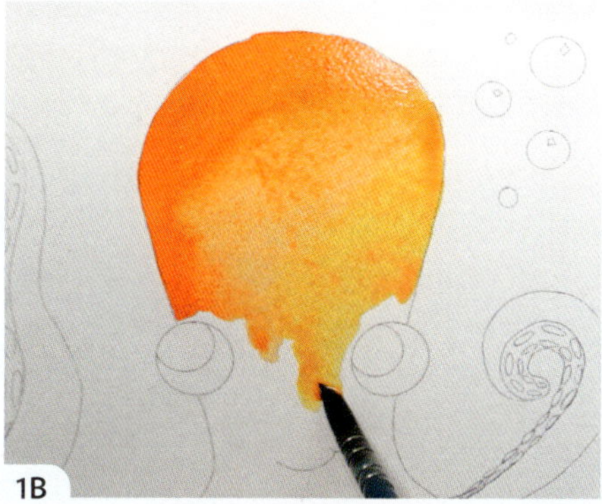

1B

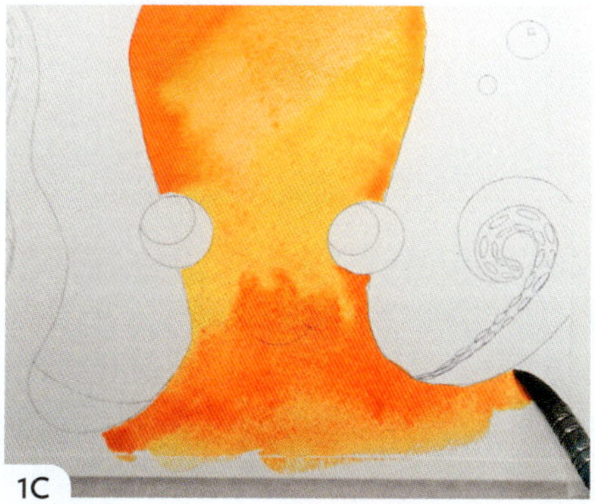

1C

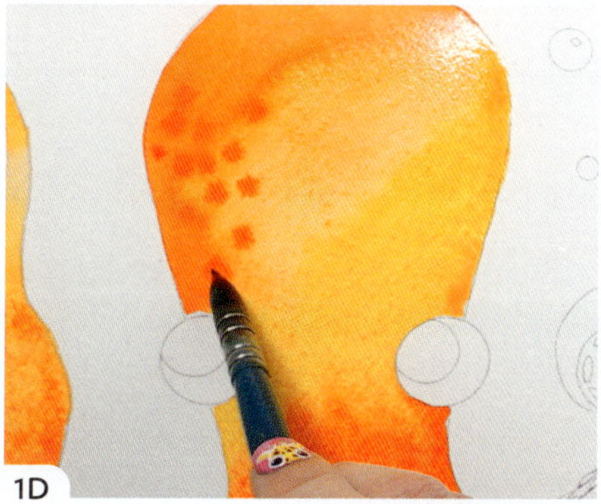

1D

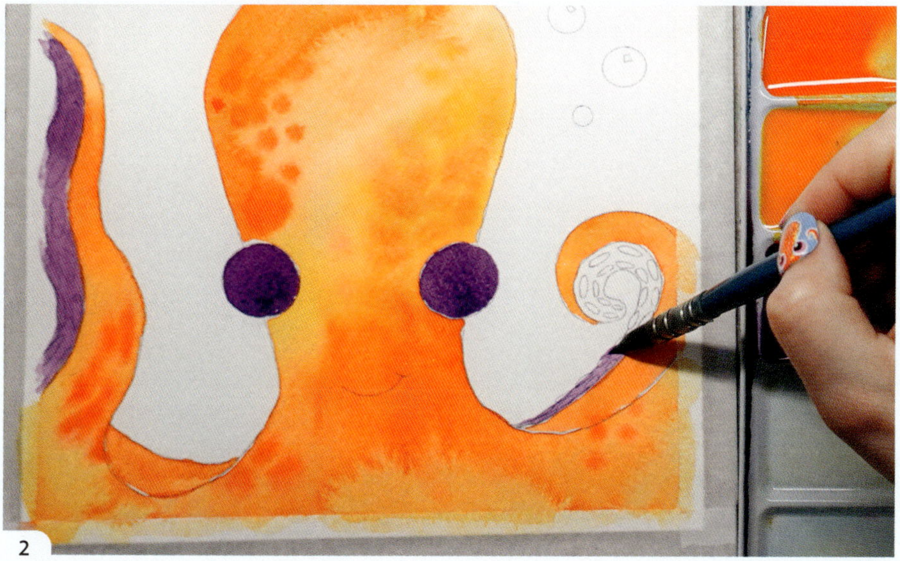

2

Step 1

Prepare for this step by mixing up two wells of fun octopus colors. I chose a saturated orange and a bright yellow.

Starting with the dark orange, or your choice of color, paint the top left part of the head (1A), making sure it stays wet, and then quickly dip your brush into the yellow color and bring that down (1B). Switch between the two colors to fill in the body and tentacles, but avoid adding these colors to the suction-cup sides of the tentacles (1C).

While this is still wet (at around the satin stage), dip your brush directly into orange, red, or pink and drop this in randomly on the body to create a fun texture (1D)! Make sure to repeat this step for the tentacle in the background. Let this dry or make it dry!

Step 2

Mix up a large puddle of a purple color and use that purple to paint in the eyes and the suction sides of the tentacles. Let this dry or make it dry!

Step 3

Mix up a generous amount of some blue and teal colors, enough to cover the background, and use a messy wash to paint in the entire background. Remember, we'll be cleaning things up with white outlines later. Let this dry or make it dry!

Step 4

Dipping straight into a black color, fill your brush and paint in the pupils of the eyes. Let this dry or make it dry!

Step 5

Using a white gel pen, outline the body and suction cups, and add in the mouth, bubbles, and highlights in the eyes!

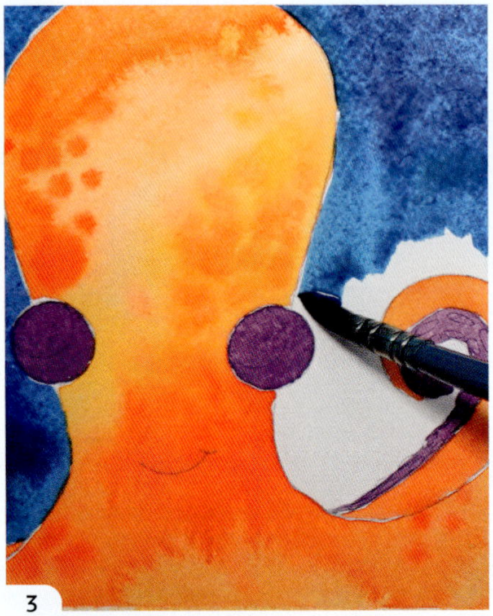

3

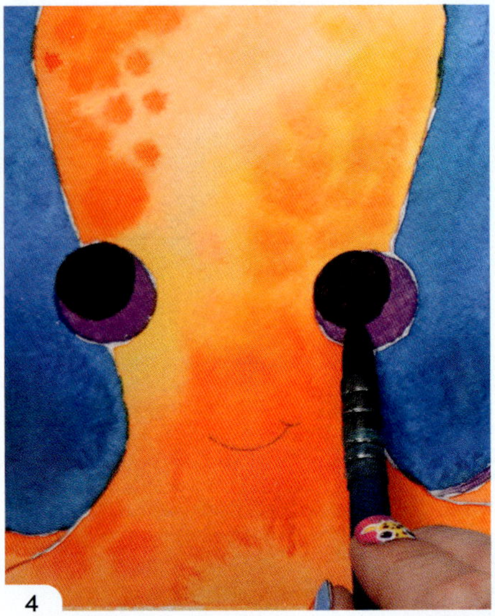

4

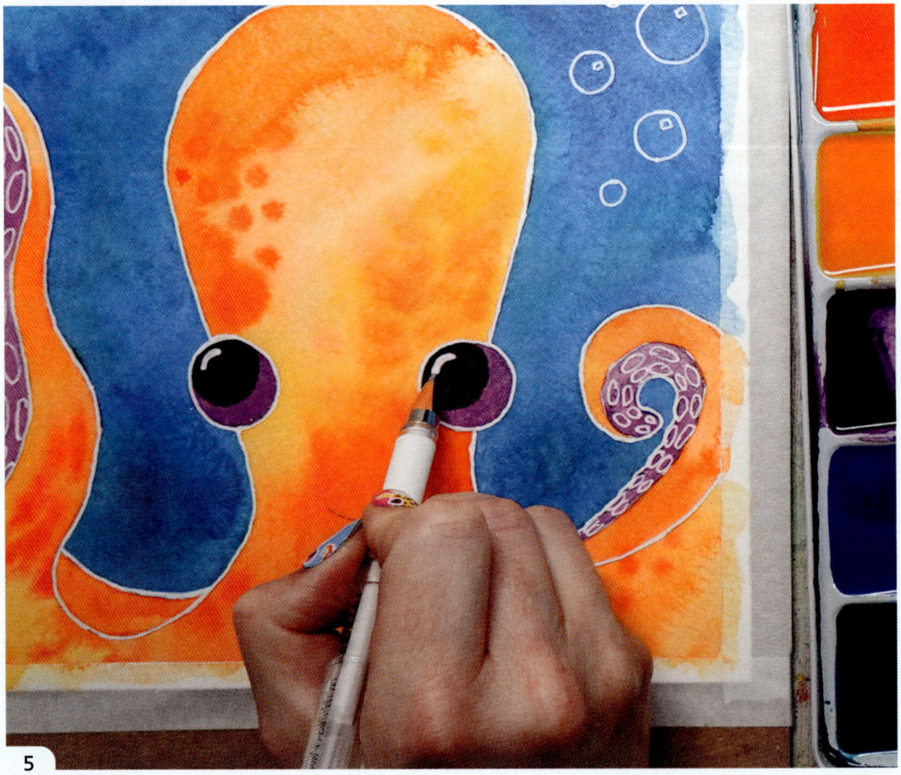

5

PADMA THE PIGEON

If you've been to a city, seeing a pigeon is an ordinary experience—but these birds are anything but ordinary. For thousands of years, pigeons have been used to carry messages and navigate long distances, and they can do it relatively quickly with their average flight speed of 50 to 60 mph (80.5 to 96.6 km/h)! They are super smart and can be trained in many ways, including pattern recognition! I love watching pigeons because of their beautiful color-shifting feathers that shine with greens and purples. The color variation is super fun to paint with watercolor!

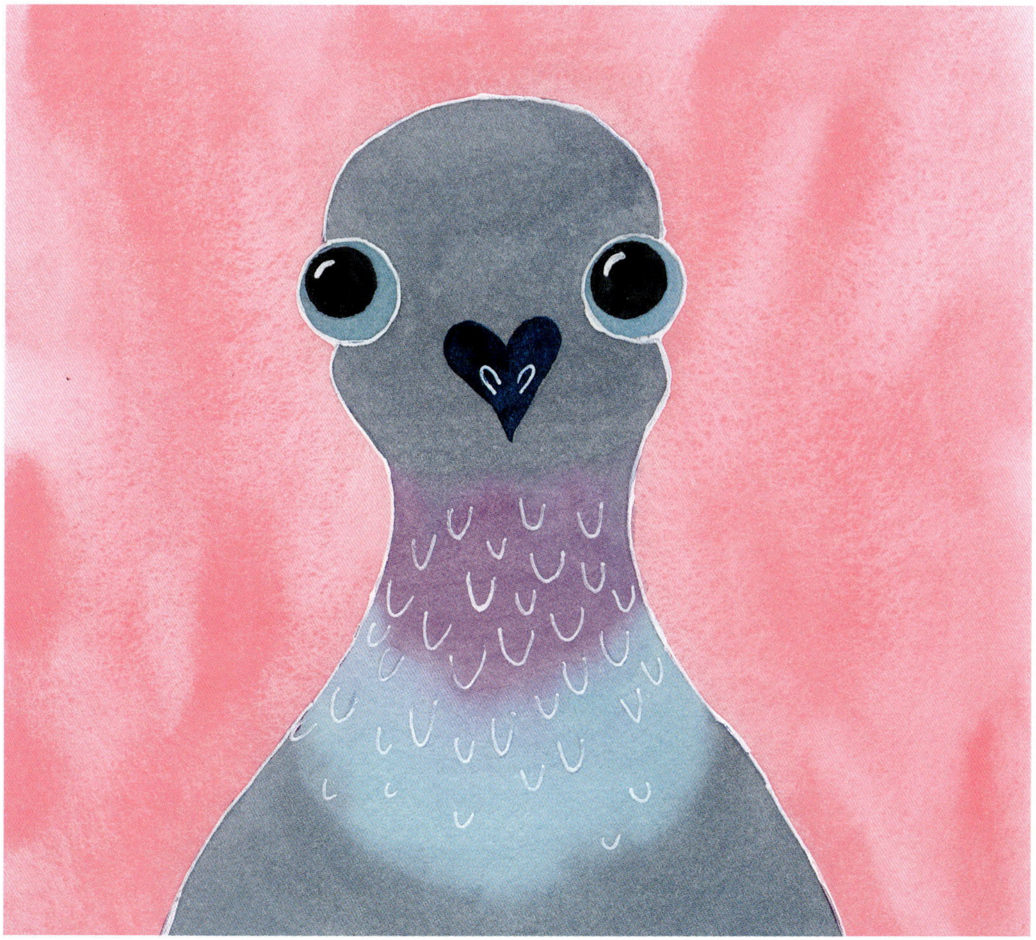

Color Palette

Teal

Gray

Purple

Black

Pinks

Techniques

Layering, page 29

Watercolor Washes, page 24

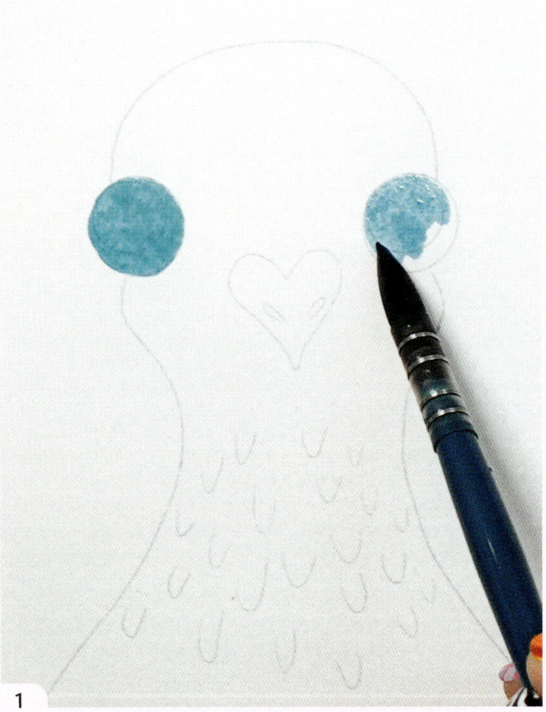

1

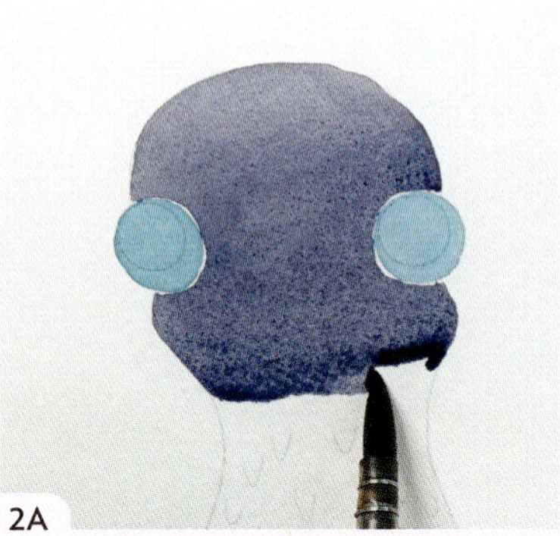

2A

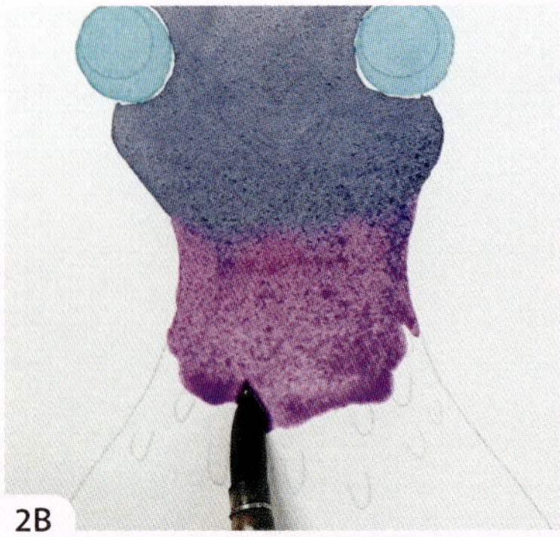

2B

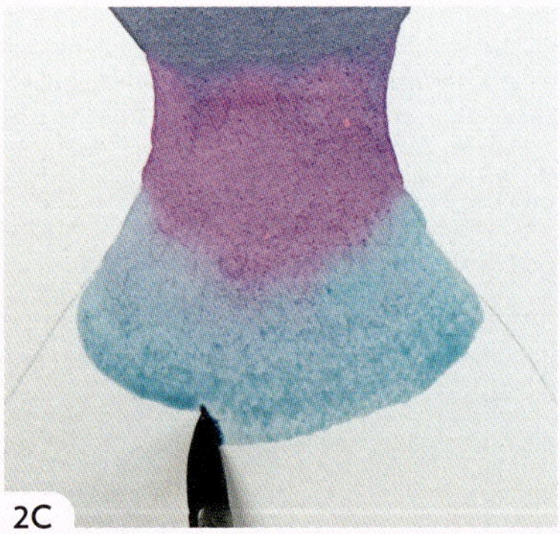

2C

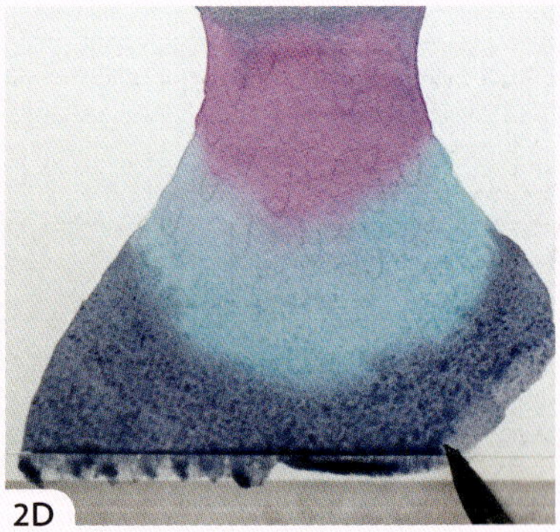

2D

Step 1

Start by mixing up a puddle of a teal. Make sure you have enough of this color for steps 1 and 2. Then fill your brush with it and paint the insides of the eyes.

Step 2

Mix up a large puddle of gray. I chose to mix a little blue into my gray to make a lovely blue-gray color. Mix up a smaller puddle of a purple color, enough to re-dip your brush a few times.

Then wash your brush and load it with the gray color. Fill in the top of the head and reload your brush as you bring it down to about where the colorful feathers start; leave an edge with a drip of the gray color (2A).

Wash your brush and fill it with purple, and then swipe across the drip of the gray color, pulling it down and creating a gradient between the two colors. Refill your brush and swipe it down a few times, making sure you leave a wet drip of purple at the bottom (2B).

Wash your brush and fill it with your initial teal color and then, touching the tip of the brush to the previous wet drip of purple color, pull it down, refilling your brush as you go to transition to the teal color until you're about two-thirds down the body (2C). Leave a wet edge of color here.

Refill your brush with the gray color you started with, grab that wet edge, and bring this color down the rest of the body, refilling your brush as you go so you don't run out of color (2D). Let this dry or make it dry!

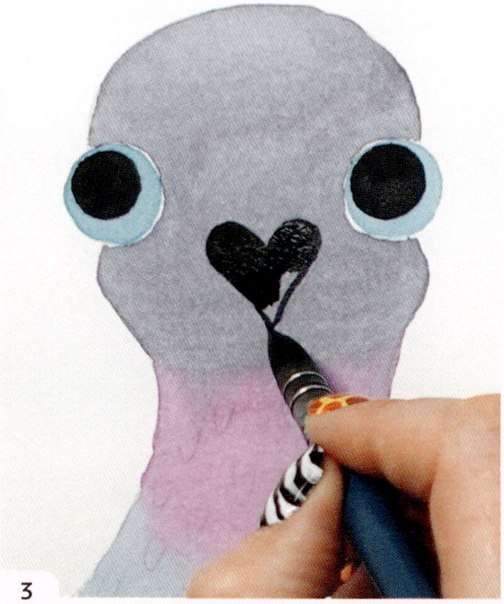

3

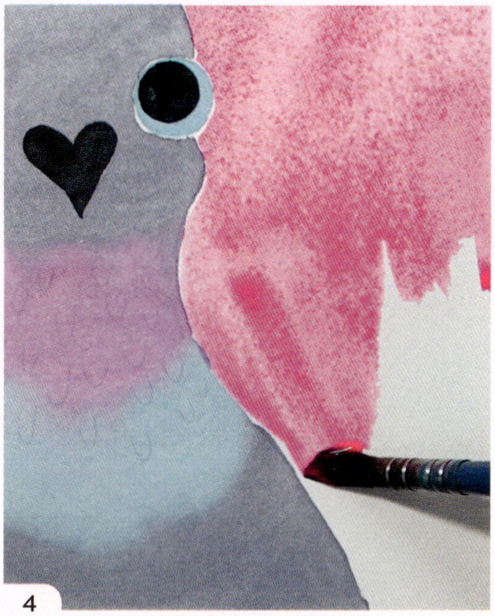

4

Step 3

Wet your brush, and then dip it directly into your pan of black and paint the eyes and beak with black. Let this dry or make it dry!

Step 4

Mix up a few large puddles of pinky colors. I like to make some of mine more saturated than others. Paint a messy wash on the background. I like to switch between different colors as I add them to the background so there's built-in variation, which I find more forgiving. Don't worry about this being perfect! Let this dry or make it dry!

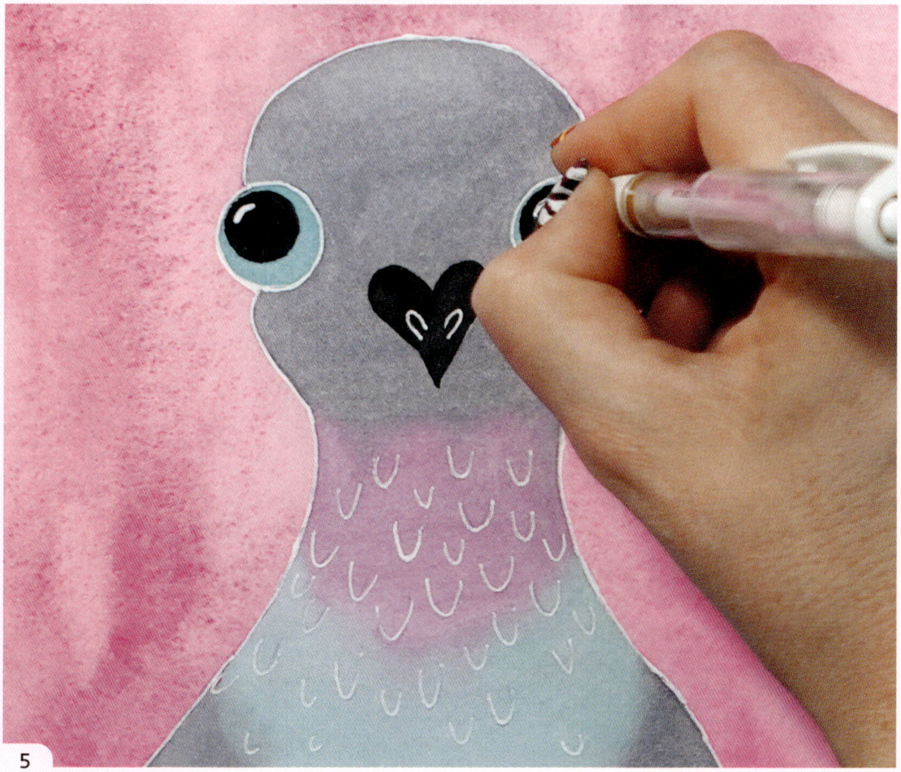

5

Step 5

Grab your white gel pen and outline all the segments of the pigeon, as well as add back in the fun details, like feathers, nostril holes, and, of course, the highlights of the eyes!

Color Palette

Purple

Medium Brown

Dark Brown

Yellows

Black

Techniques

Layering, page 29

Lifting, page 26

Watercolor Washes, page 24

PAOLO THE PLATYPUS

Many years ago, while studying for my master's degree at the University of Sydney, I developed a fascination with the platypus—especially the one at the Taronga Zoo. Each time I visited, I hurried to the platypus exhibit, only to find the tank empty and a sign that said: "Can't spot the platypus? Perhaps he's in his adjoining habitat, check there!" In my determination to spot him, I'd rush to the other portion of the exhibit only to find no platypus and the same sign. After several visits, with this same experience, I was nearly convinced the zoo was pulling a fast one and there was no platypus—just a clever display with signs. On my final visit before moving home, I finally spotted the platypus! Since then I've learned that platypuses are typically nocturnal creatures, which explains my trouble spotting him!

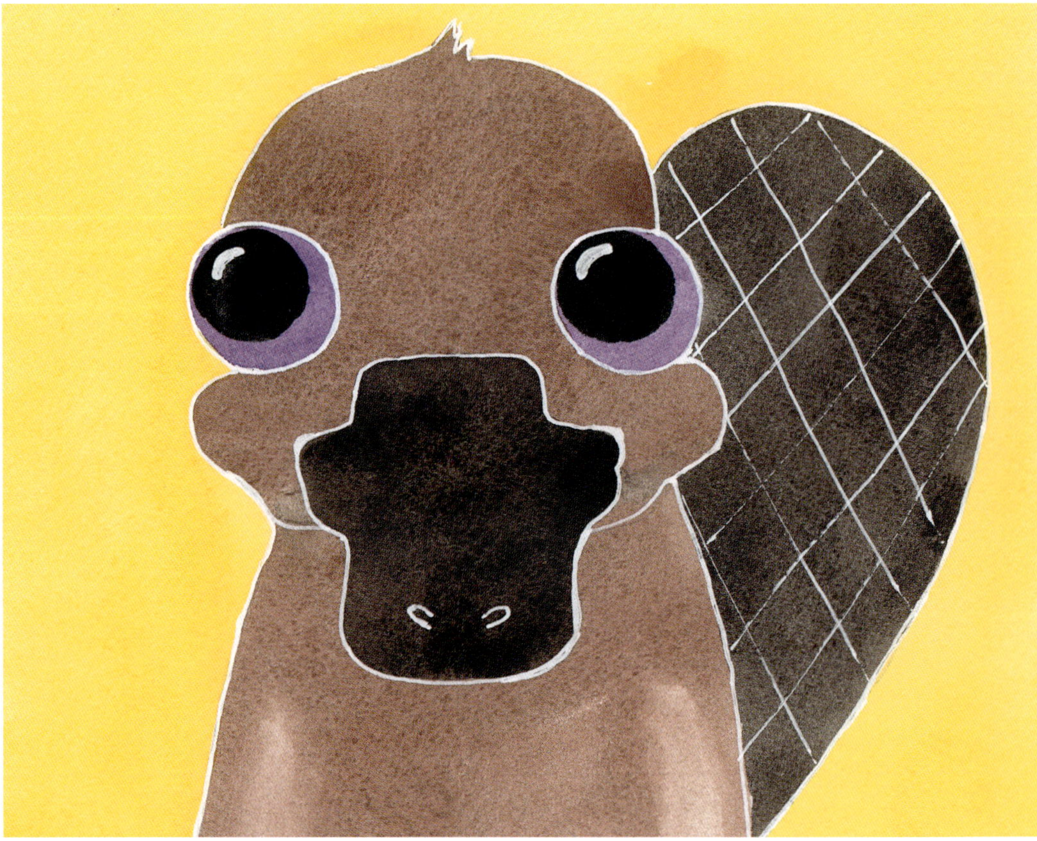

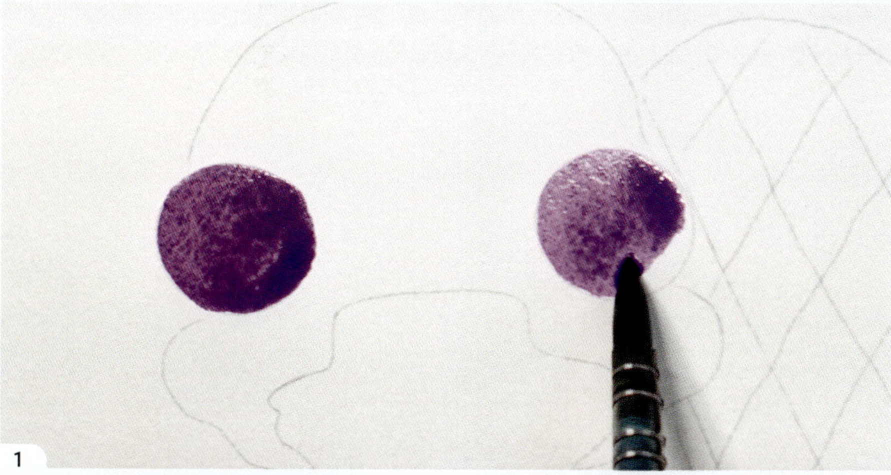
1

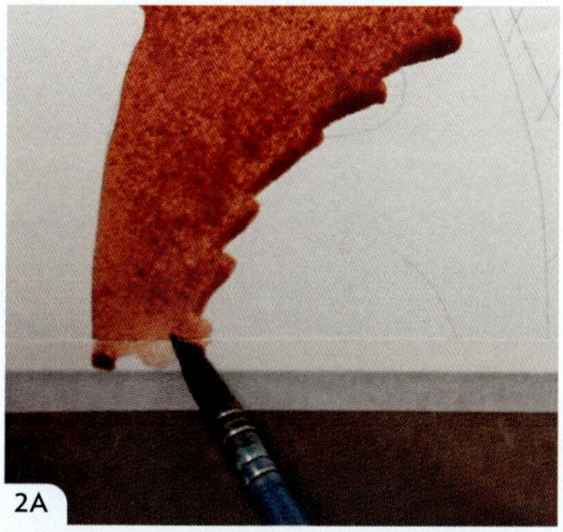
2A

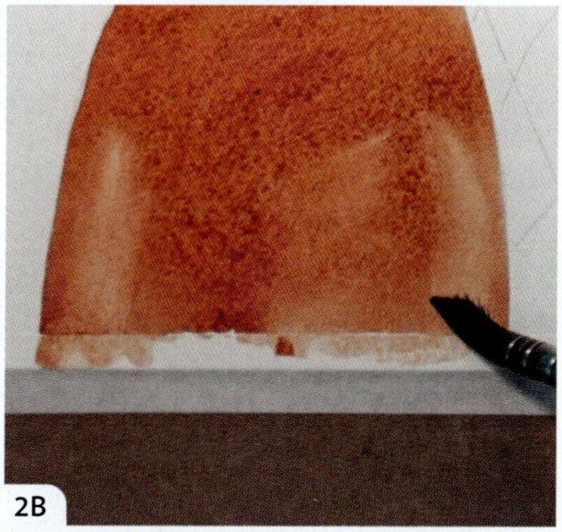
2B

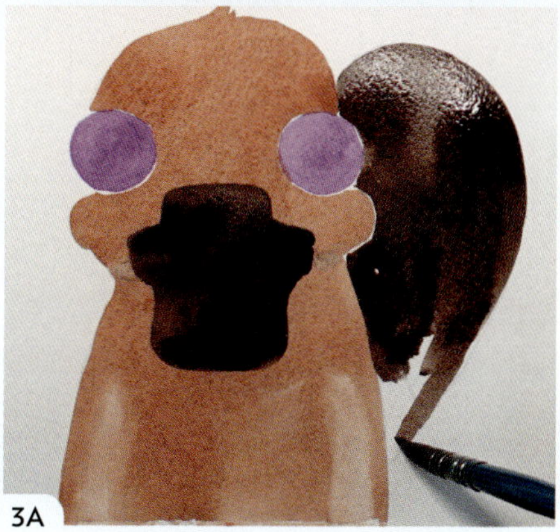
3A

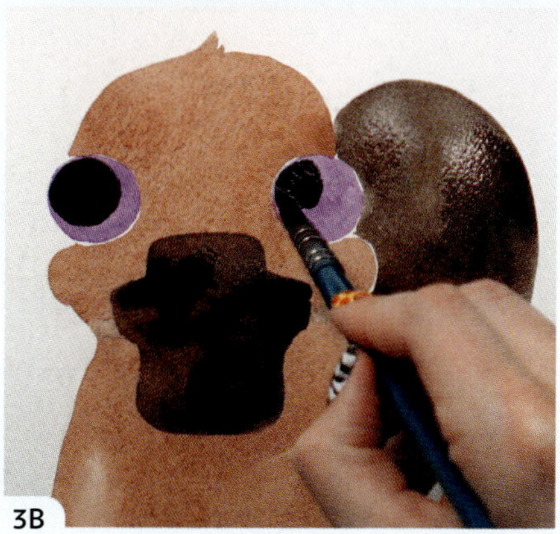
3B

Step 1

Mix a small puddle of light purple. Fill your brush with this color and then fill in the circles of the eyes. Let this dry or make it dry!

Step 2

Mix a large quantity of a medium brown color, aiming for a middle saturation here. Platypuses in real life are dark brown, but you don't want the color to be so dark you won't be able to see the sketch underneath. Make sure you mix lots of this color—you'll modify the leftovers for the next step.

Fill your brush with this color and paint in the entire head and body, leaving the tail bare (2A).

While the paint is still wet, dry your brush off and then drag it along both arms to lift some of the color to add a little dimension (2B). Let this dry or make it dry!

Step 3

Use the remaining brown as the base for a very dark brown. You can make a much darker brown by adding black into the original color until it's the desired color.

Paint this dark brown color over the bill and the tail (3A).

Load your brush with black and paint in the pupils of the eyes (3B). Let this dry or make it dry!

Step 4

Mix up large quantities of a few yellow colors, or your preferred background color. Then complete a messy wash on the background (4A). I like to switch between different colors so there's built-in variation, which is more forgiving (4B). Don't worry about this being perfect! Let this dry or make it dry!

Step 5

Grab your white gel pen and outline all the sections of the platypus and add in fun details like a checkerboard on the tail, nostrils on the bill, and, of course, the highlights in the eyes!

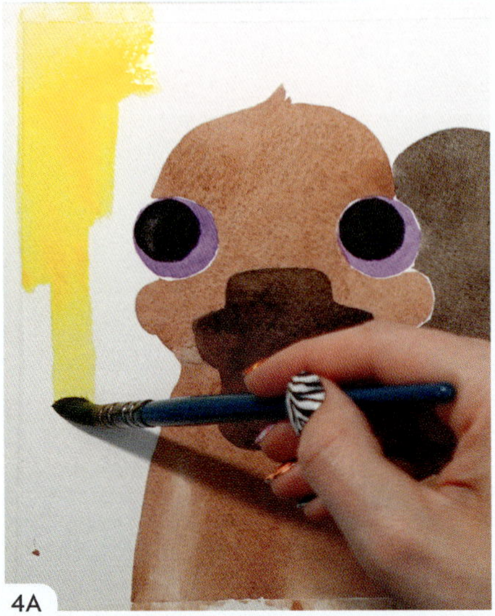

4A

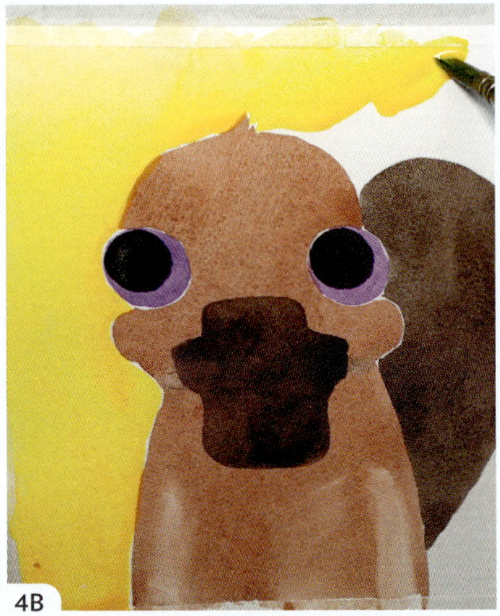

4B

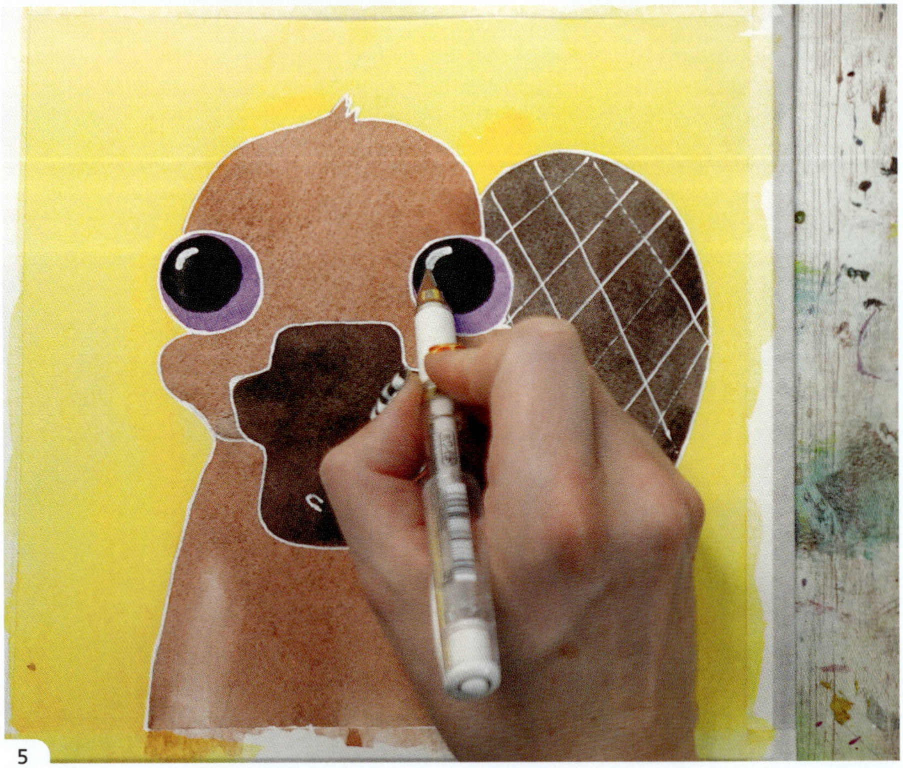

5

TAVISH THE TIGER

Similar to giraffe spots, no two tigers have the same stripes. Their stripe patterns are as unique as fingerprints. Even more amazing, a tiger's stripes don't just appear on its fur—they're also visible on its skin. This tiger is super fun to paint and a great way to explore layering, as well as building in some gradients!

Color Palette

Green

Orange

Black

Pink

Blues

Techniques

Layering, page 29

Lifting, page 26

Watercolor Washes, page 24

Wetness Stages, page 14

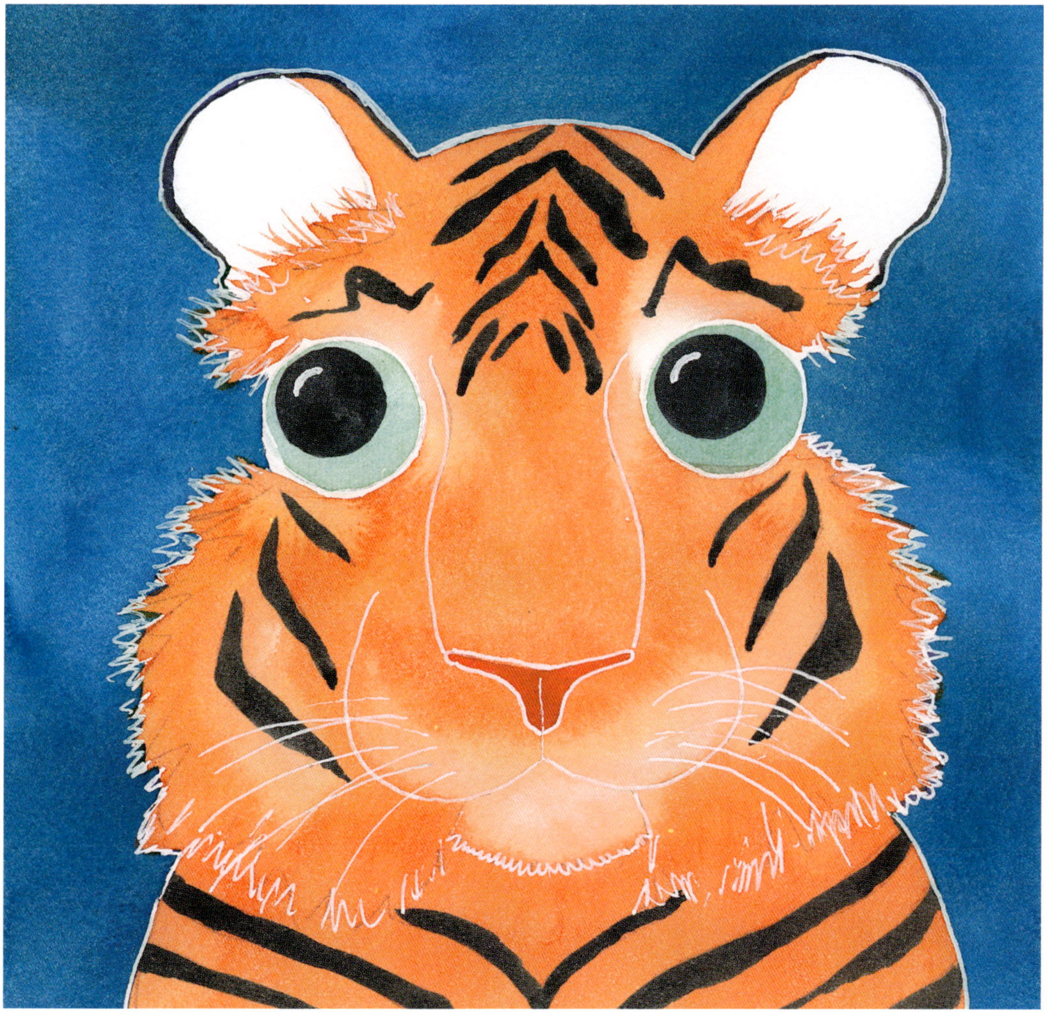

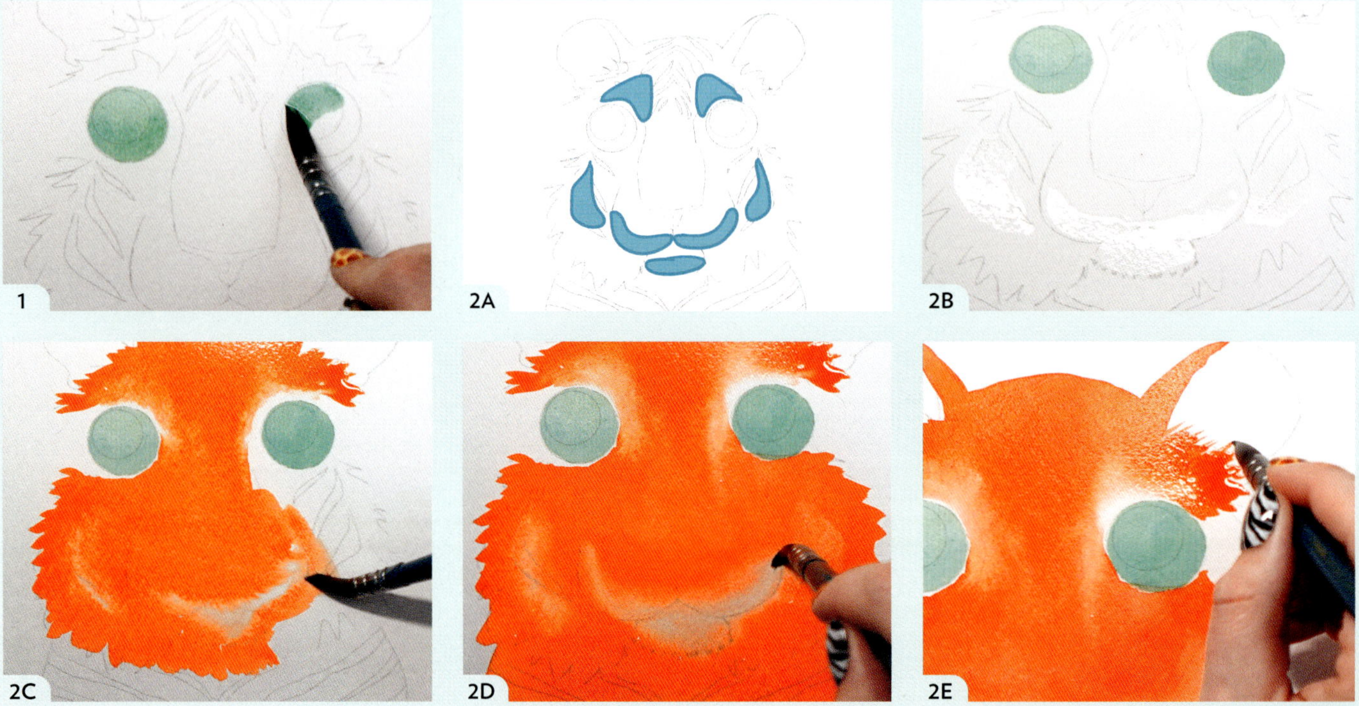

Step 1

Mix up a light green color and paint in the eye circles. Let this dry or make it dry!

Step 2

Mix up a large quantity of a bright orange color.

Wash your brush and fill it with clean water and add just water to the spots indicated on the diagram (2A). In order to build in some gradients to get natural color differences, these spots need to be wet to the gloss or satin stage. The best way to check this is to hold your page up to a light source at different angles until you can catch the reflection to check how wet they are (2B).

While these areas are still wet, fill your brush with the bright orange color and paint in the face and body of the tiger. When you get near an area you pre-wet with clean water, touch just the tip of your brush to the area (2C). The goal here is to create areas on the tiger's face of different saturations, and having excess water in some areas will help achieve this. You'll notice that some areas are brighter, and in some areas you can see more water.

If you want even more variation between the bright orange and desaturated orange, lift some color off of those areas while the orange color is still wet. To do this, wash and dry your brush, then swoop it along the areas where you wish to lift color from (2D).

While the paint is still wet, fill your brush with some more of the orange and use the tip of your brush to lightly flick thin strokes around the ear areas to create some fluff (2E). Let this dry or make it dry!

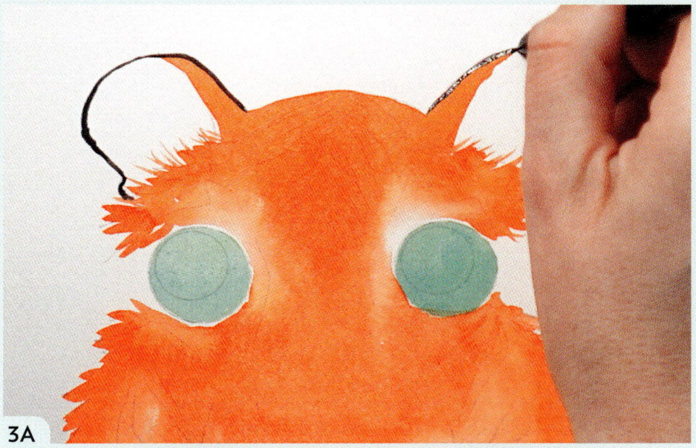
3A

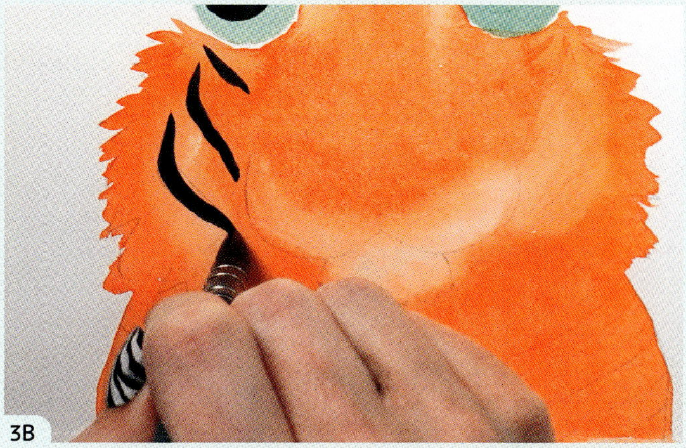
3B

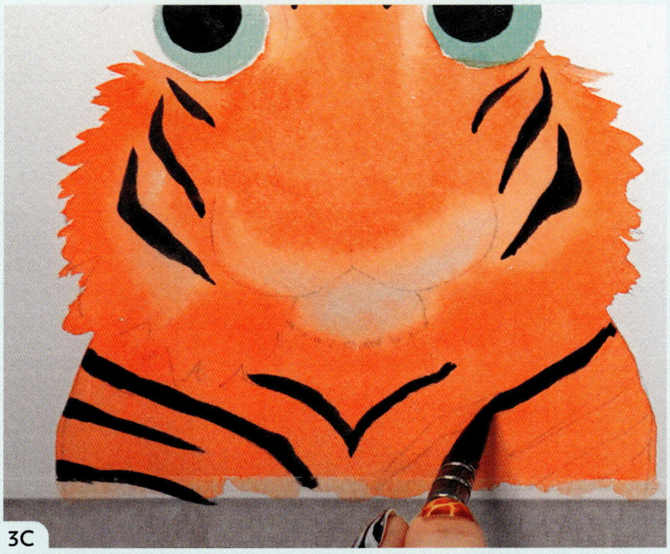
3C

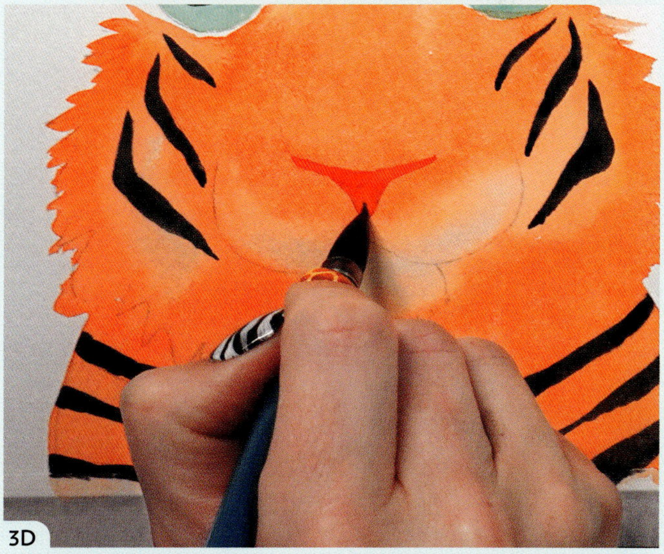
3D

Step 3

Mix up a large puddle of a dark black color. You'll need enough to cover all the stripes and the pupils in the eyes.

Outline the outsides of the ears using the tip of your brush (3A). If this isn't perfect, that's OK—the white gel pen at the end will help clean this up!

Then start filling in the stripes and the pupils of the eyes (3B). I like to work moving diagonally from the top left toward the right bottom (3C). I do this because I am right-handed, and it means less chance of smudging my recently added areas. If you're left-handed, you should work from right to left instead!

Finally, mix up a pinky color and paint in the nose (3D). Let this dry or make it dry!

Step 4

In two mixing wells, mix up two different blue colors. Switch between these colors as you create a messy wash on the background (4A). Painting around a complex shape with fur sticking out can be tricky, so don't worry if there's a little white showing. The best way to get good coverage is to move your paper around as you fill in the background, so the pointy tip of the brush can fit into the little nooks more easily (4B). Let this dry or make it dry!

Step 5

Using your white gel pen, outline all the main shapes of the tiger. On the edges where there is fur, you don't have to follow the lines exactly; just scribble up and down to get a furry effect! Don't forget to add the highlights to the eyes and, if you want an extra cute touch, make some long, swooping whiskers!

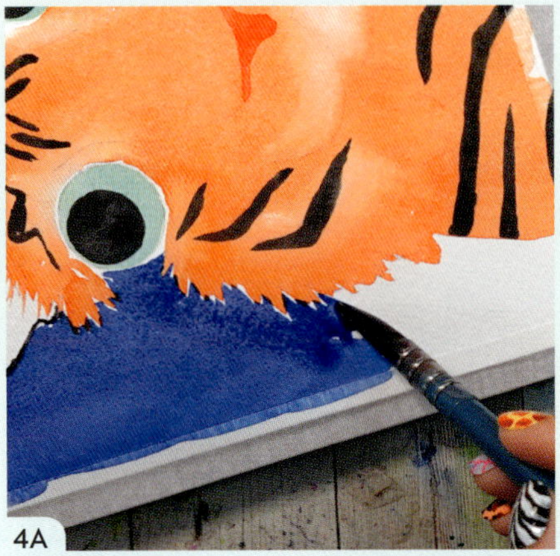

4A

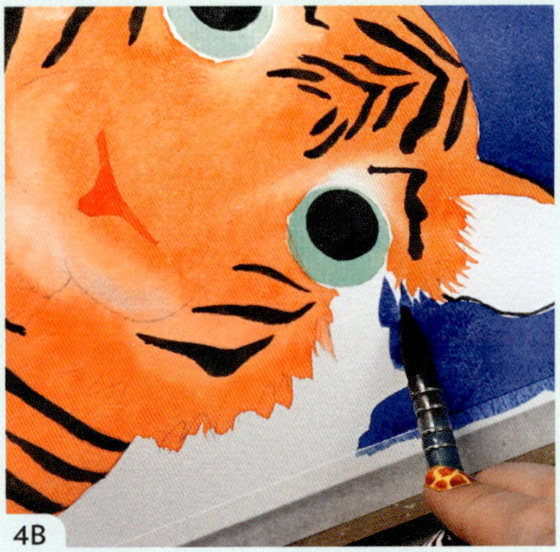

4B

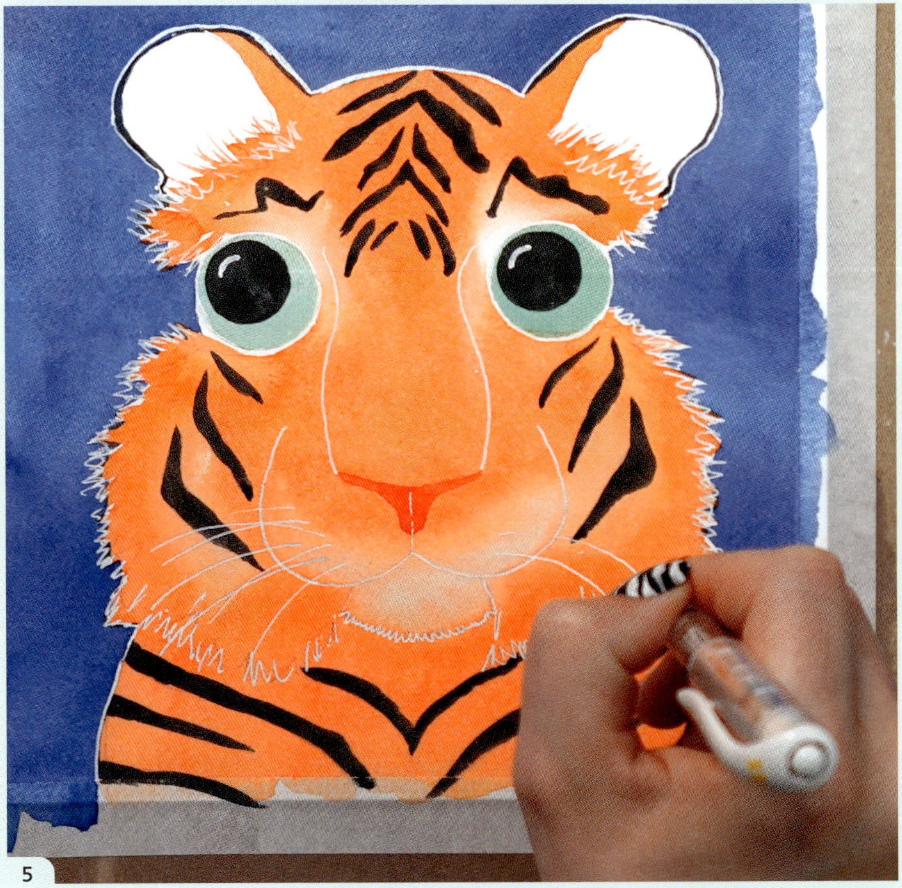

5

HAL THE HAMMERHEAD SHARK

Hammerhead sharks have a distinctive look, with their eyes placed on the sides of their aptly named hammer-shaped heads. The strategic placement of their eyes makes them a perfect fit to paint in this style! Did you know this eye placement gives them nearly perfect 360-degree vision? Their vision helps them hunt, but it does have one downfall: There's one blind spot, directly in the middle of their nose! This painting is super fun because it invites you to let colors bleed together, as well as play with a fun effect using something you might find in abundance in both the ocean and your kitchen! You guessed it—you'll need some sea salt or other coarse salt for this painting.

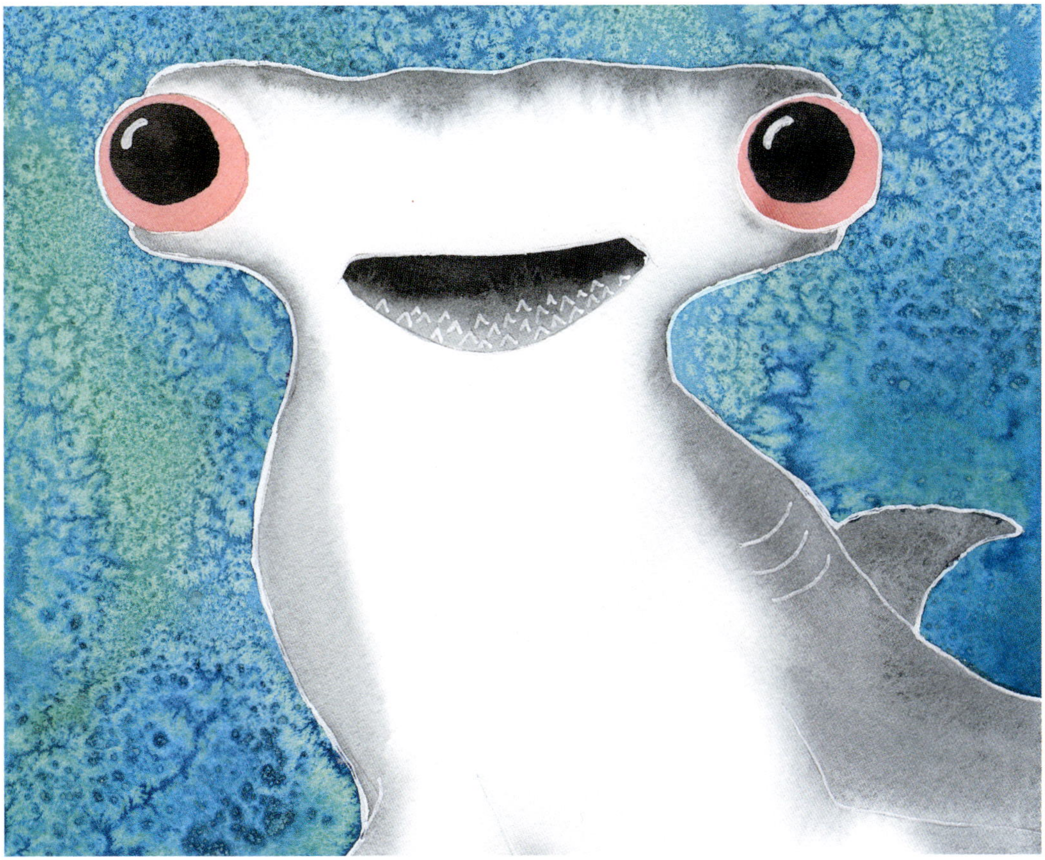

Color Palette

Gray
Pink
Black
Blue
Teal

Techniques

Adding Texture, page 28
Dropping In, page 27
Layering, page 29
Watercolor Washes, page 24
Wetness Stages, page 14

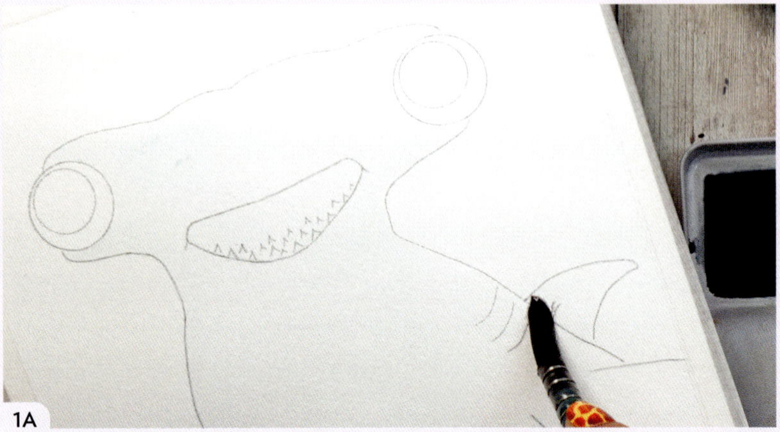

1A

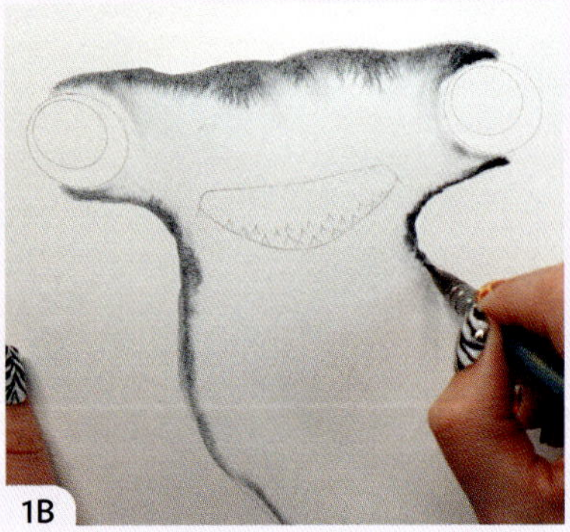

1B

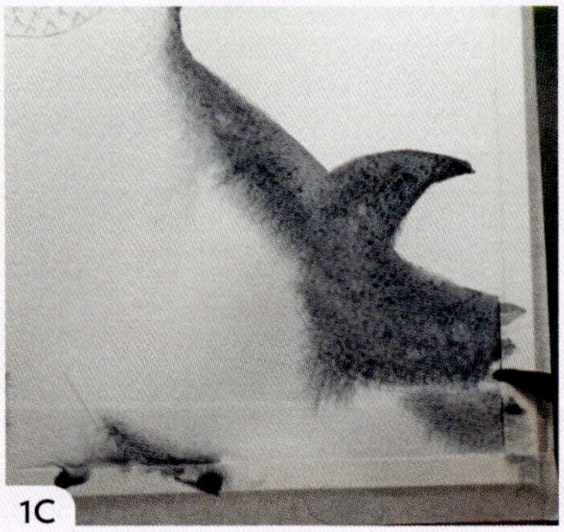

1C

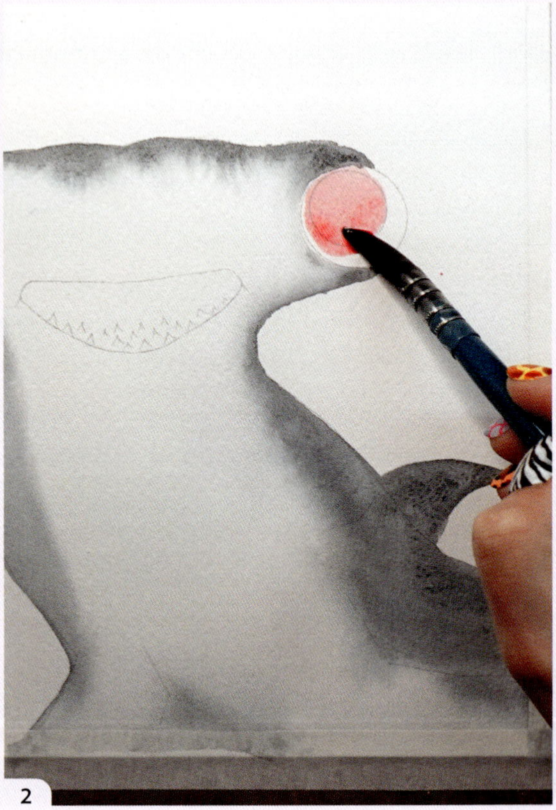

2

Step 1

Make sure you have lots of fresh clean water and mix up a little of a concentrated gray color. I opted to mix some black with a tiny bit of blue to make a cooler gray.

Fill a clean brush with lots of water and cover the entire body of the shark with an even coat, avoiding the eyes (1A). You may need to refill your brush a few times to maintain an even coating while applying the water. You want to achieve a gloss or satin stage of wetness. Remember, the reflection from a light will help you keep track of where the water has been applied!

Once the water is at the gloss or satin stage, fill your brush with the gray color and drag the tip of your brush along the outsides of the shark's body, dropping a little color along all the sides (1B). Refill your brush and then paint in the fin and a little of the body that attaches to the fin (1C). For best results, allow this to sit for a minute or two for the water and the gray color to mingle on their own before you let this dry or make it dry!

Step 2

Mix up a light pink color, or any color you want, to paint in the eyes. Let this dry or make it dry!

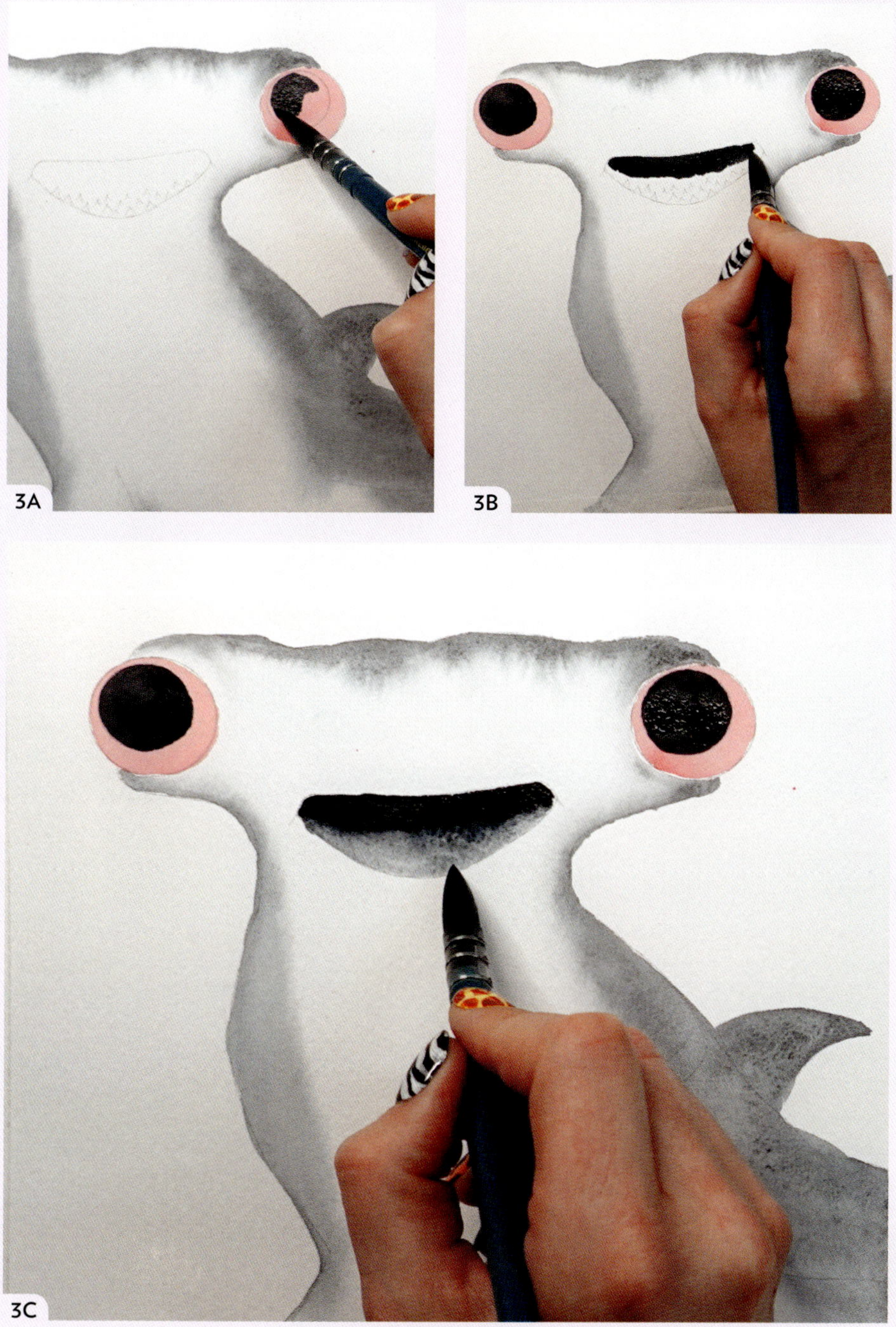

Step 3

Mix up a puddle of a black. Fill in the pupils of the eyes with the black color (3A). In the shark's mouth, paint a strip of the dark black color along the top (3B). Wash your brush and fill it with a medium amount of water and then grab that color and pull it down to the bottom to create a gradient (3C). Let this dry or make it dry!

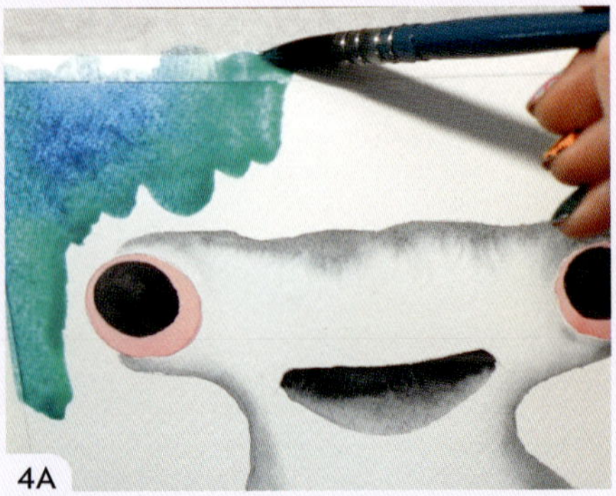

4A

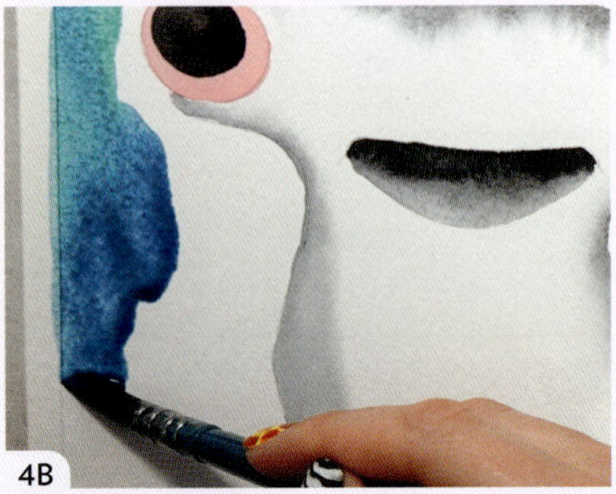

4B

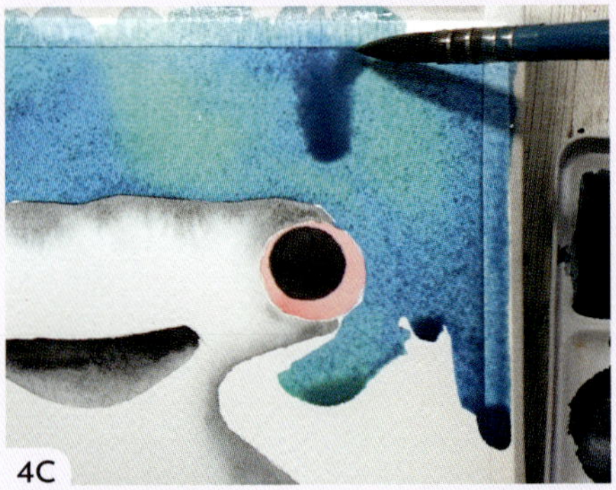

4C

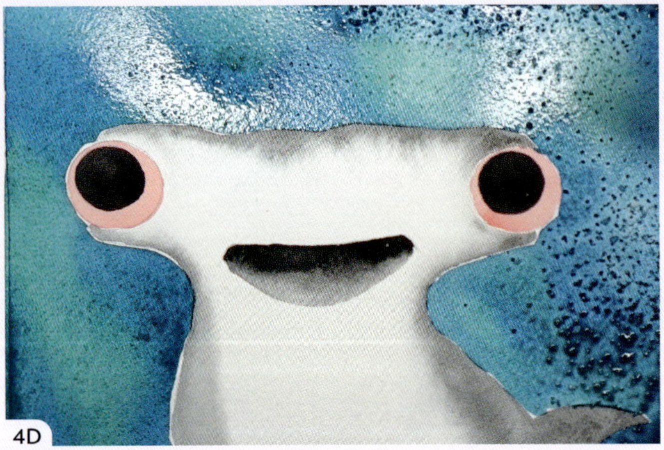

4D

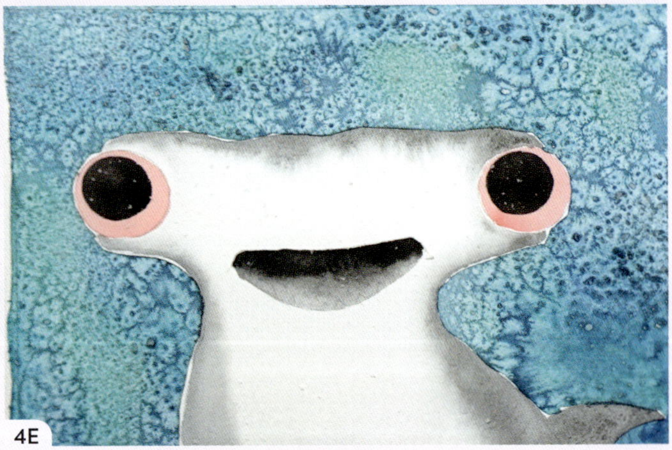

4E

Step 4

Be sure to prepare for this step, because timing and wetness is key. Mix up larger quantities of a few blue or teal colors, enough to fill the background. Also, grab some salt—you'll want that handy in a minute! The type of salt you use will create different effects. I like to use sea salt or coarse ground salt for my favorite effects.

Create a messy wash across the background. Use lots of water, erring on the side of a flood level of wetness (4A). While I work, I like to move a little in one direction, then work in another direction, and go back and forth so that each edge stays wet (4B). If necessary, as you work or when you've covered the background, go back and drop more color and water on (4C). The next effect works better on paper that is too wet rather than too dry.

Grab your salt and, while things are still nice and wet, sprinkle it on (4D). Let this dry on its own for a few hours for best results. I like to check back frequently, though, because it's fun to see how much the effect changes over time. It starts off looking just a bit grainy, but then blooms form and it creates a beautiful texture (4E)!

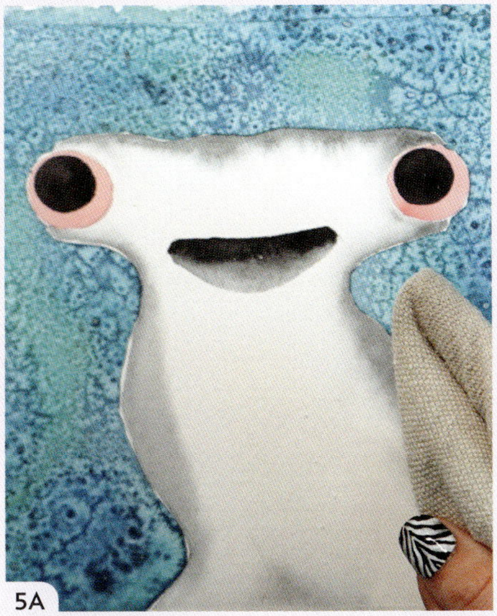

5A

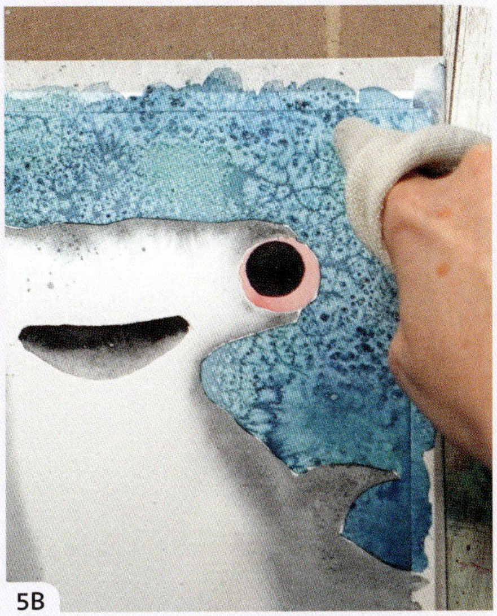

5B

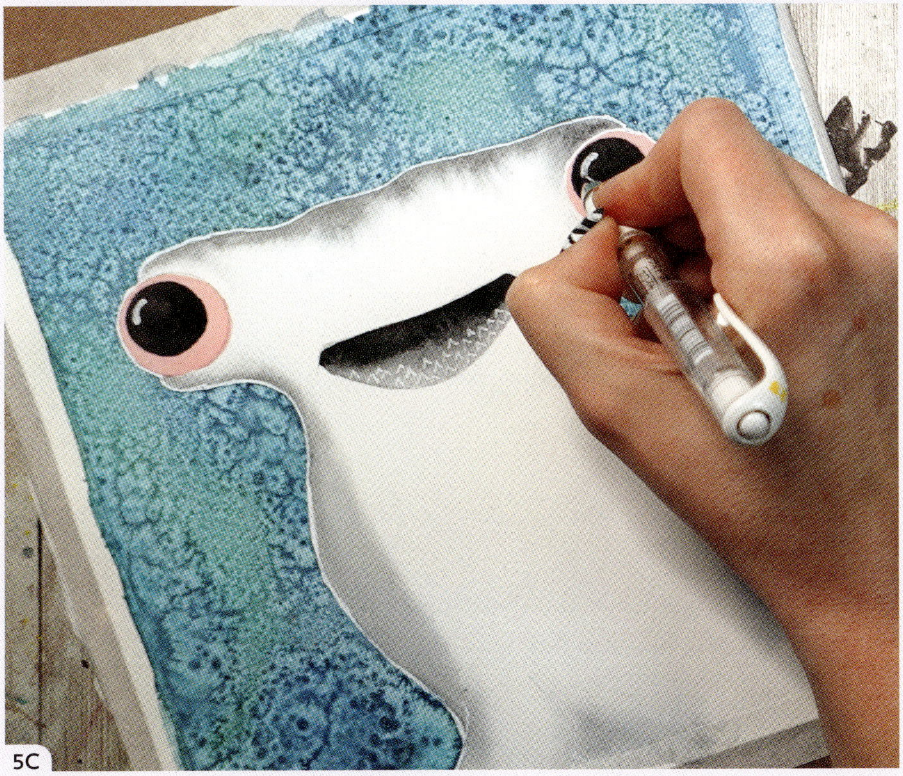

5C

Step 5

Once this is fully dry, it's time to remove some of the salt. Please note that it is very hard to remove 100 percent of the salt, so aim to remove just the bigger or loose bits. Be gentle, as being too rough at this stage could smear some of the pretty effects created by the salt.

To remove the salt, I like to wrap my finger in a cotton cloth (5A) and then gently swirl it on the paper to remove the salt that wants to be removed (5B). Take care to remove the big salt crystals near the edge of the design so that you can still go over the outline with a gel pen.

Once the salt has been removed, grab your white gel pen and outline the body and add in the remaining details like the gills, lots of teeth, and highlights in the eyes (5C)!

MAI THE MANATEE

Color Palette

Teal
Pink
Black
Gray

Techniques

Adding Texture, page 28
Charging, page 27
Layering, page 29
Lifting, page 26

Choosing a favorite animal is a tough challenge for me, but manatees are definitely one of my favorites! Manatees are voracious sea plant eaters. They can eat up to 5 to 10 percent of their body weight each day—and they can weigh up to 3,000 pounds (1,360 kg)! Can you imagine eating 300 pounds (136 kg) of sea grass each day?! This manatee is super fun to paint, with another opportunity to play a bit more with salt and use lifting to create a light ray effect in the background!

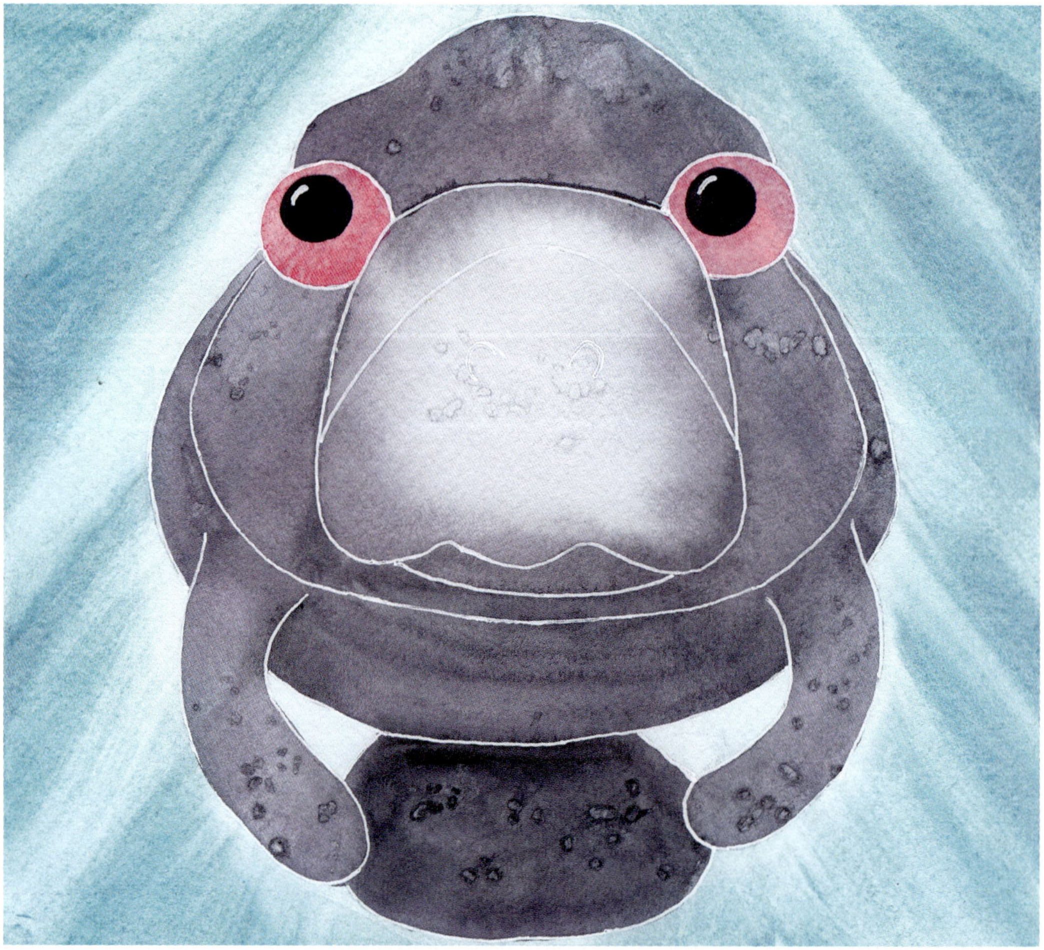

Paint along with me Scan the QR code to watch a video where I paint Mai the Manatee.

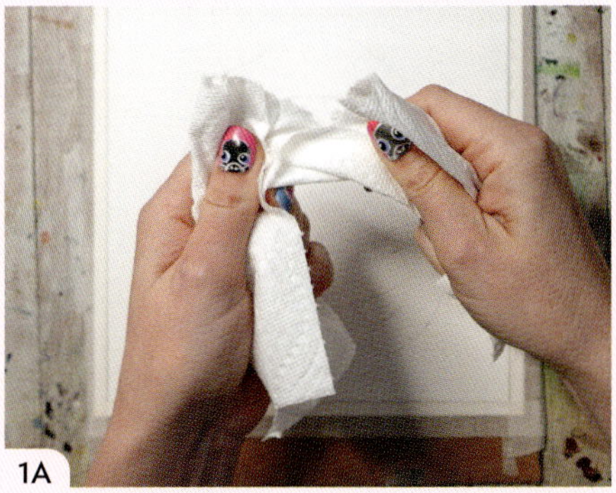

1A

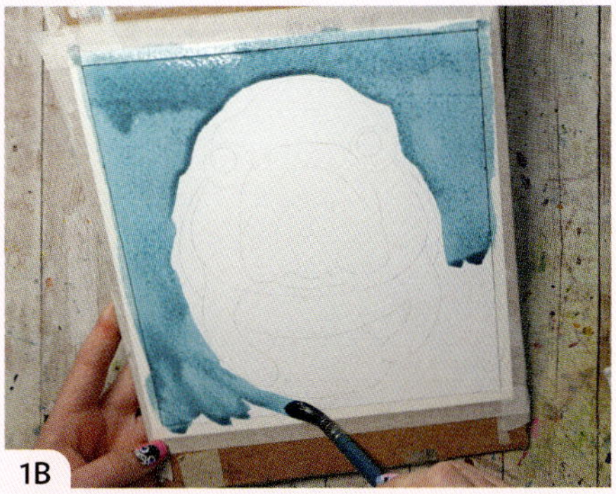

1B

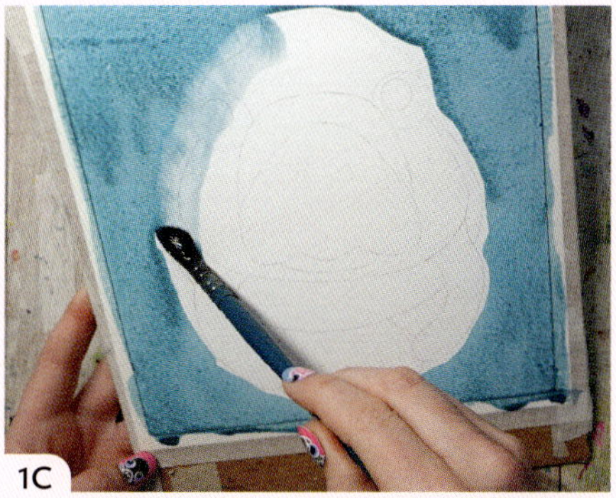

1C

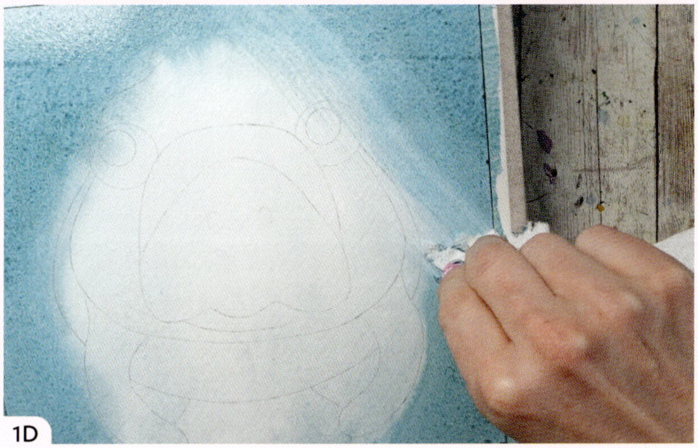

1D

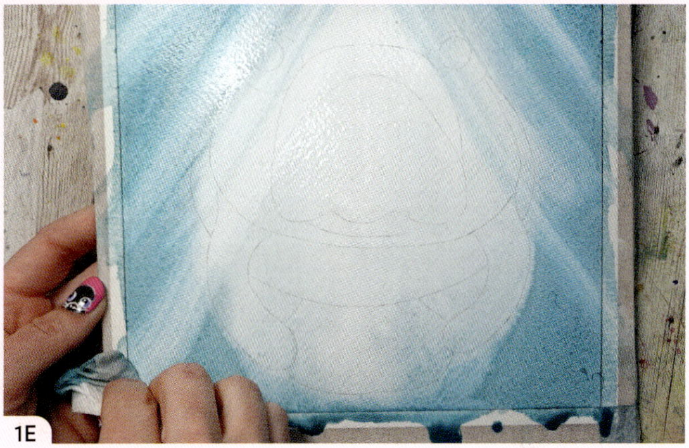

1E

Step 1

Unlike most paintings in this book, this one starts with the background. Mix up a fun blue or teal color for the background, and make sure you have plenty of clean water to dip your brush into.

Before starting the background, grab a paper towel and scrunch it up a bit, then rip it so you have a natural ripped edge (1A).

Then fill your brush with the teal color and start painting around the manatee (1B). Replace the teal color in your brush with water and paint in the manatee's body with water. Refill your brush with the teal and paint it around the manatee (1C). Some of the teal will bleed in and that's fine, but it should be a bit lighter in the middle. Work as quickly as you can here, because you want this to be wet. If you need to, you can always re-drop some color or water on your page as you go to keep areas wet that are drying faster than you'd like.

While this is still wet, use the paper towel you prepared and start from the top center of your paper, dragging the ripped edge out at an angle toward the outer edges of the paper (1D). This creates some light rays shining around the manatee (1E). Repeat this to make more light rays, and if your paper towel isn't lifting color, tear off the wet part to get a fresh, dry segment to lift. Once you're happy with your rays, let this dry or make it dry!

Step 2

Mix up a small puddle of pink and paint in the biggest circles of the eyes. Let this dry or make it dry!

Step 3

To prepare for this step, have some salt on hand, make sure your black color is activated, and mix up a large quantity of a gray color—enough to fill in the manatee.

Grab a dark black color with your brush and fill in the pupils of the eyes (3A).

Next we're going to paint the manatee, while also creating texture using salt. This works best while things are still wet, so I recommend working in sections. Start by adding gray to the top of the manatee's face (3B), then quickly sprinkle some salt on just the top of the head (3C). Next wash your brush and paint water onto the nose (3D), refill your brush with the gray, and add some to the sides of the body and quickly sprinkle some salt (3E). Finally, paint in the main body with gray (not the tail or flippers yet).

While the head and body are still wet, dip the tip of your brush into some black and drop in some shadows around the nose, mouth, and sides of the body (3F). Working in sections ensures things don't dry too fast to add in the shadows.

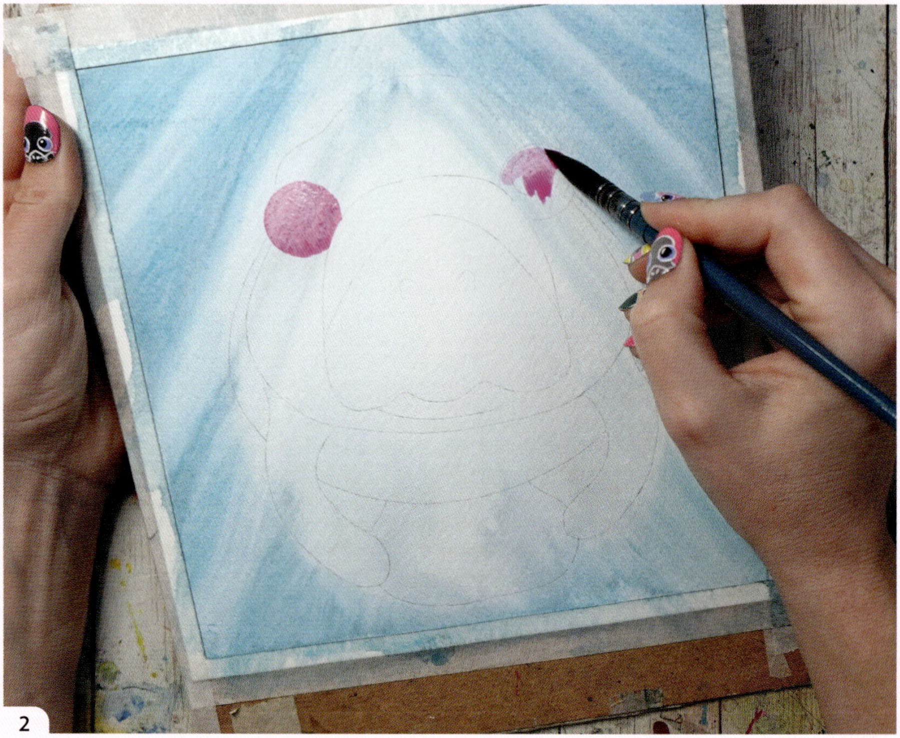

2

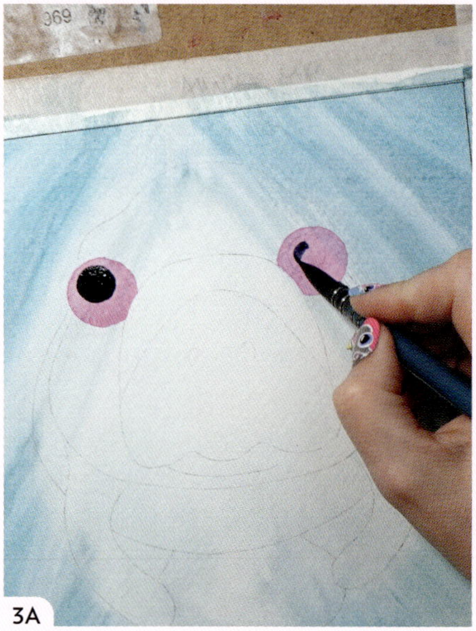

3A

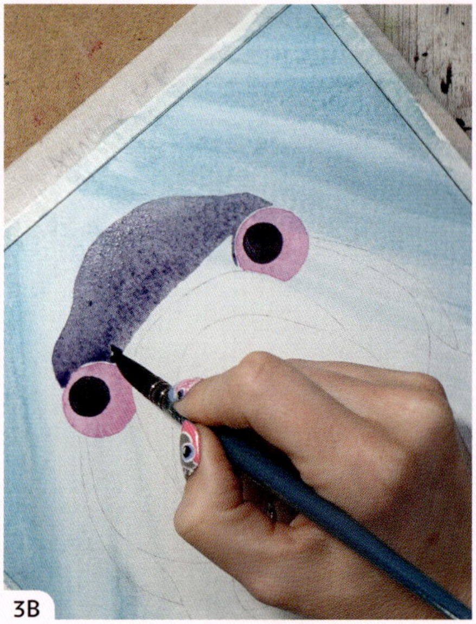

3B

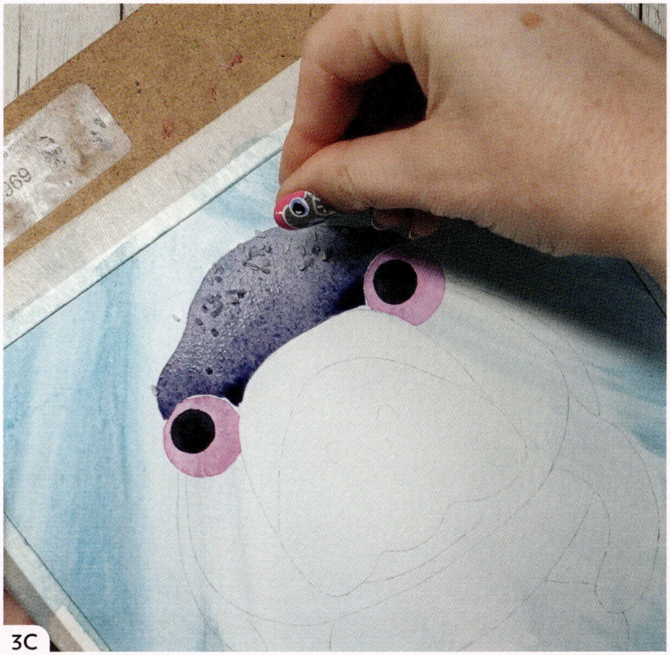

3C

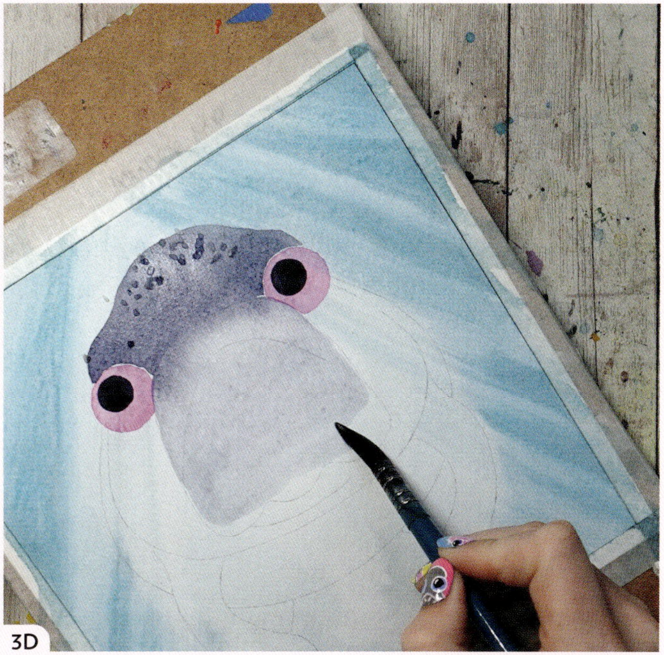

3D

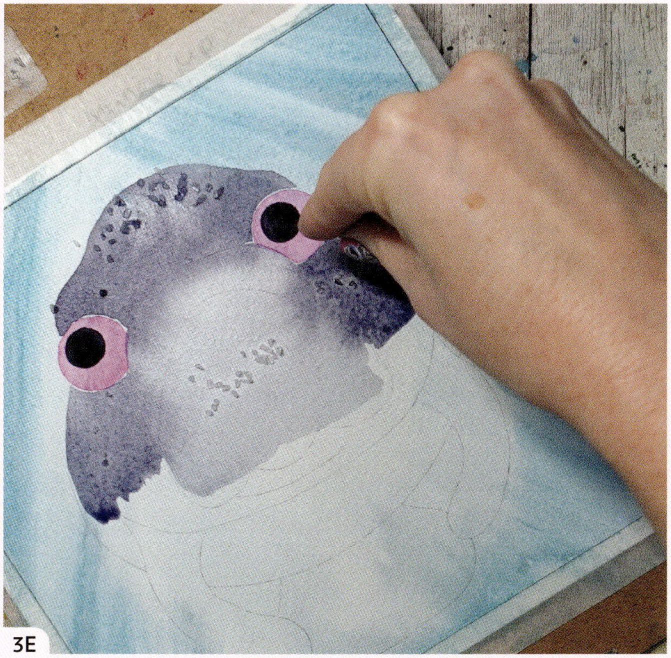

3E

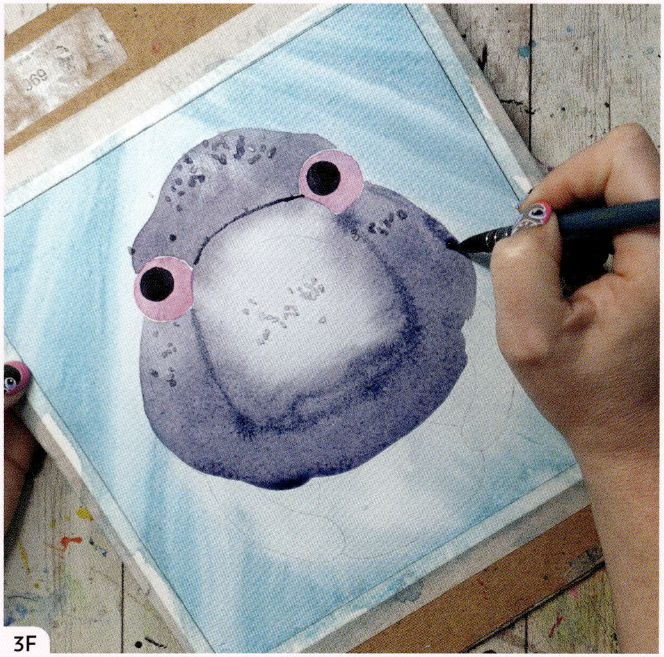

3F

Step 4

Next, paint in the flippers with gray and sprinkle some salt (4A), and then paint the tail. While this is still wet, dip the tip of your brush into some black and drop in some shadow colors under the body. Concentrate on the tail to make it look like it's further back and in shadow (4B). Sprinkle more salt on the tail.

Let this dry on its own so the salt has some time to create the fun textures.

Step 5

Once the manatee has dried, remove as much of the salt as you can so you can add the white outlines. I like to wrap my finger in a cotton cloth or paper towel and then gently rub the salt off in circular motions (5A).

Create the white outlines around the body of the manatee, nose, eyes, flippers, and tail, and then add in the finishing details like the nostrils and highlights in the eyes (5B).

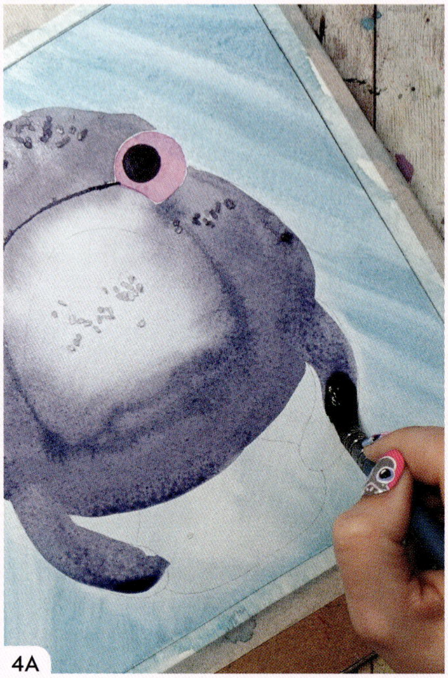
4A

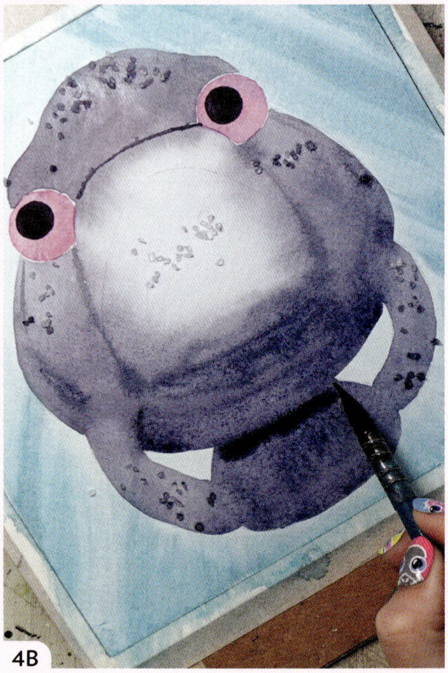
4B

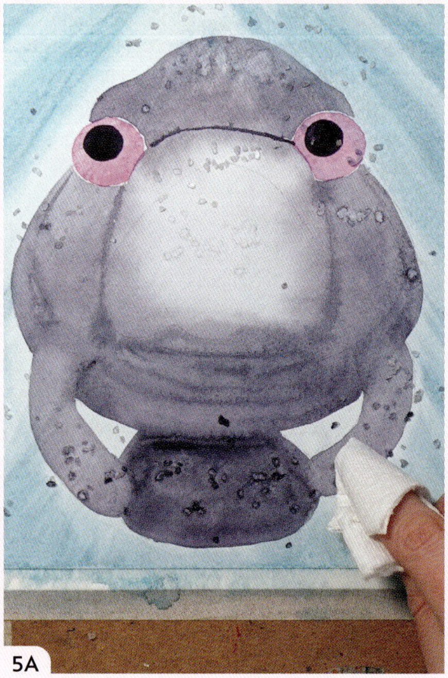
5A

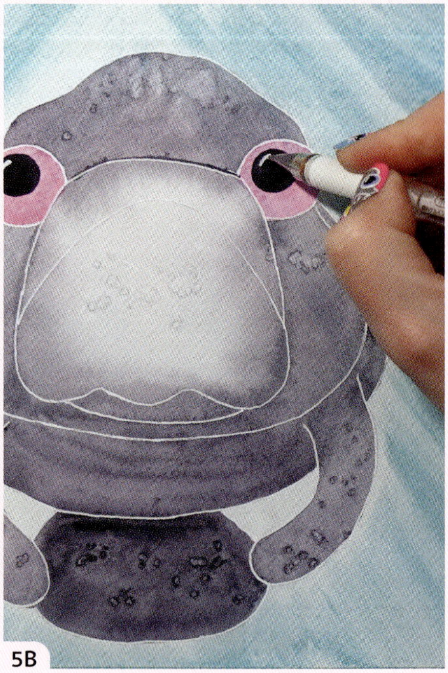
5B

SALMA THE SILKIE

Silkie chickens are possibly the cutest chickens, with their fluffy plumage. Did you know that when chickens cluck, they're not just making sounds? They have a wide range of unique vocalizations to communicate with each other, including sounds for danger, food location, or even how they are feeling! This silkie is fun to paint because after dropping in color, you'll just scribble on the top—so the process is super freeing!

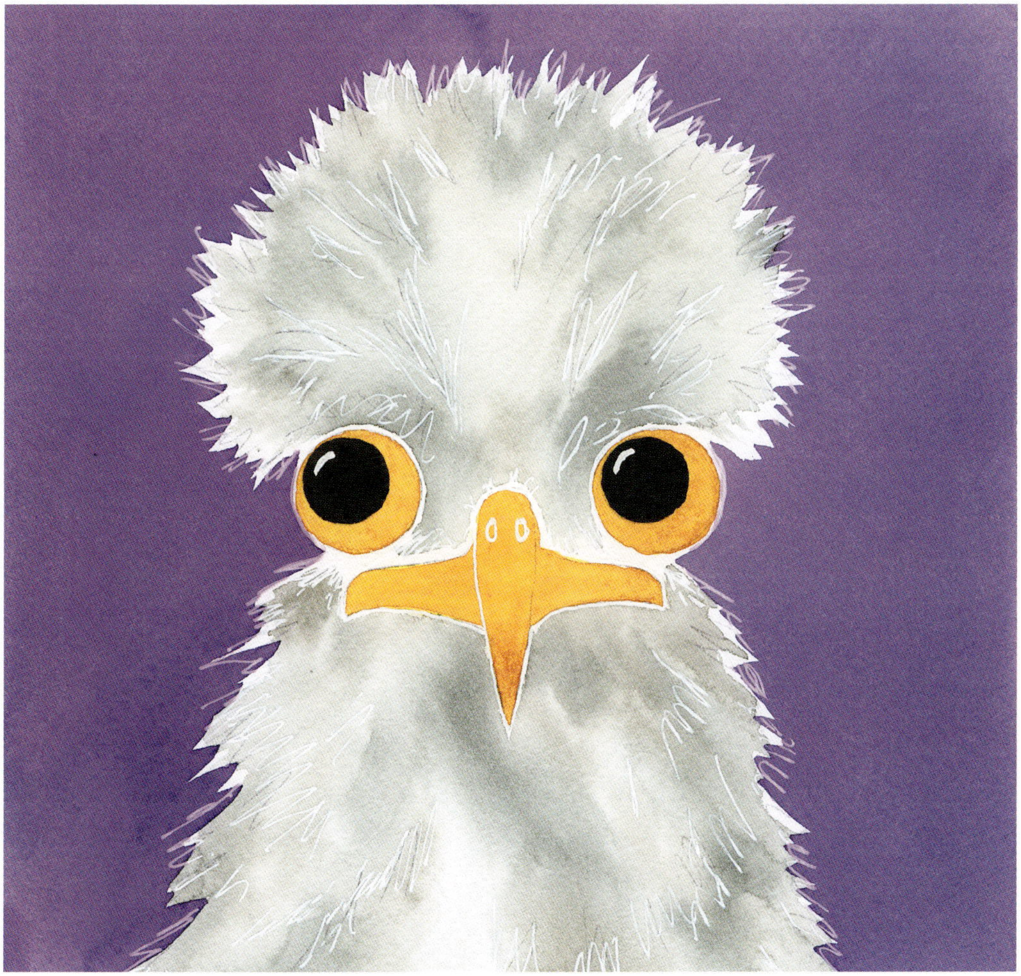

Color Palette

Yellow

Grays

Black

Purples

Techniques

Dropping In, page 27

Layering, page 29

Watercolor Washes, page 24

Wetness Stages, page 14

Paint along with me Scan the QR code to watch a video where I paint Salma the Silkie.

Step 1

Mix up a puddle of a yellow color and paint in the eyes and beak. Let this dry or make it dry!

Step 2

Mix up two puddles of grays. I made one of my grays a little blue and one a little brown.

Wet the head of the chicken with a nice, even coat of clean water until it's about the gloss or satin stage of wetness (2A).

While it's wet, drop in the two gray colors with random intentionality: Randomly switch between colors, but make intentional brushstrokes in lines that swoop out from the center of the head (2B). Let these sit for a minute to spread out in the water (2C). After you drop these colors in, wait and observe for a minute. Sometimes colors will flow together so much that you can no longer see any variation. If you notice this happening, you can drop in more colors in some areas to increase the variation (2D). Keep an eye on the wetness of the chicken's head, as you want it to dry a bit more but not too much. If yours is drying too fast, skip ahead to step 4 to lift out some highlights.

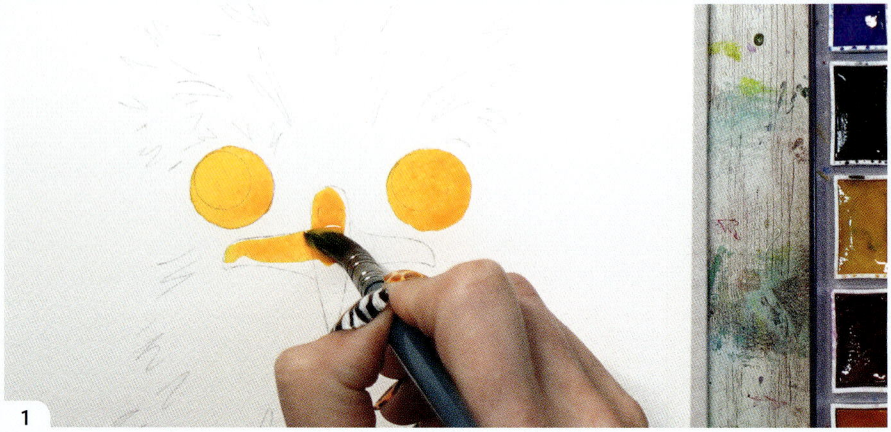
1

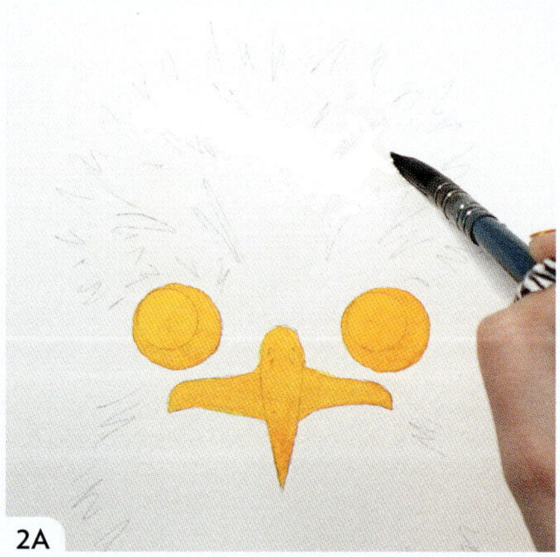
2A

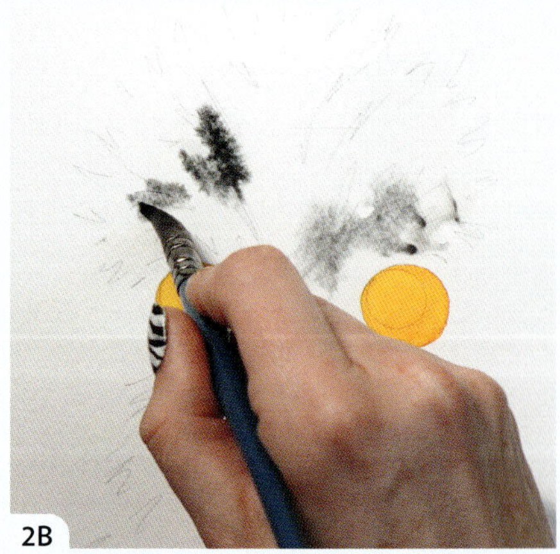
2B

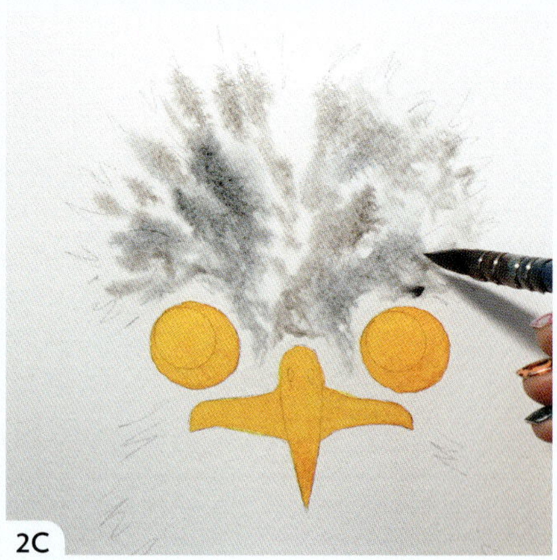
2C

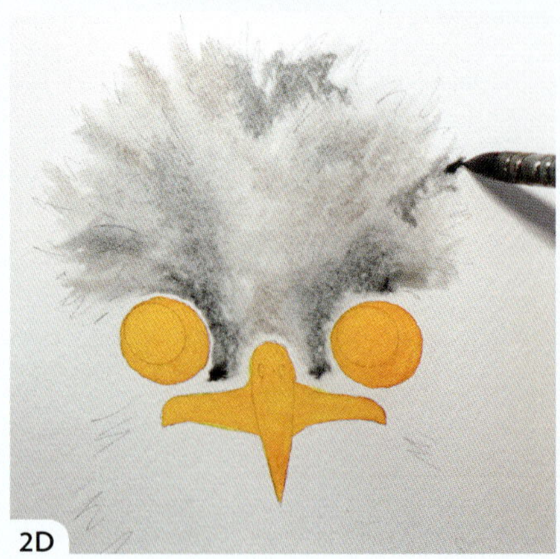
2D

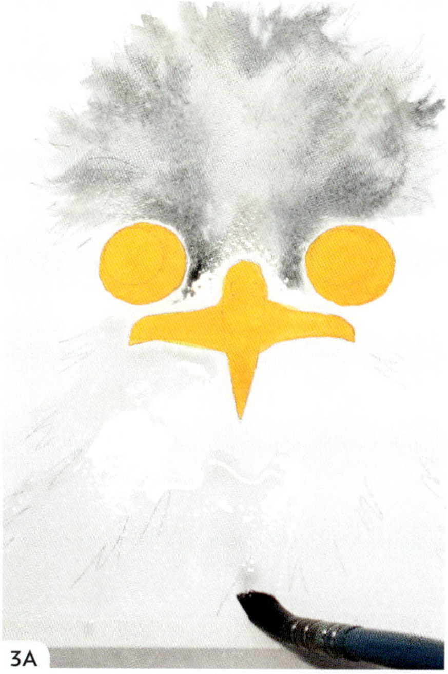

3A

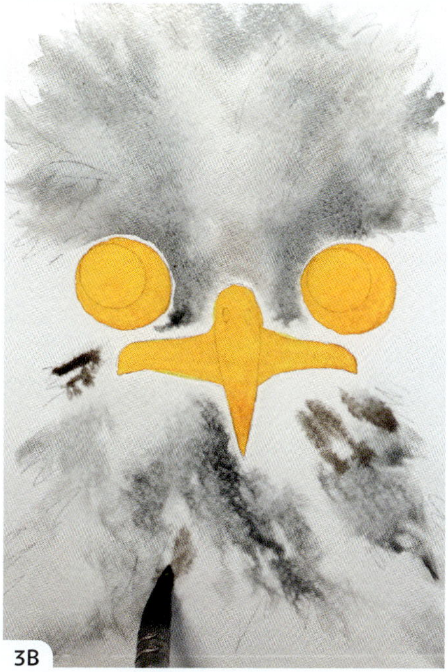

3B

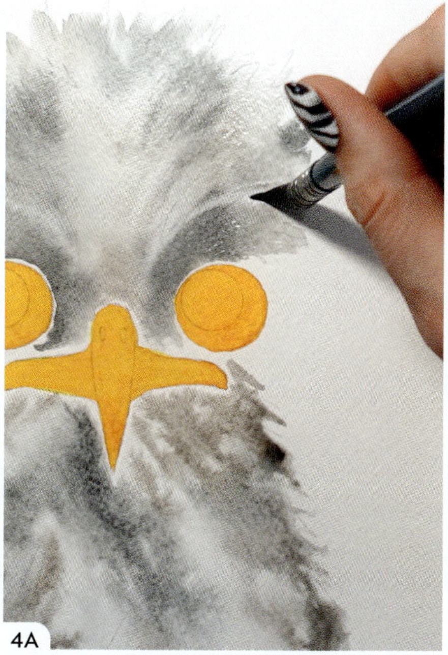

4A

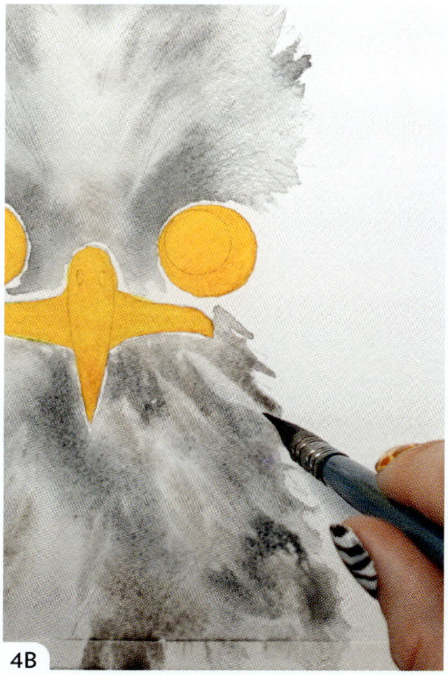

4B

Step 3

While the head is softening together, wet the body of the chicken with clean water to the gloss or satin stage (3A). Again, drop in the two gray colors somewhat randomly, swiping your brush from the bottom of the beak out toward the edge of the body on either side (3B).

Step 4

Move back to the head of the chicken, which should still be at the satin or damp stage of wetness, wash and dry your brush off, then drag the dry brush in arching motions along both sides of the head to create some lifted highlights (4A). While the body is still wet, check to see if you want to drop some more colors in, and then wash and dry your brush and lift out some swoops from the body (4B). Let this dry or make it dry!

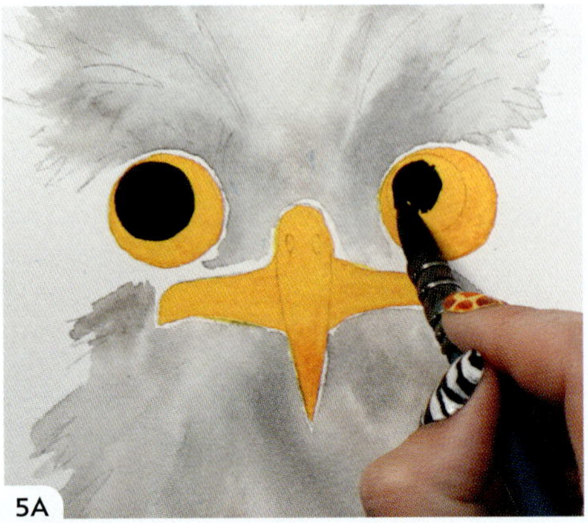
5A

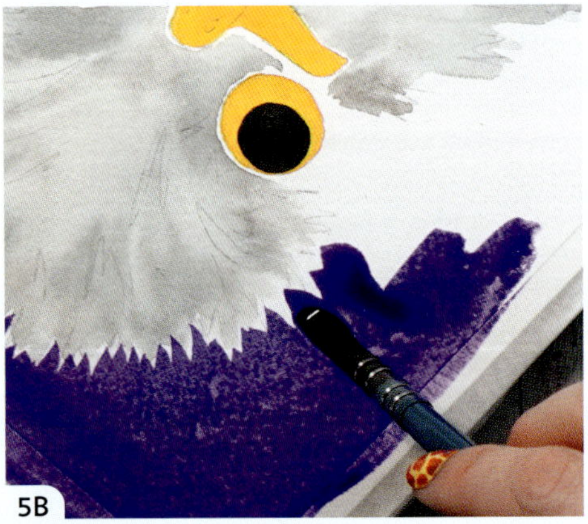
5B

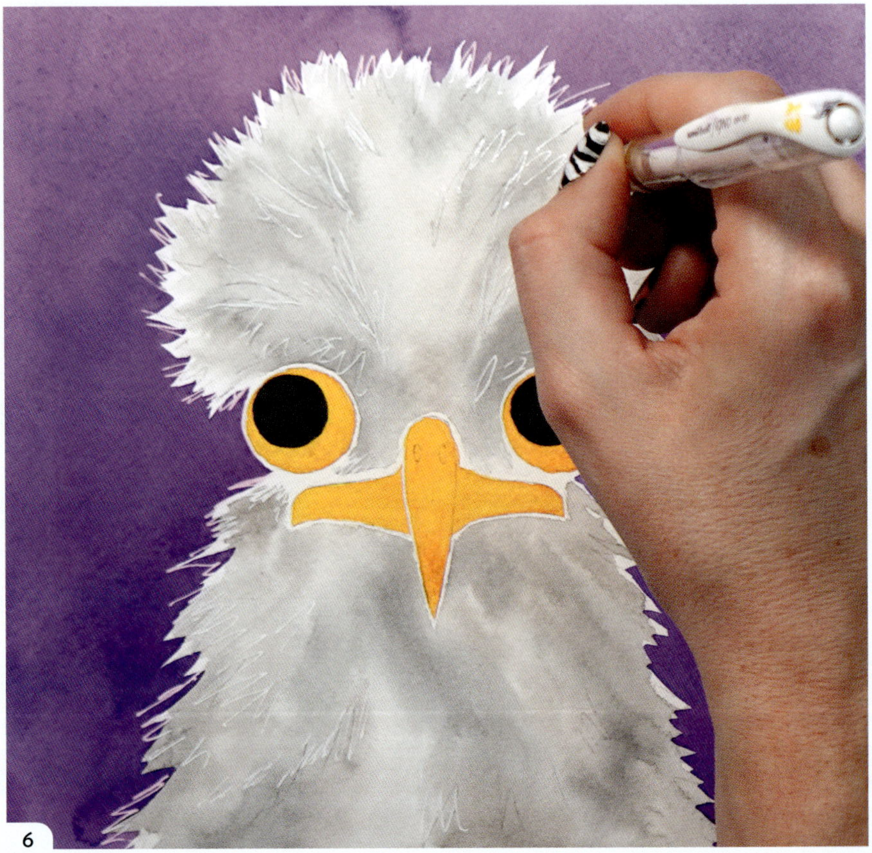
6

Step 5

Make sure your black watercolor is activated so you can easily grab the color. Mix up a large quantity of purple or multiple purple colors. Adding purple in the background will complement the golden yellow color of the eyes and beak!

First grab some black watercolor with your brush and paint in the pupils of the eyes (5A).

Next create a messy wash of color for the background. Because the edges of this animal are fluffy, don't worry too much about getting it perfect. I like to rotate my page while I paint this in so that I can easily angle my brush to get little spikes into the fluffy feathers (5B). As I paint around the background, I continue to spin the paper so it's easier to place my brush where needed. Let this dry or make it dry!

Step 6

Grab your white gel pen and scribble around the head and body of the silkie. Really go to town scribbling to create a super fluffy look. I also added some additional scribbles on the head and body to emphasize the fluffiness. Then outline the eyes and beak and add in the finishing touches: The nostrils and highlights of the eyes!

CLIVE THE CAPE BUFFALO

The Cape buffalo is one of five subspecies of buffalo found in Africa. Buffalo are proficient swimmers and often cross rivers, as well as wallow in mud, to help kill the insects and parasites that try to make their skin home. This painting utilizes a technique that relies on the natural qualities of watercolor to create texture, so have fun exploring this!

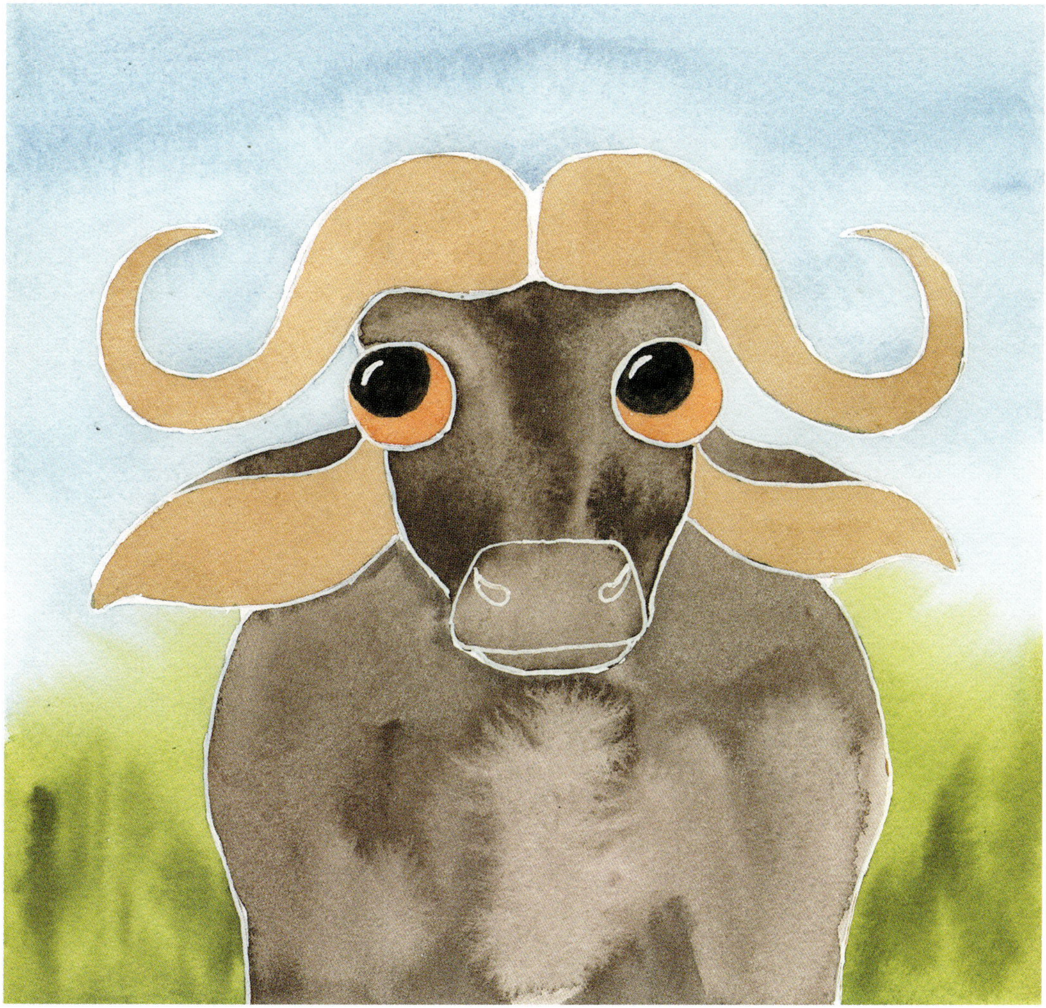

Color Palette

Orange
Tan
Dark Brown
Black
Blue Gray
Greens

Techniques

Adding Texture, page 28
Charging, page 27
Layering, page 29
Watercolor Washes, page 24
Wetness Stages, page 14

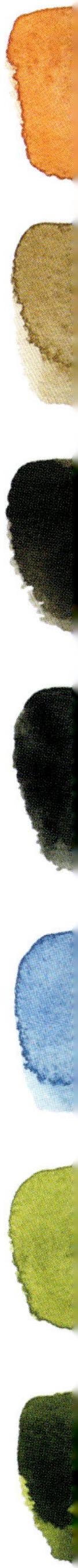

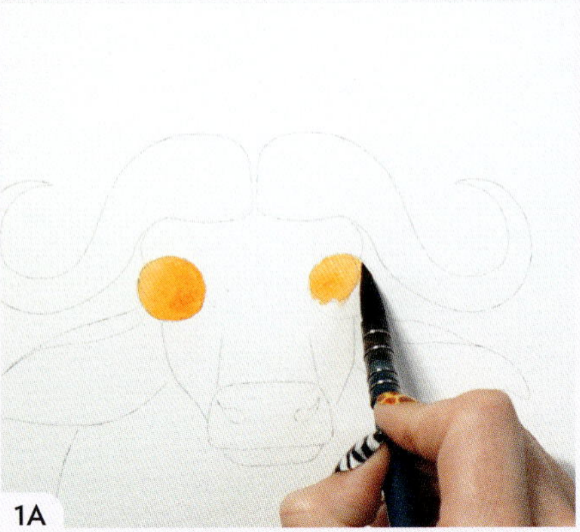

1A

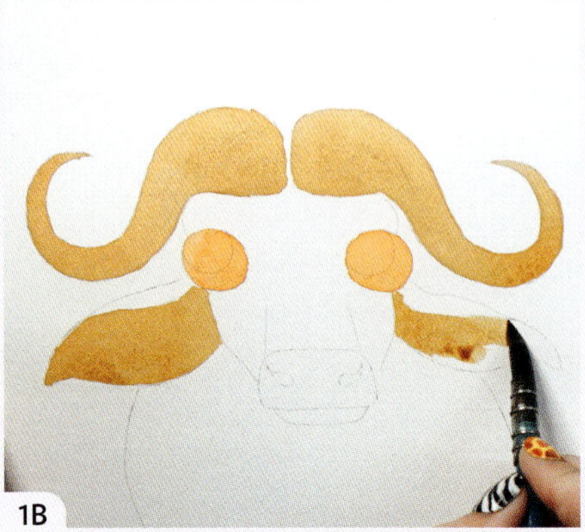

1B

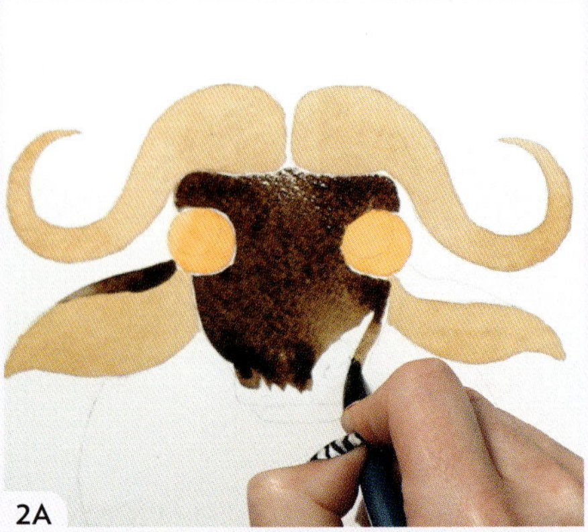

2A

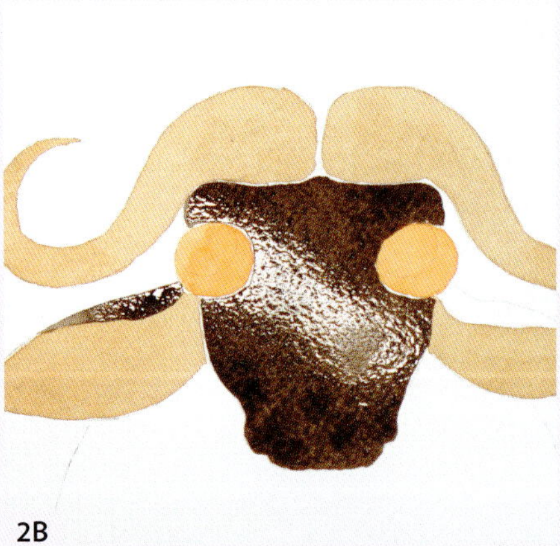

2B

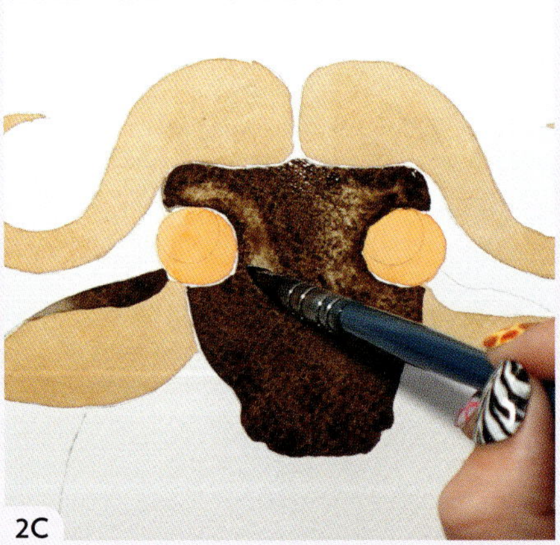

2C

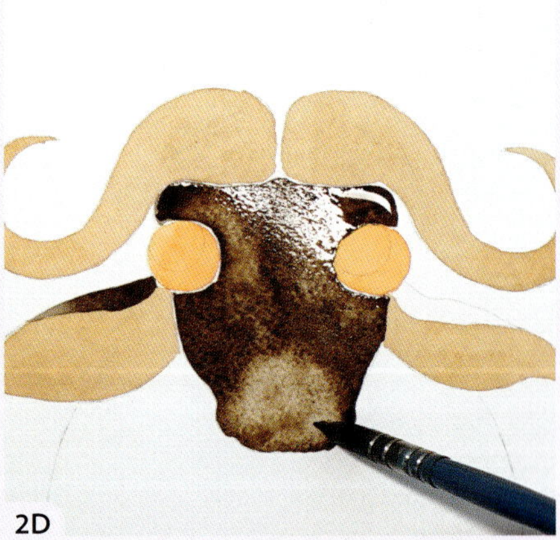

2D

Step 1

Mix up a small puddle of an orange color and a larger amount of a tan color. Using the orange color, paint in the eye circles (1A).

Wash your brush and fill it with the tan color and paint in the horns, as well as the inner parts of the ears (1B). Let this dry or make it dry!

Step 2

Mix up a large quantity of a dark brown color. I chose to mix together some brown, black, and a tiny bit of blue to get my dark brown.

Fill your brush with the dark brown color and paint in the head carefully, avoiding the eyes and horns (2A). Make sure to fill your brush with enough color to get a good wet coat of color, as it needs to stay wet for the next step. Let this soak in until it's around the gloss or satin stage, when you can start to see the texture of the paper showing through (2B).

Wash your brush, and when you pull it out of the water, lightly press it on the side of your water container to remove that big drip of water, but keep some water loaded in the brush. We're going to strategically create blooms to add texture and make

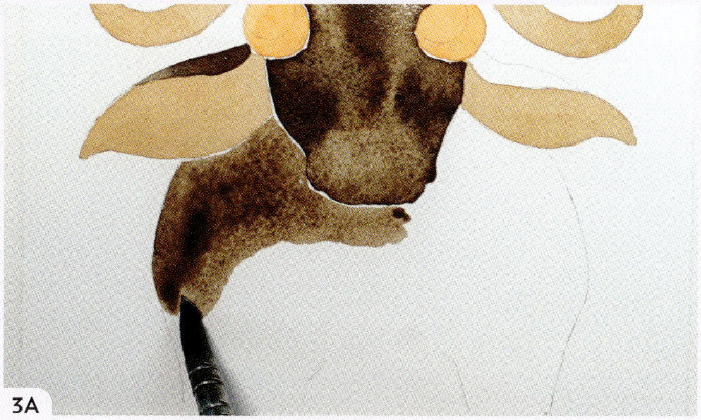

3A

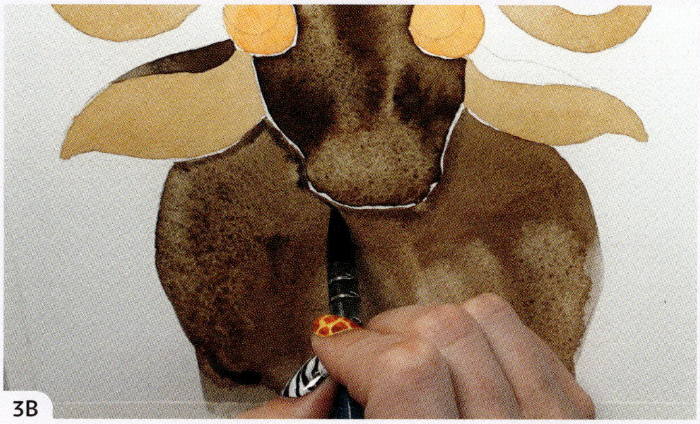

3B

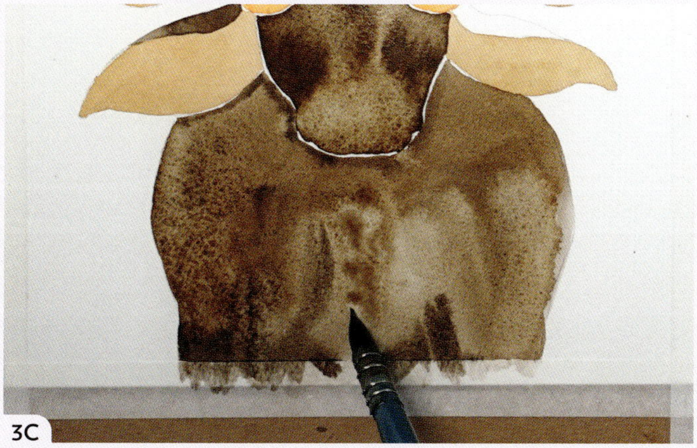

3C

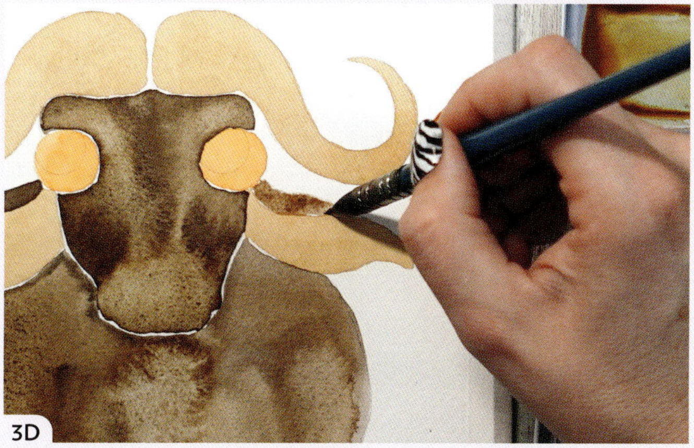

3D

certain areas lighter. To do this, drag your wet brush around the eyes to drop some water there, forming the brow bones (2C). Then move down to the mouth and drop a larger quantity right on the mouth (2D). If you end up with way too much water there, dry your brush and then lightly grab some of the excess. Blooms are sneaky and grow on their own, so err on the side of them being too small.

Step 3

Refill your brush with the dark brown color and paint the body. I didn't want my blooms and color placement to move into the body, so I was careful to leave a small gap between the body and head (3A). Then dip the tip of your brush into a dark black color and lightly drop that along the line between the head and body and around the legs to create a little shadow effect (3B).

While the body is still wet, wash your brush and fill it with clean water. Drop a little water down the middle of the chest to give it some texture (3C). Remember, blooms grow more than you might think, so be patient for them to form! While you're waiting, make sure you've painted in the tops of the ears with the dark brown color (3D). Let this dry or make it dry!

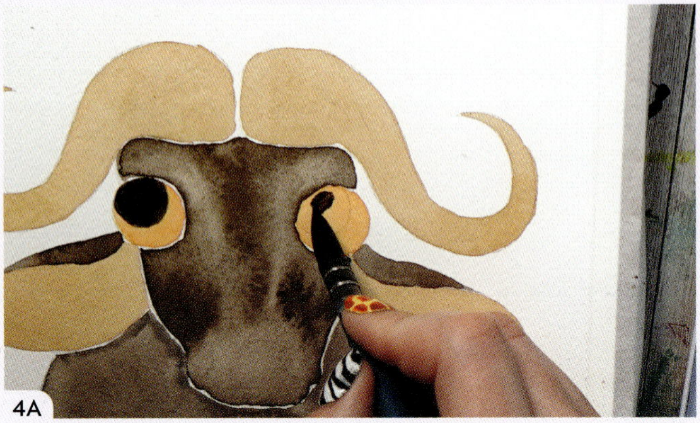
4A

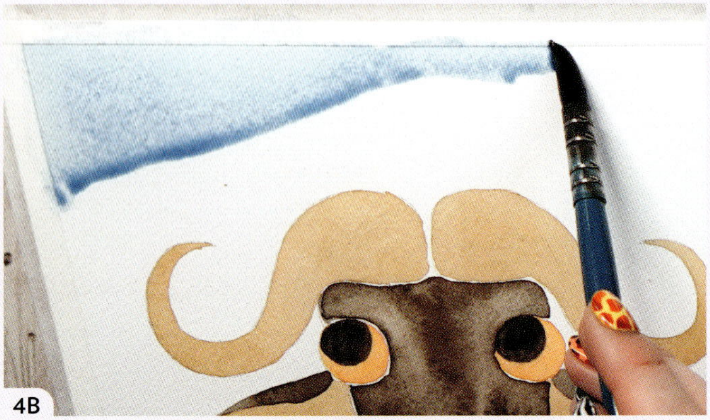
4B

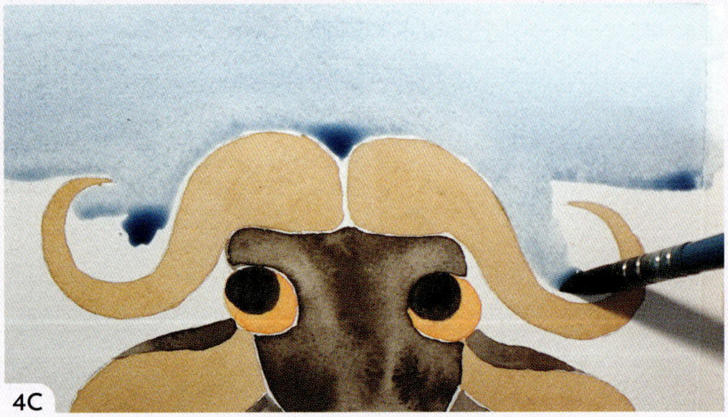
4C

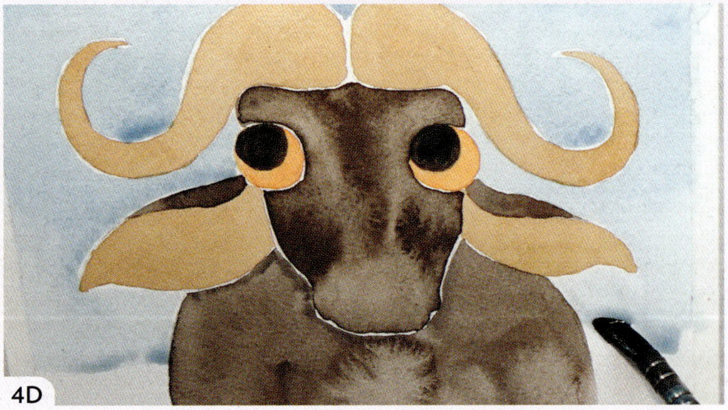
4D

Step 4

Make sure your black watercolor is activated so you can dip directly into it. Then mix up a large quantity of a light blue-gray color and a large puddle of green.

Grab some black watercolor and paint in the pupils of the eyes (4A).

Next make a messy gradient background to simulate the sky and grasslands, following the technique of a drip line.

Start by holding the page at an angle, allowing gravity to help (this is easier if you tape your painting to a board). Fill your brush with lots of the light blue-gray color and start at the top, making strokes across the page, leaving a little pool of water at the bottom of your strokes (4B). Refill your brush and continue pulling the drip line down. Working around the horns can get tricky, so it's okay if you get some backruns—they can serve as clouds in the sky!

Notice that as I move around the different parts of his head, I leave little puddles that I can grab and pull down so no area dries before I can move back to it (4C). When you get to just under the horns, instead of refilling your brush with the blue gray, start filling it with clean water and continue moving down until you have reached to just under his shoulders (4D).

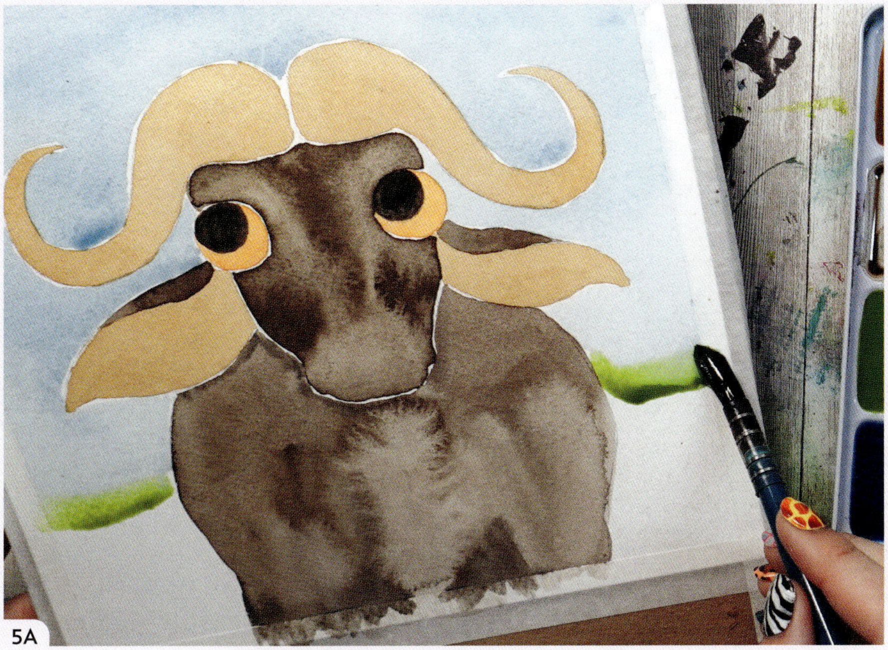
5A

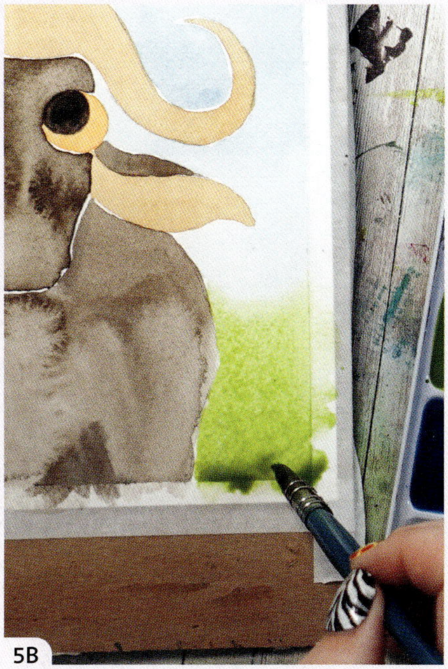
5B

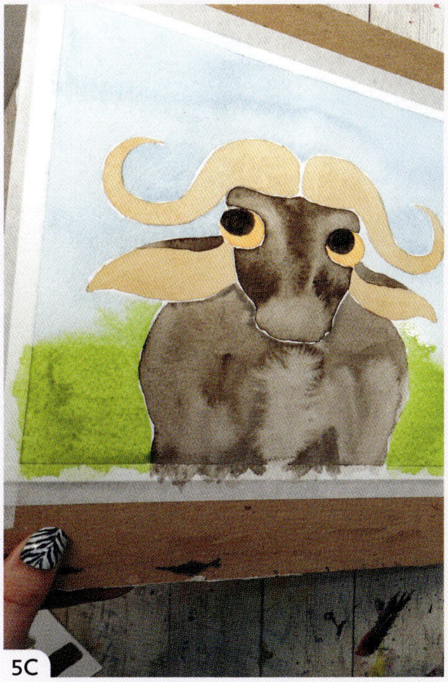
5C

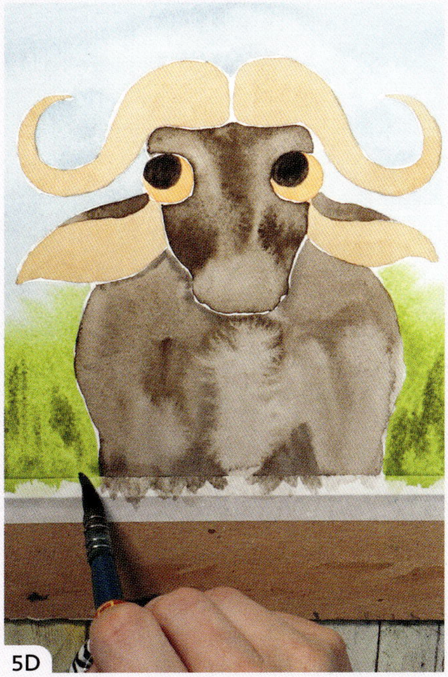
5D

Step 5

Once there, grab your green and pull that down to the bottom to make the gradient (5A)! To further embrace some of the fun, flowy nature of watercolor, load more green onto the bottom of the painting (5B) and then tilt the page back and forth to encourage some of that extra green to flow around and create fun shapes (5C). While it is still wet, touch your brush onto a pan of green and drop it into the green foreground to give it a little variation (5D). Let this dry or make it dry!

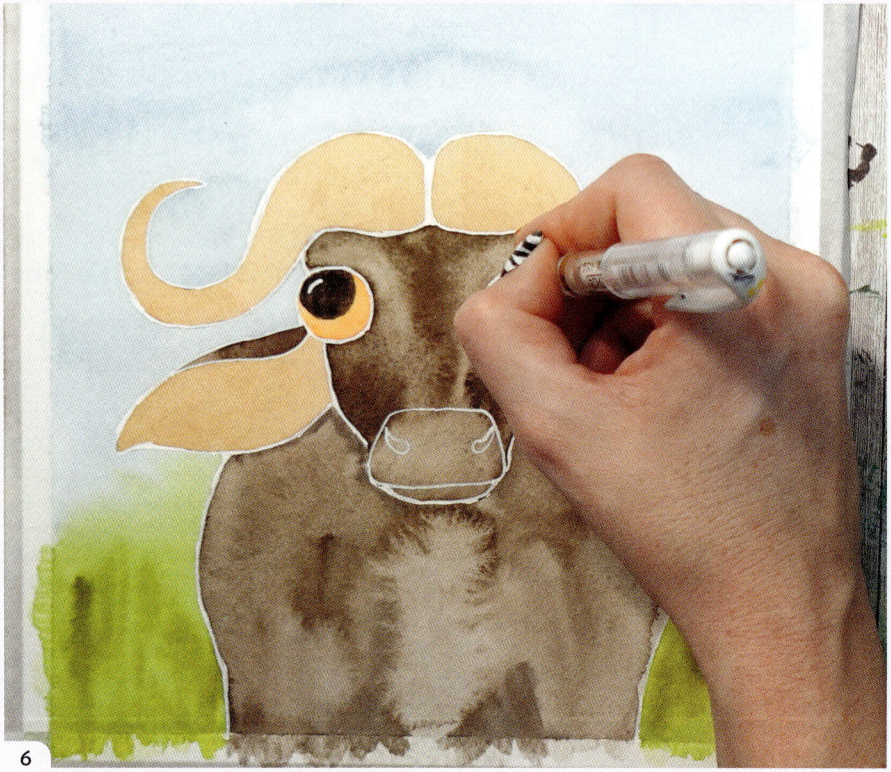

6

Step 6

Grab your white gel pen and outline the body, head, ears, and horns. Then add in the finishing touches like the nostrils and highlights in the eyes!

Mix up enough color

You might notice that the right side of the body in my painting gets a bit lighter—this is a cautionary tale about not mixing enough color. I ran out of color and had to supplement by refilling my brush with water. In this painting, it doesn't matter much, though, because we want color and texture variations, so I didn't fix it. But if I was going for a smoother coat, it would have caused big problems.

BELINDA THE BAT

You might be surprised to learn that bats play a vital role in pollination. Hundreds of species of fruits rely on bats to pollinate them, including bananas, mangos, figs, guavas, and even saguaro cacti. This painting is a great way to practice mixing dark colors, because we'll need quite a few!

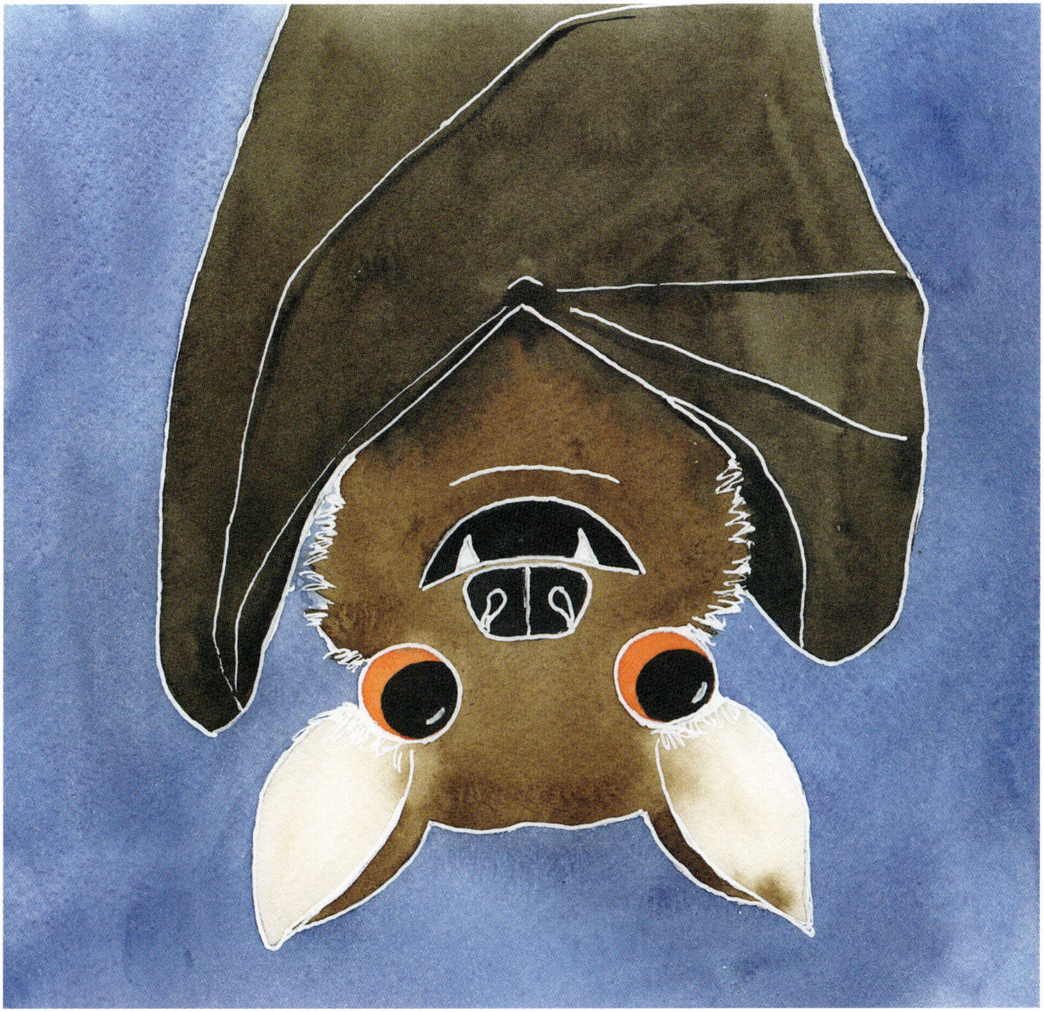

Color Palette

Orange

Dark Brown

Medium Brown

Black

Blues

Techniques

Charging, page 27

Keeping White Space, page 26

Layering, page 29

Watercolor Washes, page 24

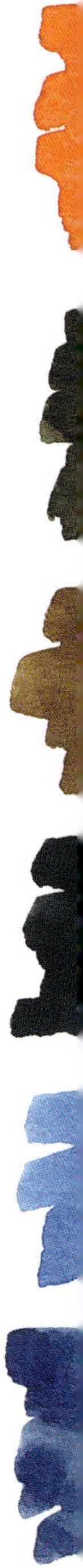

Step 1

Mix up a small puddle of a bright orange color. Grab the bright orange color and paint the eyes.

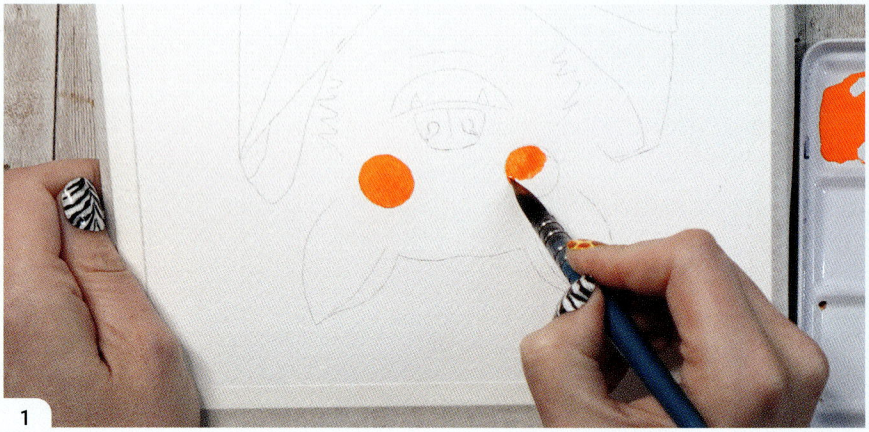

1

Step 2

Mix up quite a large quantity of a medium brown color. I paint the head and body separately but used the same base for both, modifying the leftover paint for the body color.

Paint in the head, avoiding the mouth, nose, and eyes (2A). Normally the mouth and nose would be painted on top of previous layers, but the dark paint color makes it harder to keep track of the outlines, so avoiding those areas can be helpful here. Paint in the tops (or in this case, since it's upside down, the bottoms) of the ears (2B). You want the head to be at the satin stage for the next step, so keep an eye on how wet it is.

While it's still a bit wet, touch your brush to your black watercolor and then, using the tip of your brush, lightly drop some of that color along the top of the bat's chest to create the shadow of the wings (2C).

Then lazily wash your brush so that just some of the color comes out, leaving lots of water in your brush. Mix this around on your palette to combine, and then use that desaturated color to fill in the ears and gently touch to the dark brown while it's still wet so the colors softly bleed together (2D). Let this dry or make it dry!

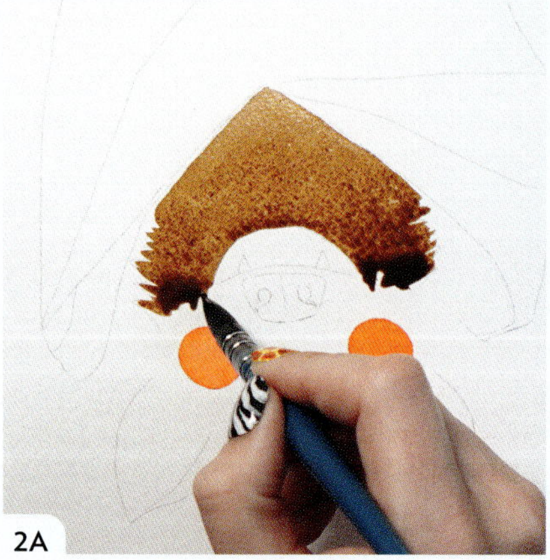

2A

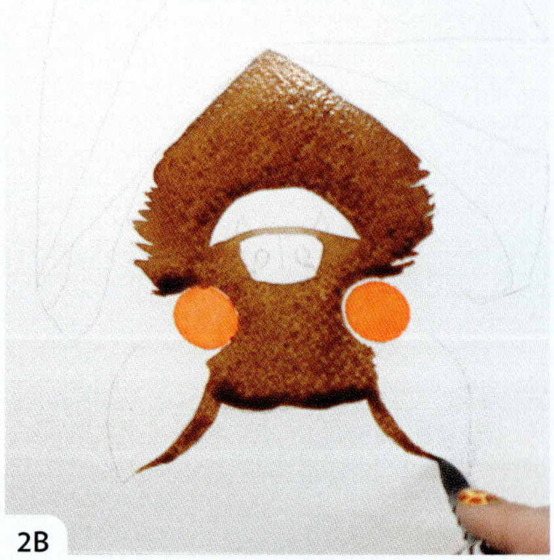

2B

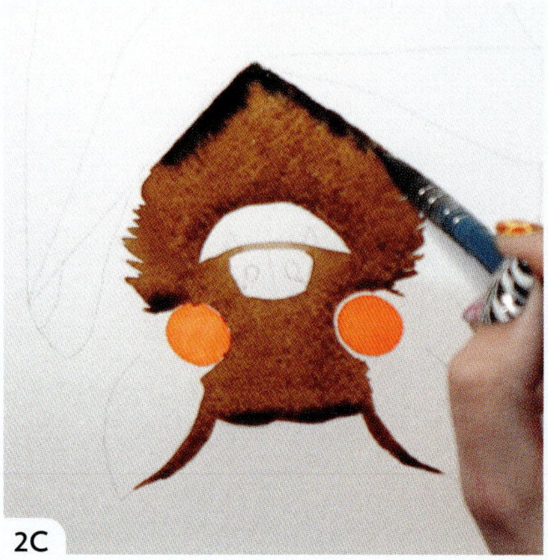

2C

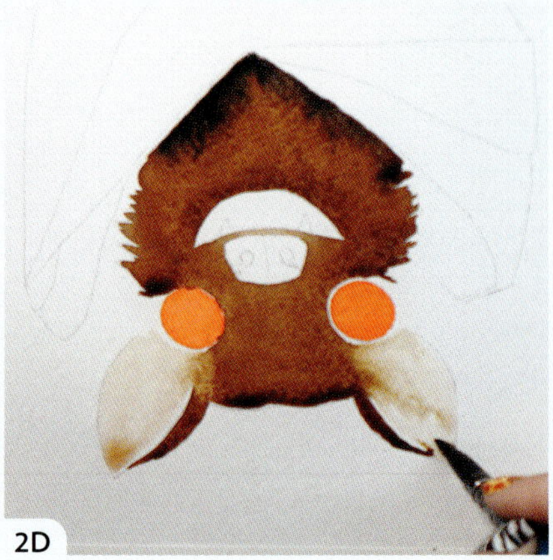

2D

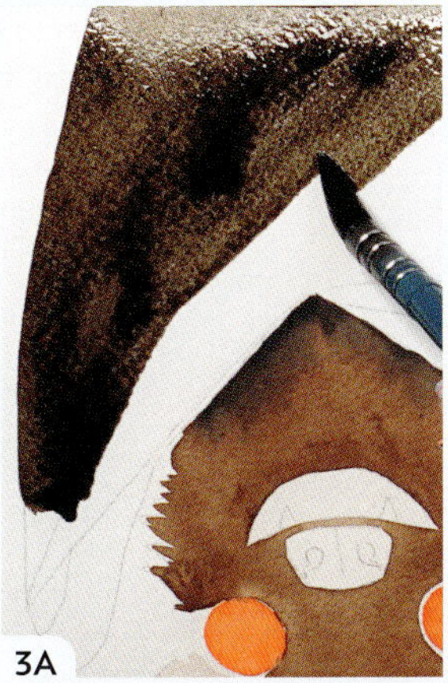
3A

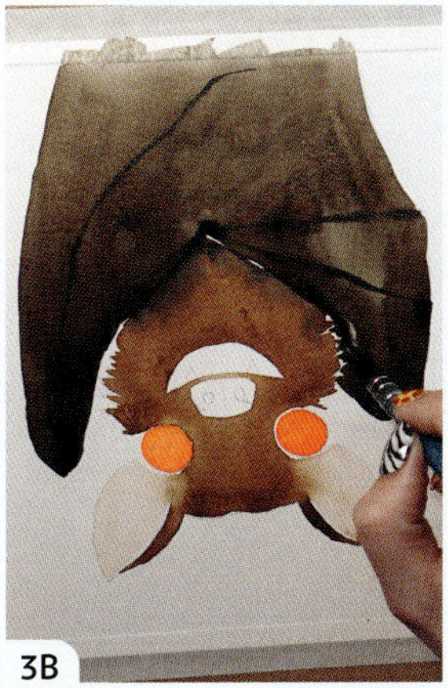
3B

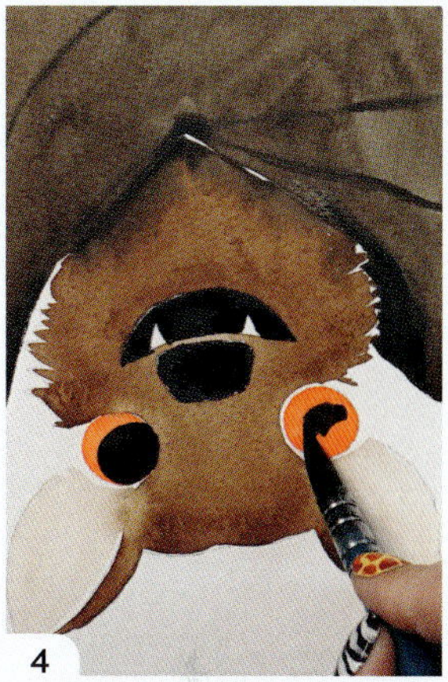
4

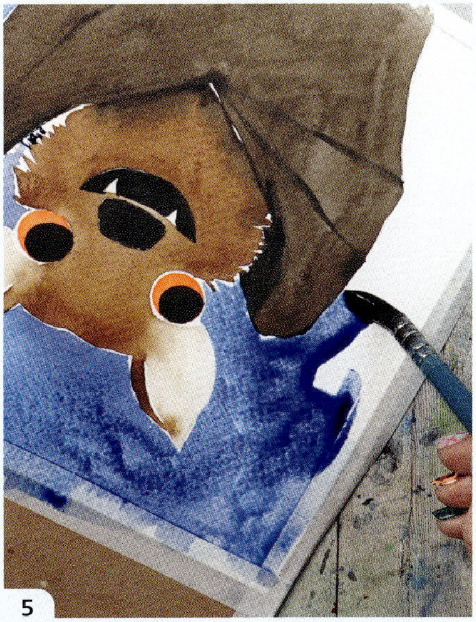
5

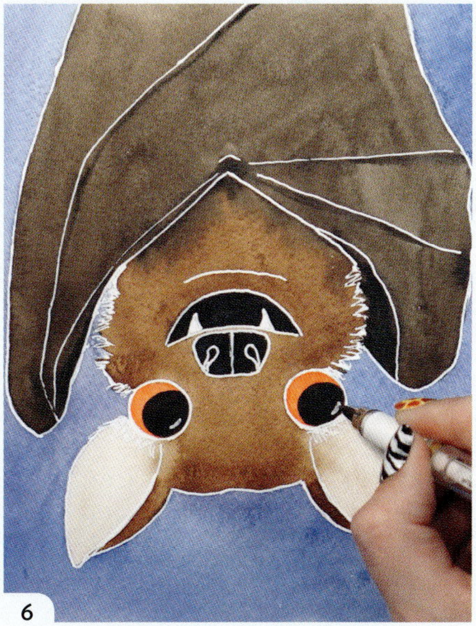
6

Step 3

Evaluate how much of the medium brown color you have left. You want to make sure you have enough to cover the wings of the bat. If you don't, add some water to the mix and start adding in browns and blacks until it's a very dark shade of brown, leaning toward black.

Paint in the wings of the bat with the dark brown color (3A). Make sure this stays at the satin stage of wetness.

Tap your brush onto your black watercolor to grab a saturated amount in the tip of your brush, and lightly add a little shadow along the lines of the wings. Grab some more of the black color and drop it along the insides of the wings near the face to create additional shadow (3B). Let this dry or make it dry!

Step 4

Refill your brush with the black watercolor and paint in the mouth, avoiding the fangs so they stay white. Paint the nose and pupils of the eyes. Let this dry or make it dry!

Step 5

Mix up a large quantity of blue, or a few blue colors if you want some variation, and then create a messy wash across the background. It helps to rotate the piece as you paint the background, so it's easier to angle the the brush and have better control. Let this dry or make it dry!

Step 6

Grab your white gel pen and outline the different body parts and add on the finishing touches, like nostrils on the nose and highlights in the eyes! If you accidentally covered the fangs in a previous step, you could re-add them with the white gel pen.

DOTTIE THE DONKEY

Color Palette

Teal

Dark Brown

Black

Pinks

Techniques

Adding Shadows, page 27

Adding Texture, page 28

Dropping In, page 27

Layering, page 29

Lifting, page 26

Watercolor Washes, page 24

I just love donkeys! Not only do they have sweet faces, but their character is also sweet. They are highly intelligent creatures and excellent communicators. The noise they commonly make is called a bray, and the call can be heard well over a mile away! This painting is fun because you get to dive into several techniques we've been practicing, like charging and some cool blooms!

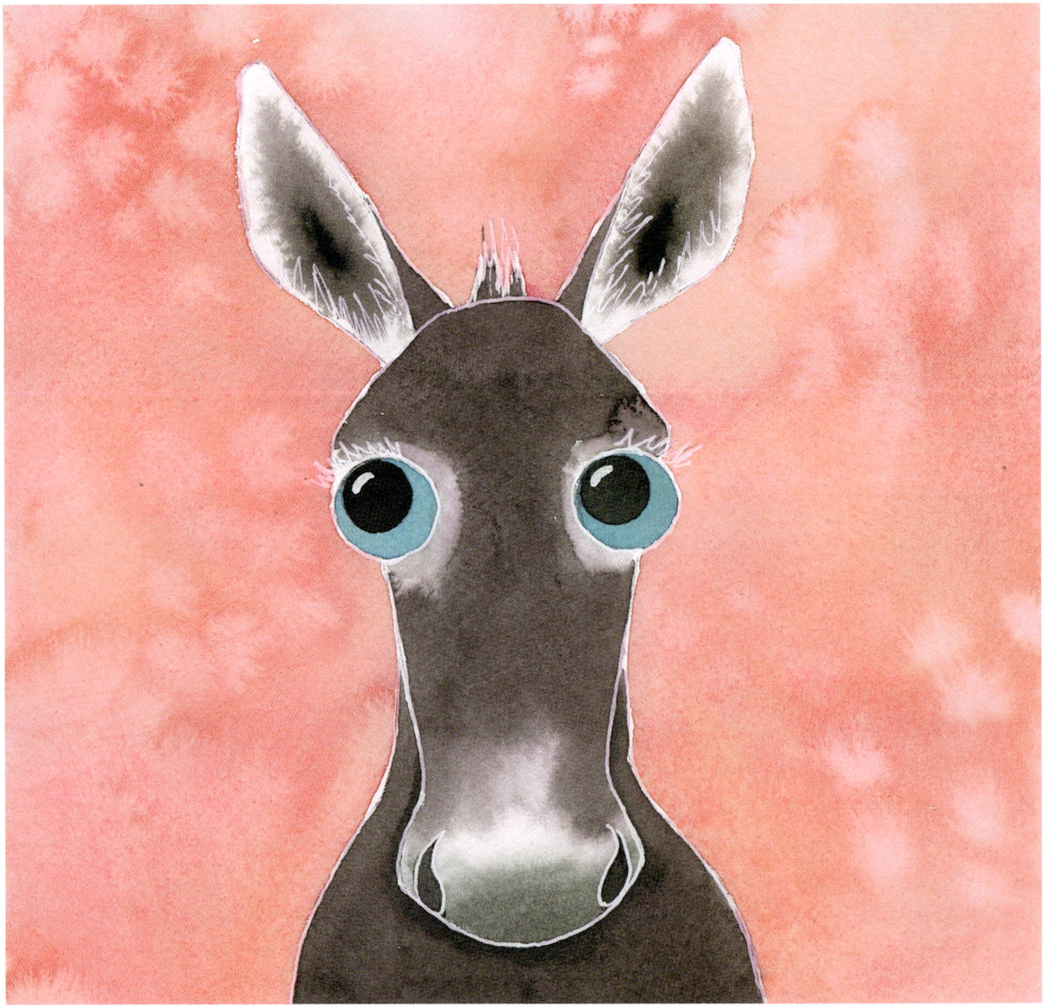

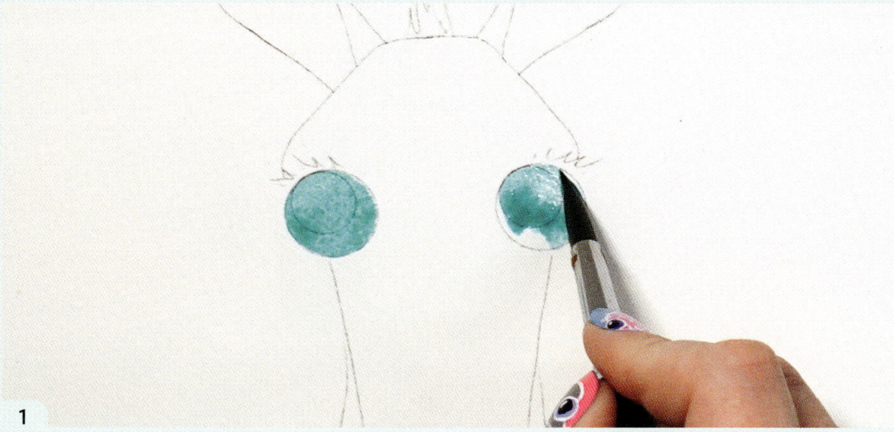

1

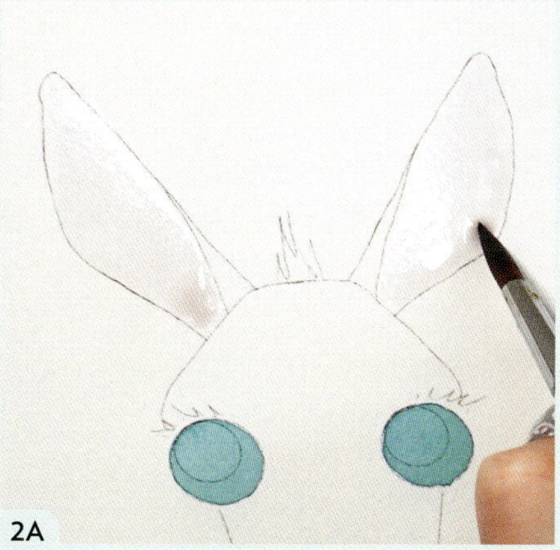

2A

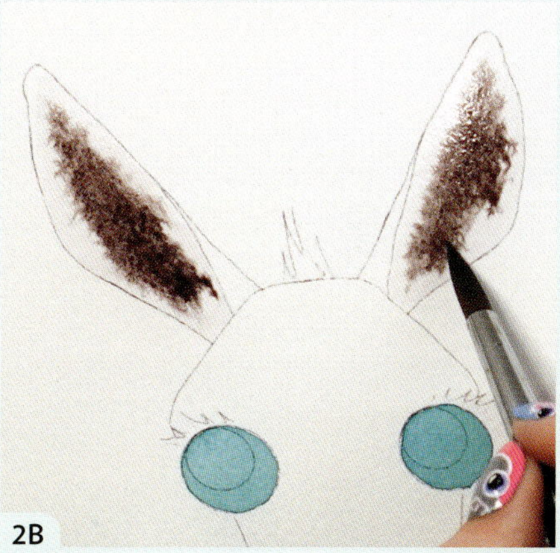

2B

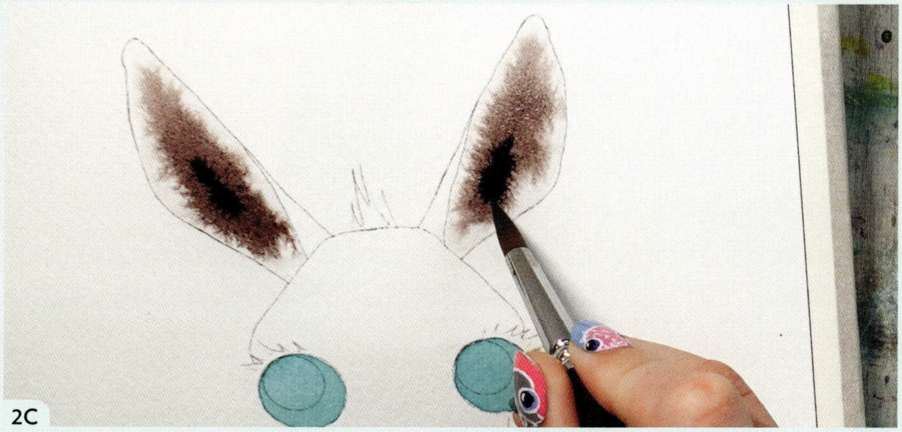

2C

Step 1

First, mix up a puddle of teal and paint in the larger eye circles.

Step 2

Mix up a puddle of a dark brown color. Then wash your brush and wet the insides of the ears until they are at about the gloss or satin stage (2A).

Once the paper has reached the desired wetness stage, fill your brush with the dark brown color and drop it into the wet insides of the ears, avoiding the edges (2B). Remember, wherever you pick up your brush will deposit the most color, so I like to pick it up in the center of the ear rather than near the edge.

Keep an eye on the wetness of the ears. The paper should reach the satin stage, or nearing damp, in order to be able to add some concentrated black in the center of the brown without it spreading too much. So, once the paper is at that satin stage, fill your brush tip with some concentrated black and gently touch it to the center of the brown to deposit a few drops (2C). Let this dry or make it dry!

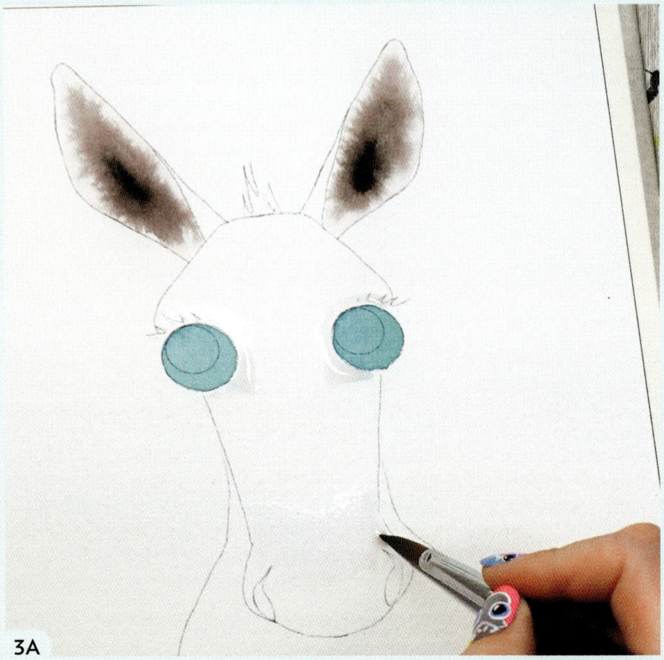

3A

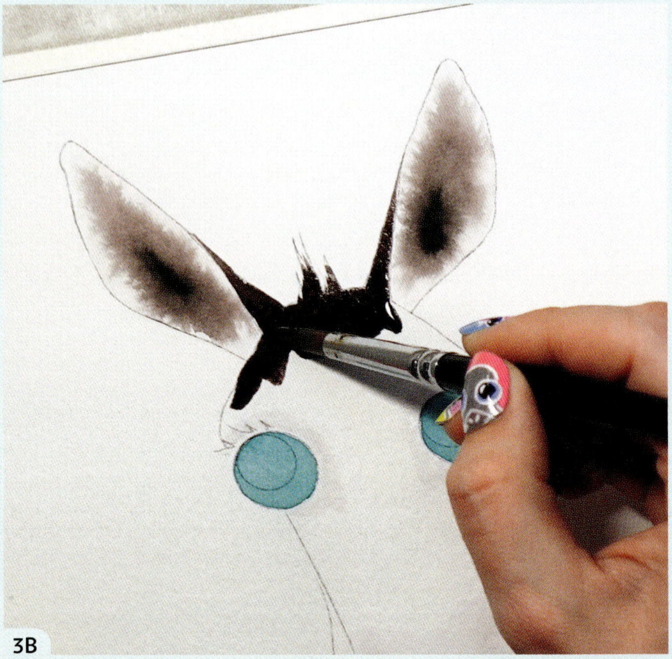

3B

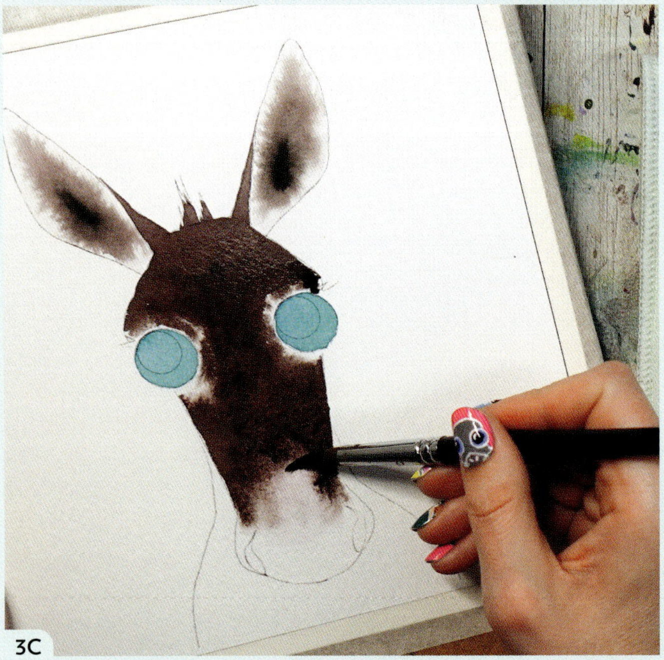

3C

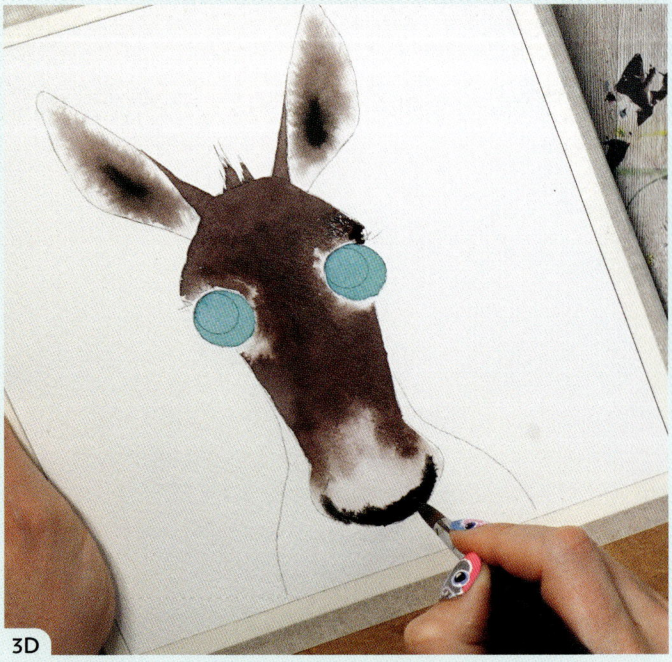

3D

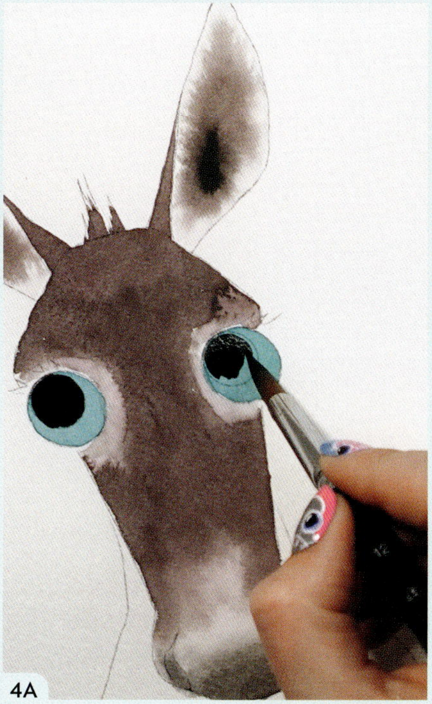

4A

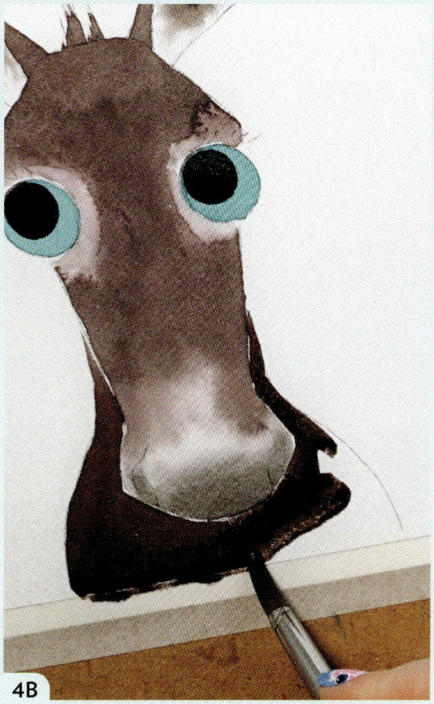

4B

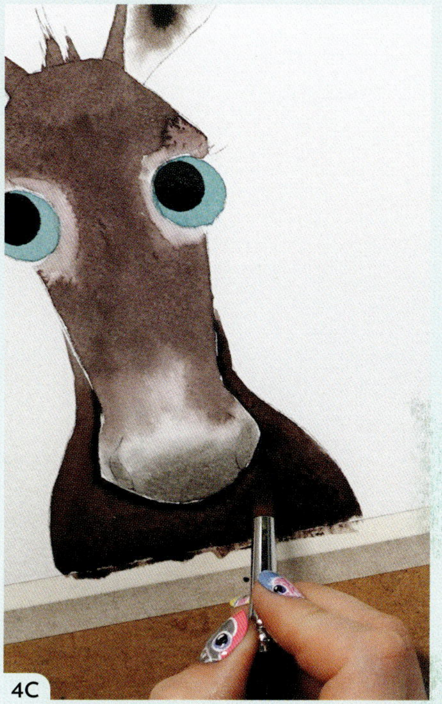

4C

Step 3

Load a clean brush with water and paint in water around the eyes, as well as on the donkey's nose (3A).

Load your brush with the dark brown color and paint in the middle-facing parts of the ears and the head of the donkey, just letting your brush graze the areas you pre-wet (3B). My color started to bleed a bit too much into the nose, so I dried my brush off and lifted some of it up to maintain the lighter space (3C).

My donkey's nose started to dry, so I washed my brush and re-wet the nose to a satin stage before filling my brush with black and dropping it along the bottom of the mouth (3D).

Before moving on, evaluate your painting. Different watercolors will have different effects. If the areas around the eyes are lighter, leave them be. My watercolors bled more than expected and didn't leave much lighter areas around the eyes. Because it was mostly dry, I used the lifting dry watercolor technique to pick up a bit around the eyes. Let this dry or make it dry!

Step 4

Fill your brush with black and paint in the pupils of the eyes (4A).

Wash your brush and fill it with the dark brown color and paint in the donkey's body (4B).

While the body is still wet, fill the tip of your brush with black and lightly drag it along the bottom of the mouth to give it a bit of shadow (4C). Let this dry or make it dry!

Step 5

Mix up two pink colors. I made one more coral colored, and one closer to just pink. Use a messy wash to paint in the background (5A). To add a little texture to the background, drop in a little water or a little darker color to the areas that are still wet to create blooms of water and color (5B). Fill your brush with black and paint in the nostrils (5C). Let this dry or make it dry!

Step 6

Grab your white gel pen and outline the different body parts, scribble some fluff in the ears, and add on the finishing touches, like eyelashes and highlights in the eyes!

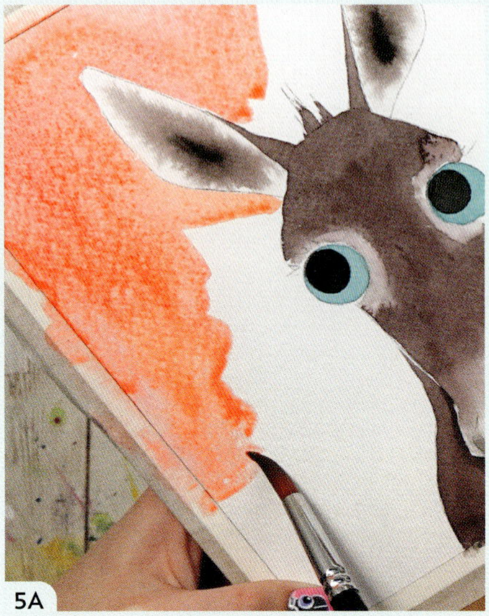

5A

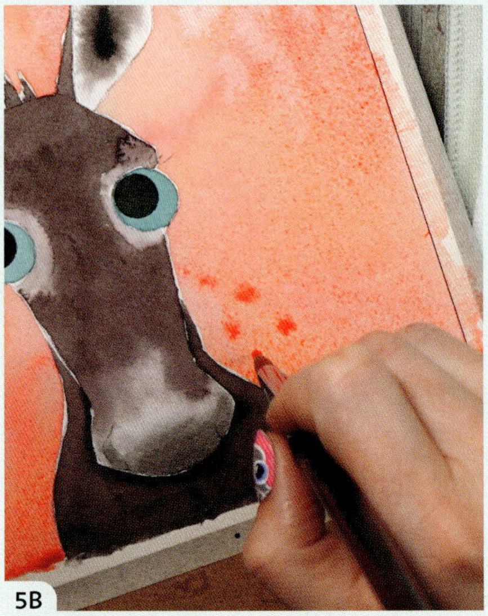

5B

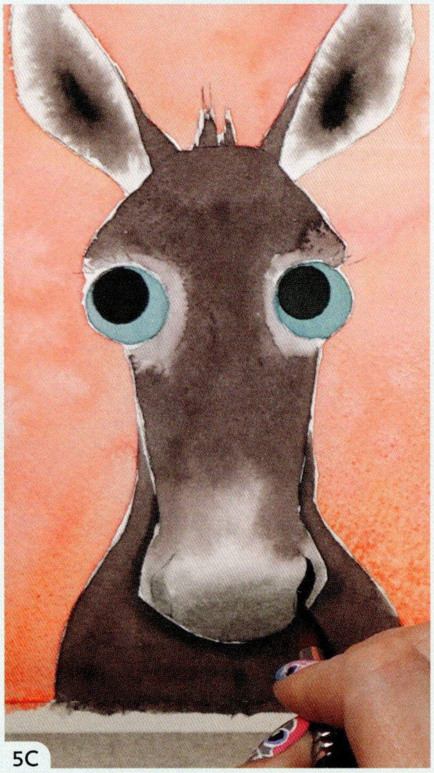

5C

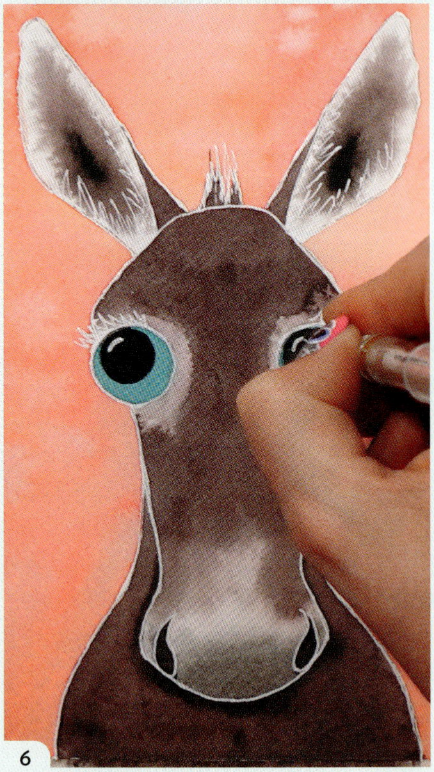

6

EMILIO THE ELEPHANT

Elephants have long been one of my favorite animals. I love things that exemplify opposites, and elephants fit that description perfectly—they have a giant, intimidating stature, but a sweet and gentle nature. One fun fact about elephants is that they are excellent swimmers. They even use their trunk as a snorkel in deep waters!

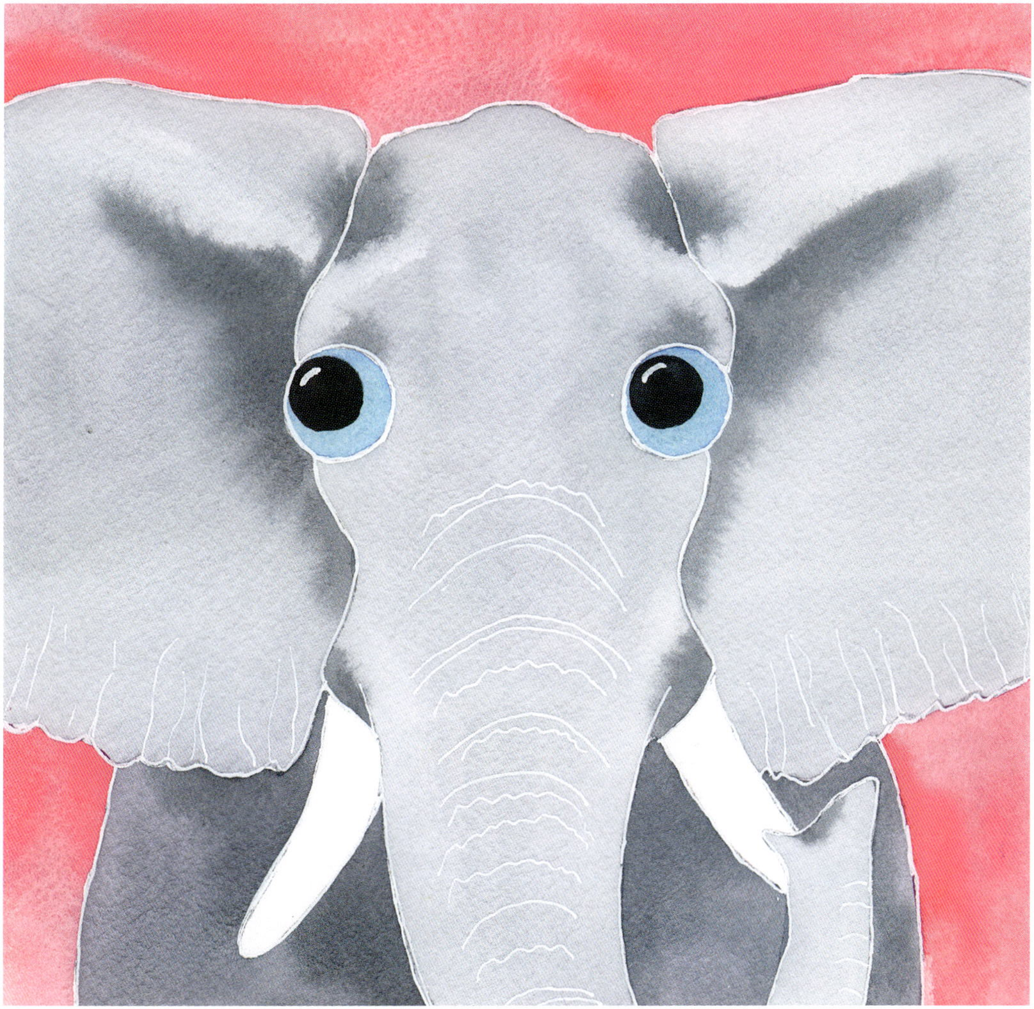

Color Palette

Light Blue

Gray

Black

Pink

Purple

Techniques

Adding Shadows, page 27

Adding Texture, page 28

Charging, page 27

Layering, page 29

Lifting, page 26

Step 1

Mix up a light blue color and paint in the larger eye circles. Let this dry or make it dry!

Step 2

Mix up a large quantity of a gray color. You need lots of this to go over the entire elephant.

Start by filling the the first ear, in my case the right ear, with the gray color, making sure it's nice and wet so you have a bit of working time (2A).

While the paint is still wet, dry your brush off, and then swipe just above the eye at an angle up and away to remove a little of the color (2B). This also makes this area drier and prevents color bleeding.

Quickly, while everything is still wet, fill your brush with black (ensure it's not too wet) and gently drop a little of the black above the line you lifted out (2C). Grab some more black and deposit along the face, under the line you lifted, and farther down the face with just a bit of paint. Repeat these steps with the second ear (2D). This gives a bit of shape to the two large ears. Let this dry or make it dry!

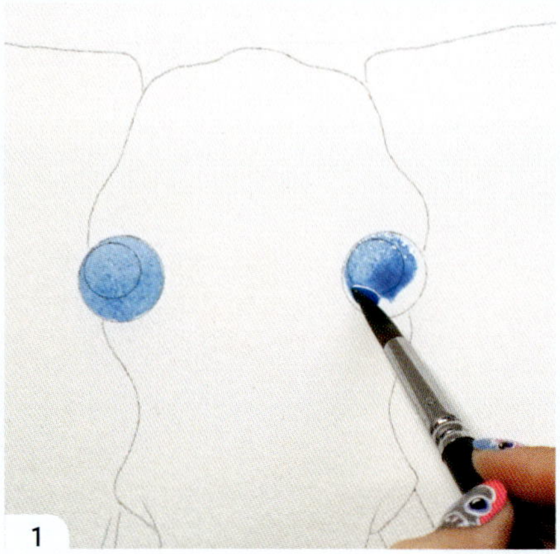

1

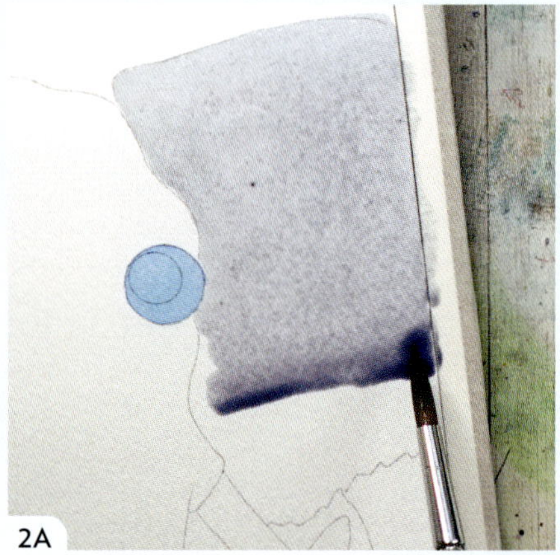

2A

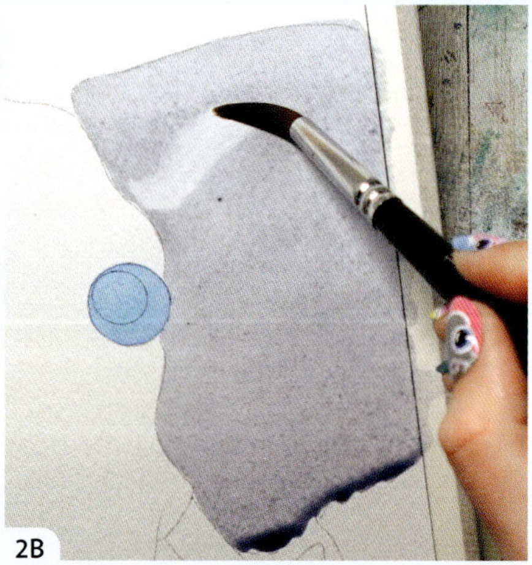

2B

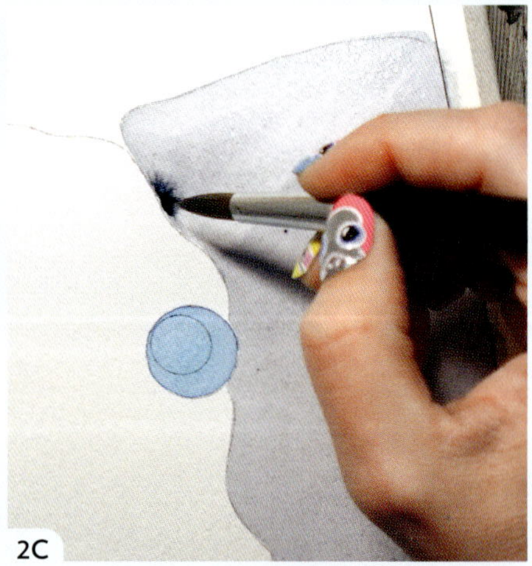

2C

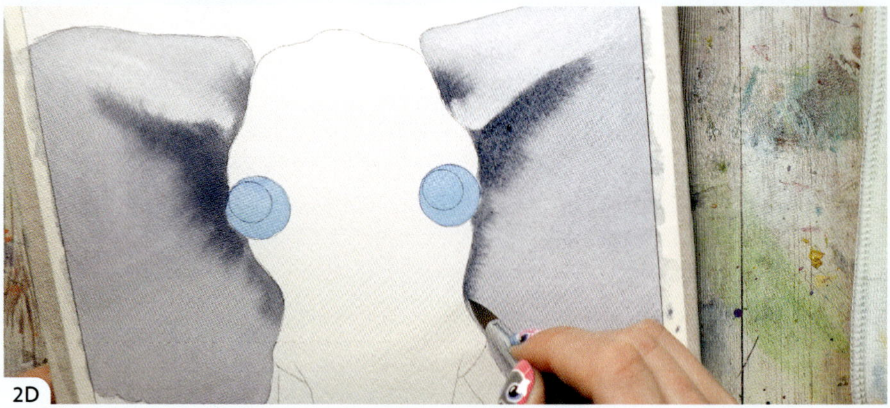

2D

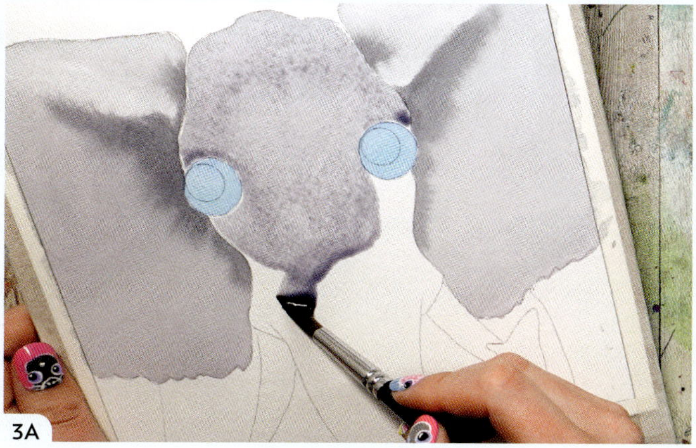

3A

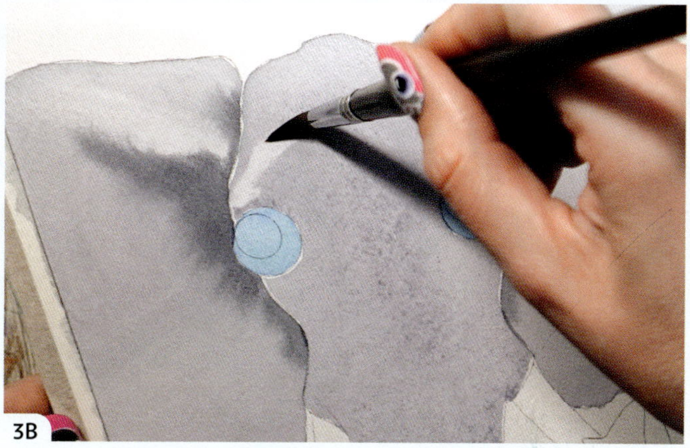

3B

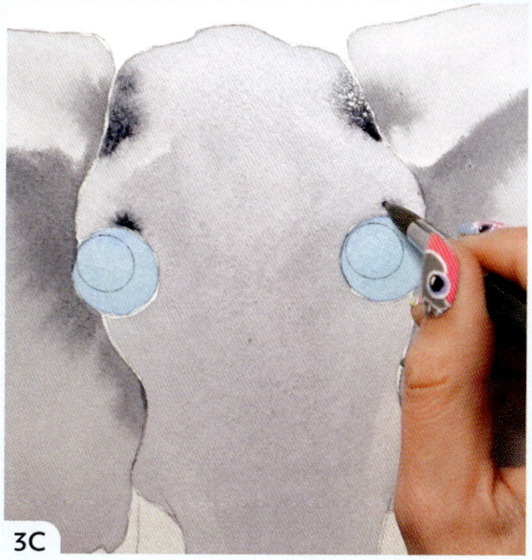

3C

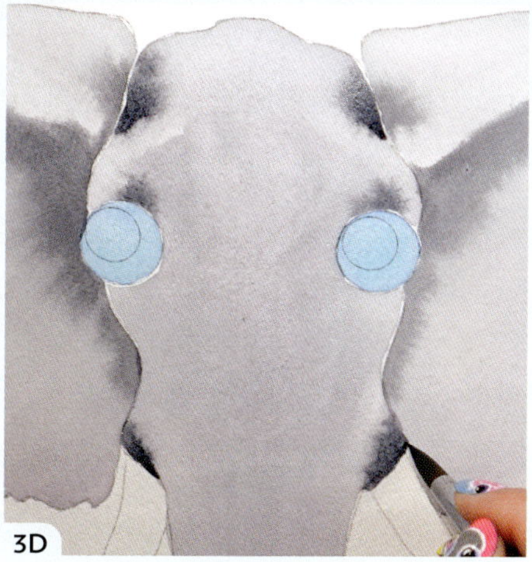

3D

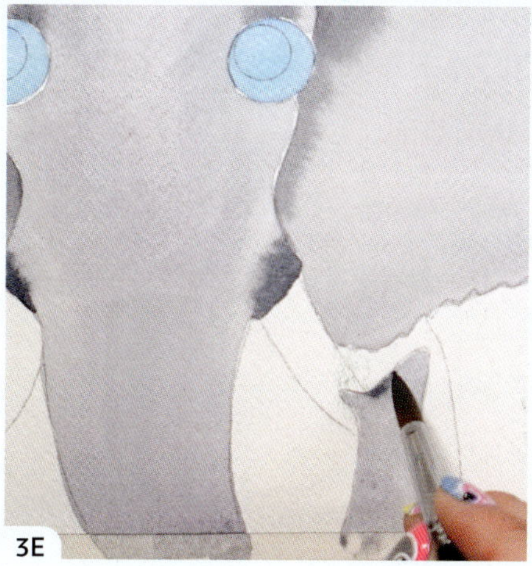

3E

Step 3

Fill your brush with gray and paint the entire face and main segment of the trunk (3A). Keep this wet as you work—you may need to go back to the top occasionally to drop a little extra color in to keep it wet.

While the paint is still wet, dry your brush off and lift from above the eyes at an angle toward the top of the head (3B).

Fill the tip of your brush with black and gently drop a little of that color above the lines you lifted, above the (3C), and right at the base of the head where the tusks connect (3D).

Paint gray into the other segment of the trunk. While it's still wet, fill the tip of your brush with black and tap it on the top of the trunk segment to deposit some color (3E). Let this dry or make it dry!

Step 4

For the body, you'll work in sections. For each of the sections, start by filling your brush with gray and paint in the area. While it's still wet, fill your brush with black paint and drop it near the top and around any features that would cast a shadow (4).

Fill your brush with black and paint in the pupils. Let this dry or make it dry!

Step 5

Mix up a couple colors for the background. I chose a pink and a pinky purple. Use a messy wash to paint the areas around the elephant. Let this dry or make it dry!

Step 6

Grab your white gel pen and outline all the main shapes of the body and add in a few details. I added some lines to the bottoms of the ears. For the trunk, I made curved lines and alternated between solid lines and squiggly ones. Don't forget the highlights in the eyes.

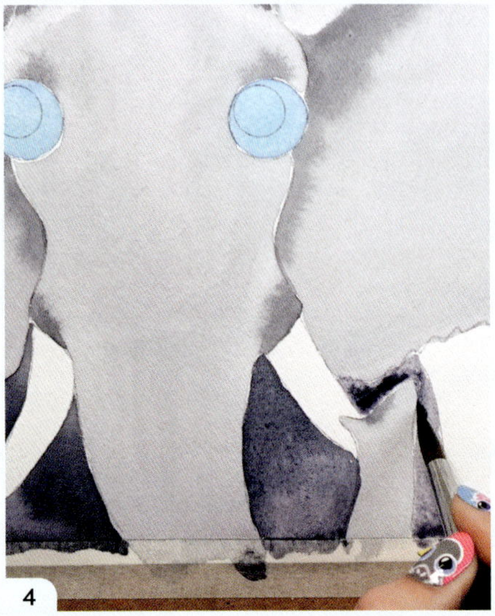
4

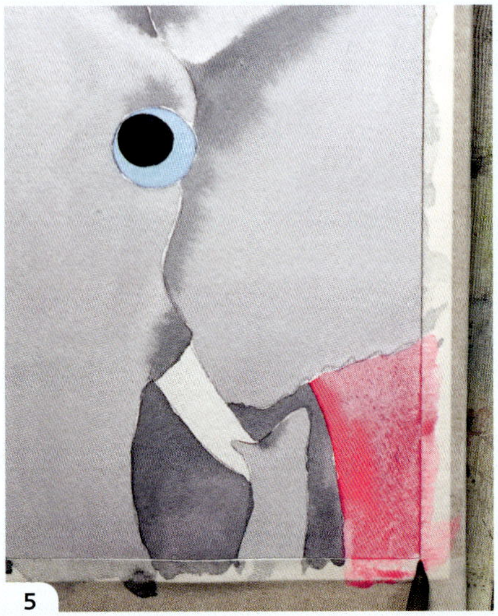
5

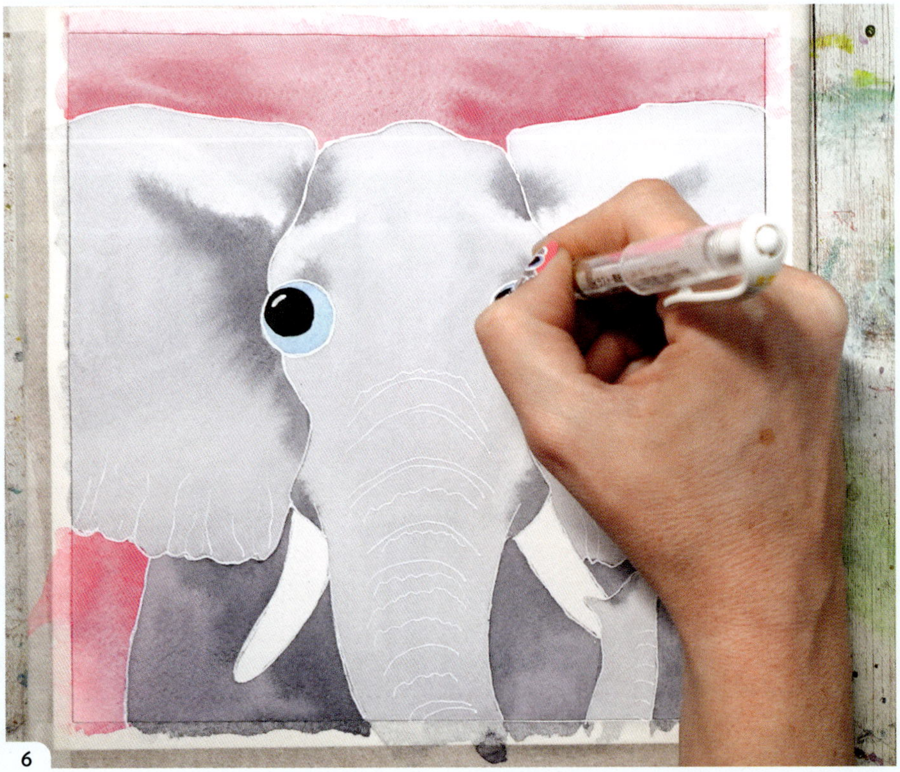
6

HEATHER THE HIGHLAND COO

These fluffy-haired cows, called *coos* in Scottish, are absolutely adorable and very sweet. I had the pleasure of getting to see them in real life, and I was surprised by how much smaller they are than the cows I am used to seeing. Fun fact: Highland cows are highly sociable creatures; they enjoy the company of humans and love making friends with other Highland cows. They even engage in play fighting with their friends! This painting turns out super cute and invites a bit of extra fun with the background!

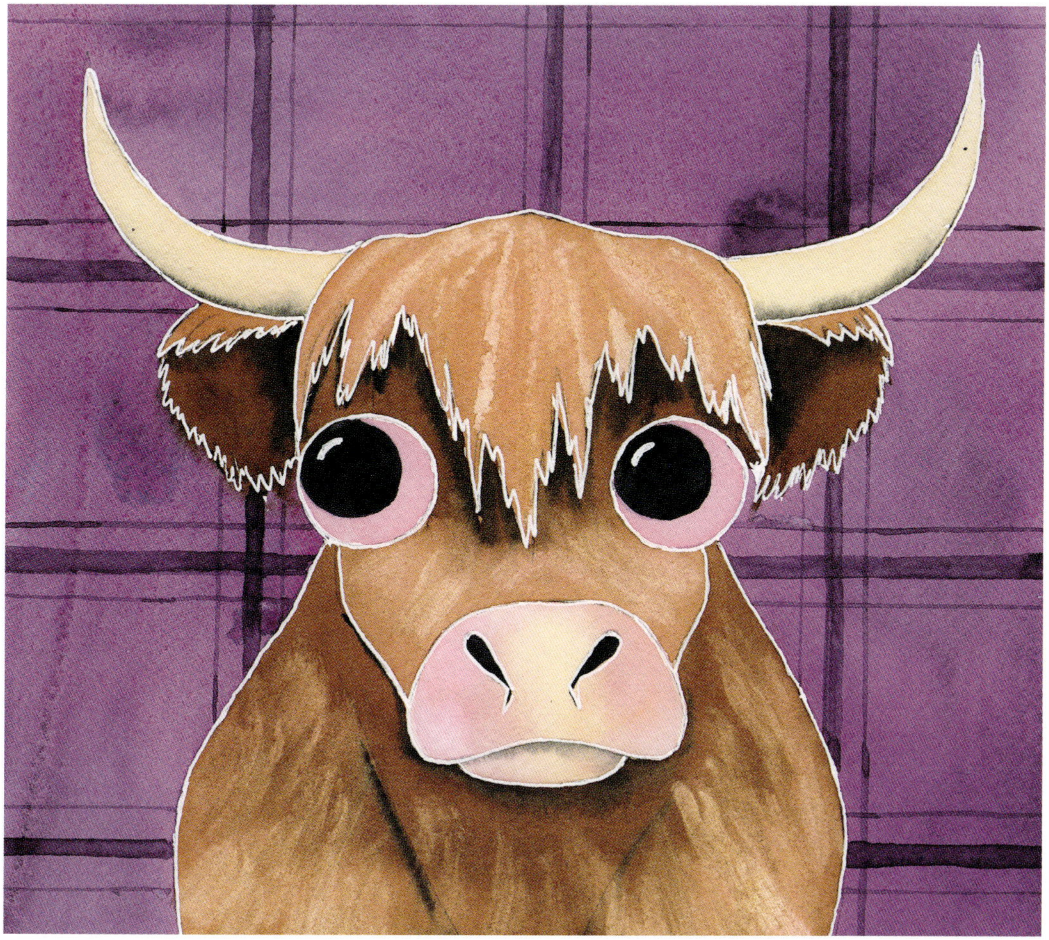

Color Palette

Light Pink
Light Brown
Dark Brown
Brown
Black
Purples

Techniques

Adding Shadows, page 27
Charging, page 27
Layering, page 29
Lifting, page 26

Step 1

Mix up a light pink color and paint in the main eye circles. Mix up a large puddle of a light yellowish-brown color, with lots of water and just a little color. Paint in both of the horns (1A).

For the nose, paint the light yellowish brown in the center and, while it's still wet, wash your brush and reload it with the pink color you used in the eyes and paint that around the yellow, just touching it so the colors lightly bleed together (1B). Let this dry or make it dry!

Step 2

Mix up a large puddle of a brown color and prepare a piece of paper towel by folding it over until it has a point (2A).

Fill your brush with the brown color and paint in the fringe (2B). While it's still wet, drag the prepared paper towel point along the fringe to lift out lines (2C).

Fill your brush with the brown color and paint in the tops of the ears. Let this dry or make it dry!

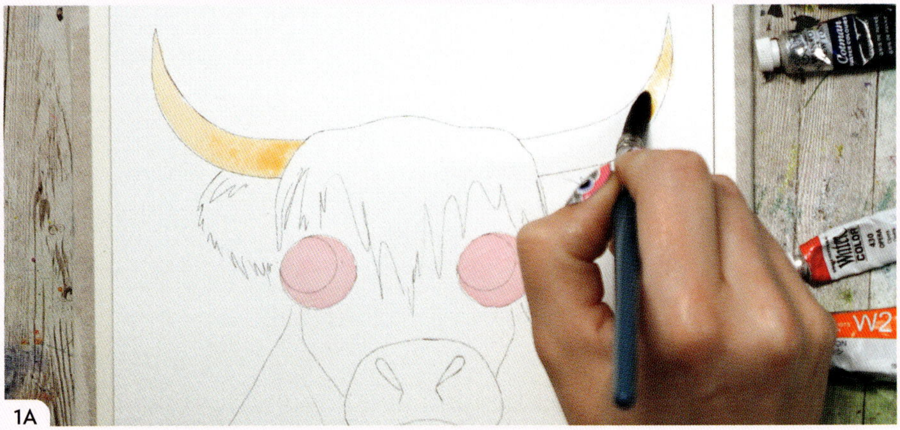

1A

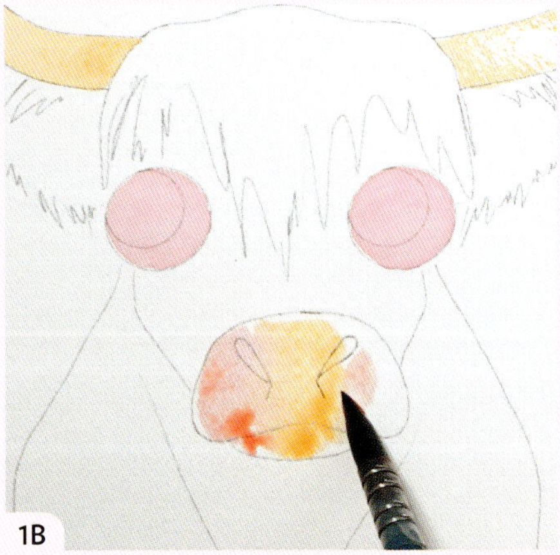

1B

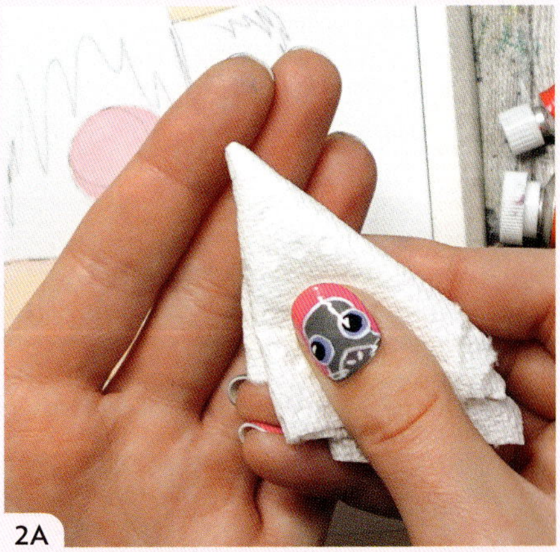

2A

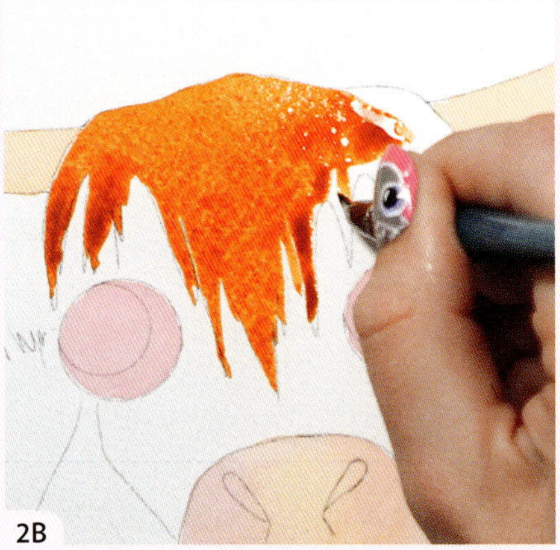

2B

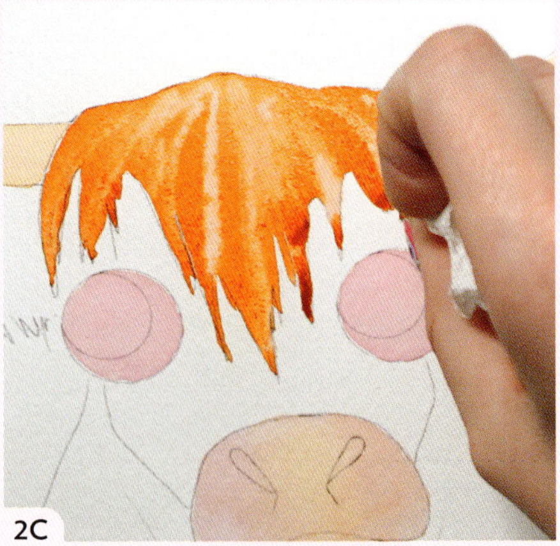

2C

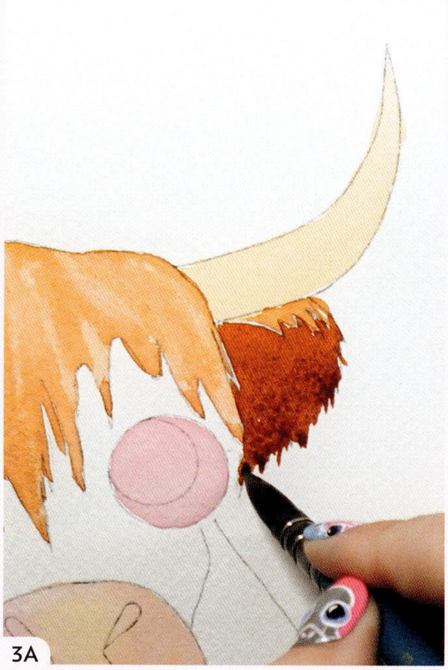

3A

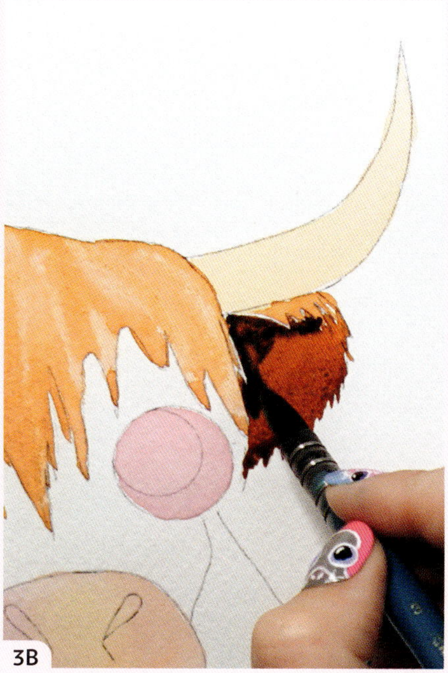

3B

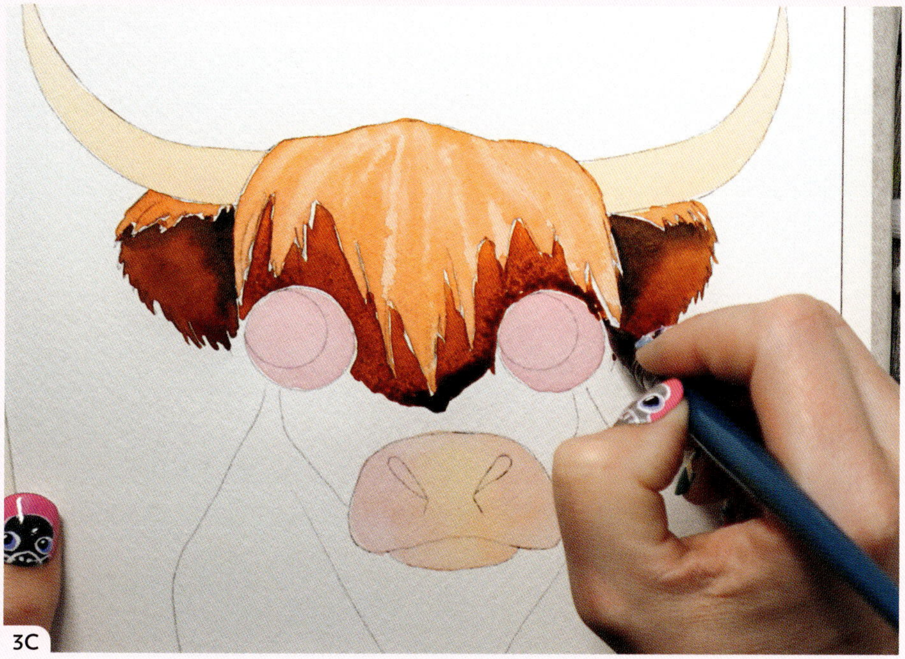

3C

Step 3

Mix up a large puddle of a second darker brown color. Paint the insides of the ears (3A). While each ear is wet, dip the tip of your brush into black and then deposit some of that color near the top and inner parts of the ears (3B).

Wash your brush, fill it with the darker brown color again, and start painting the area underneath the fringe until you get to just between the eyes; leave a drip line here so you can pull it down in a minute after adding in the shadow to the fringe (3C).

Step 4

Add the shadow for the fringe, dipping the tip of your brush in black and gently dragging it along the bottom of the fringe to deposit some of that color (4A). (I painted the face in two sections like this so the top wouldn't dry and it would flow together.)

After you've deposited the shadow color, wash your brush and reload it with brown. Grab that line of color you left wet and fill in the rest of the face (4B). While it's still wet, grab your prepared paper towel and drag it along the nose to lift out some lines that will mimic the hair (4C). Let this dry or make it dry!

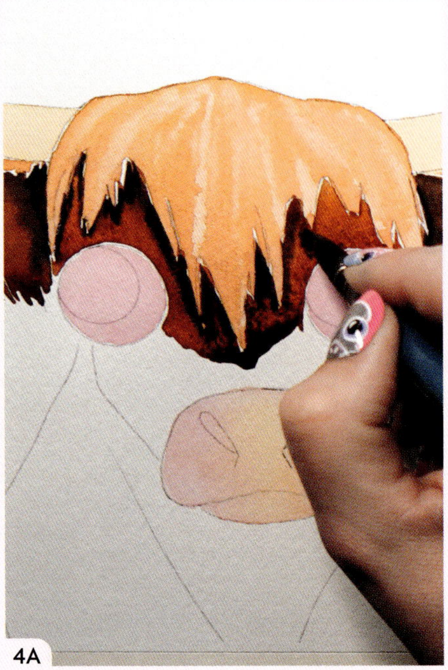

4A

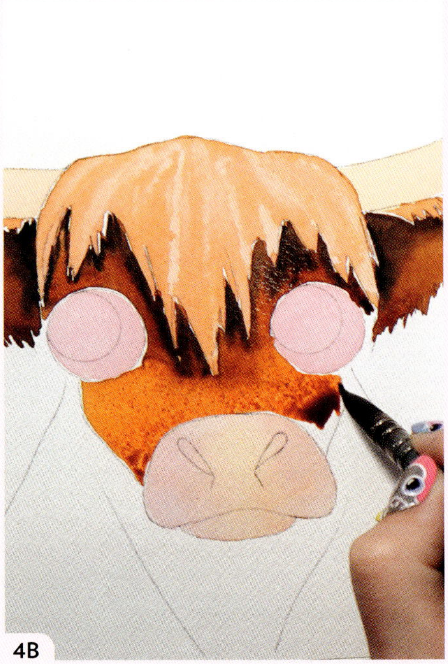

4B

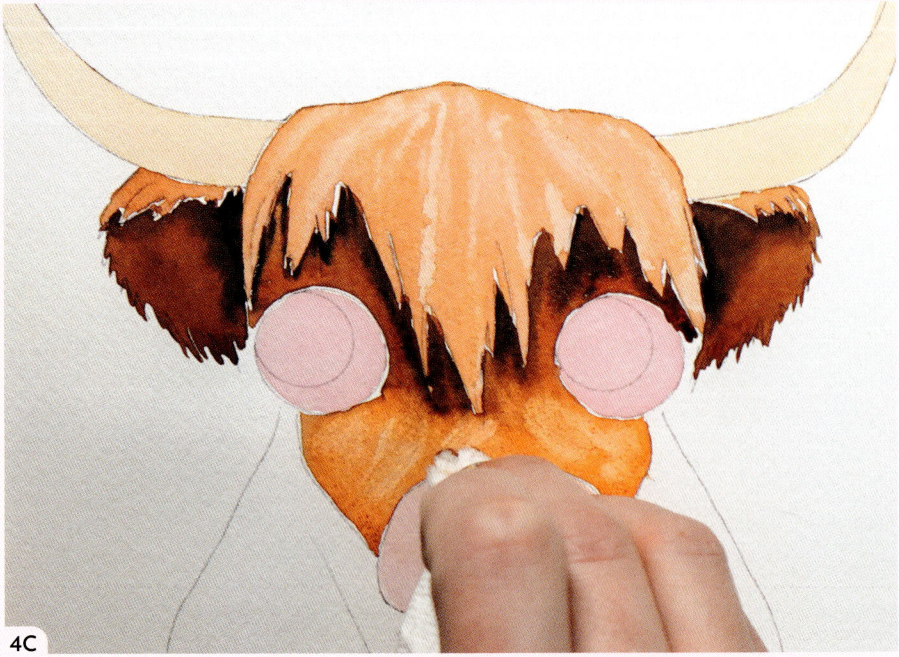

4C

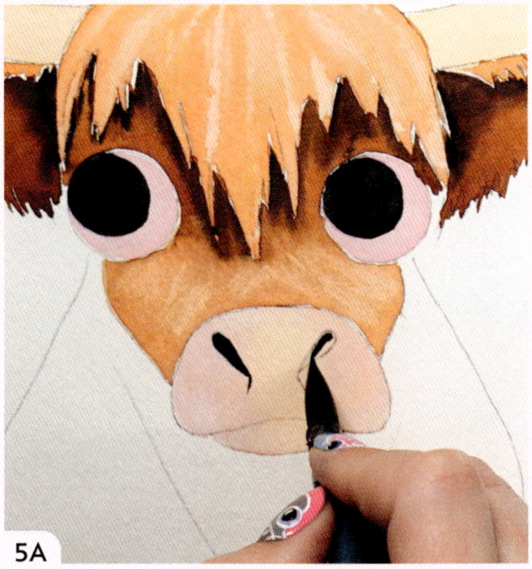

5A

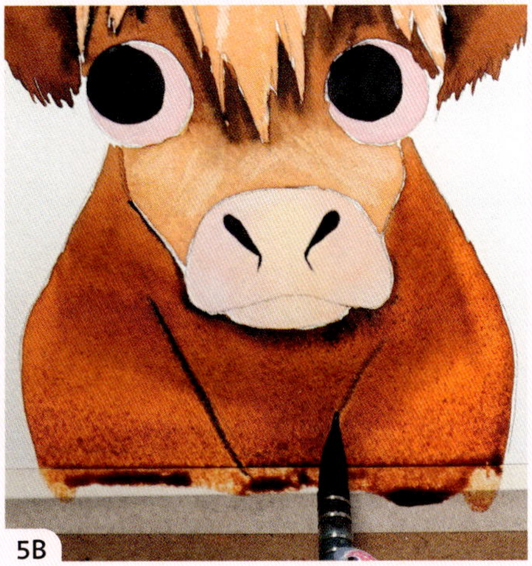

5B

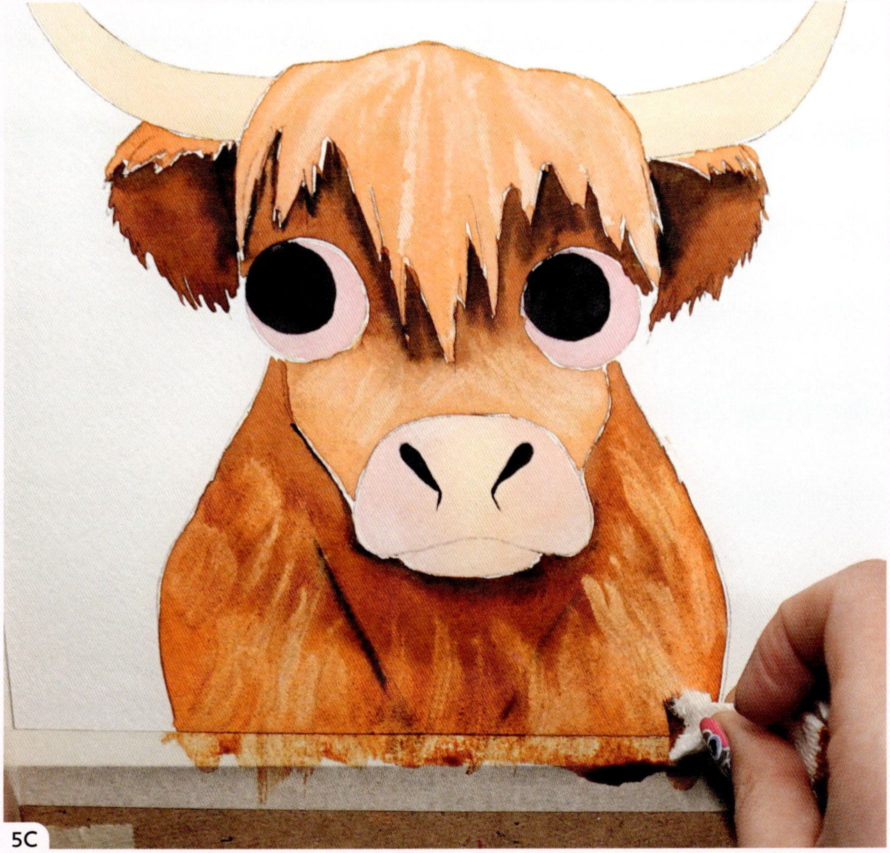

5C

Step 5

Wash your brush and then fill it with black and paint in the pupils of the eyes, as well as the nostrils (5A).

Wash your brush and then refill it with your dark brown color and paint in the body. While it's still wet, dip the tip of your brush in black and drag it along the bottom of the head, as well as the lines on the body, to give it a little dimension (5B).

While it's still wet, grab your paper towel and drag it along the wet color to make the fur texture (5C). Let this dry or make it dry!

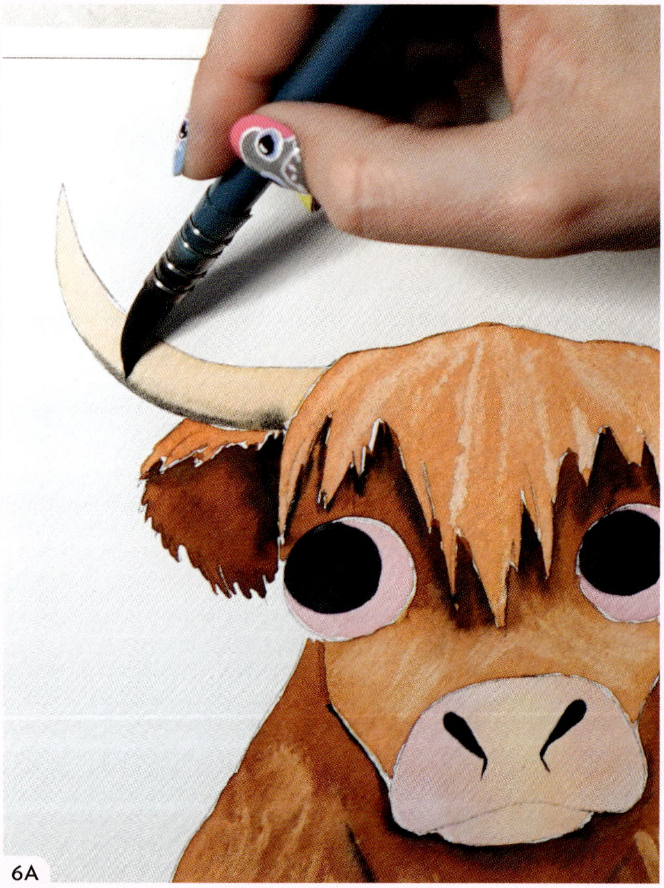

6A

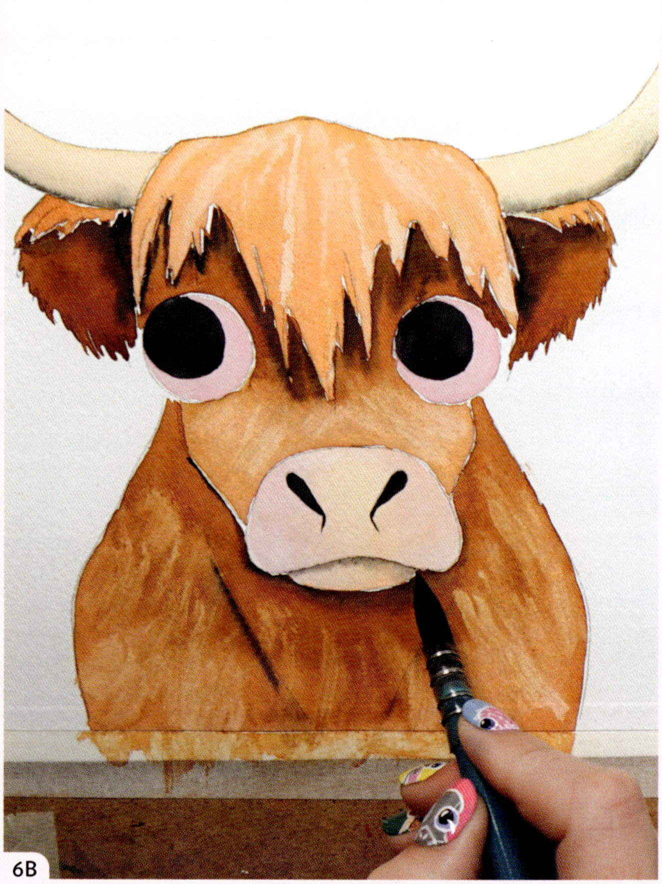

6B

Step 6

I was going to move to the background at this stage, but after looking at this for a bit, I felt like the horns and mouth lacked some of the shading and dimension I put into the rest of the body. The good news is shadows can be added after the fact, and it's always OK to change your plan mid-painting.

Wash your brush and wet each of the horns with clean water, and wait for the water to soak in a bit until it reaches the satin stage. Then dip the tip of your brush into black and lightly drag your brush along the bottom, depositing some color. Then wash your brush and swipe between the water and the color to smooth it out (6A).

Repeat this technique for the bottom part of the mouth, but instead of dropping the black along the bottom, drop it along the top (6B). I can't believe how much depth this brought to the mouth! So, if you ever have a painting you want to bring a little extra depth to, you can add shadows on a dry layer. Let this dry or make it dry!

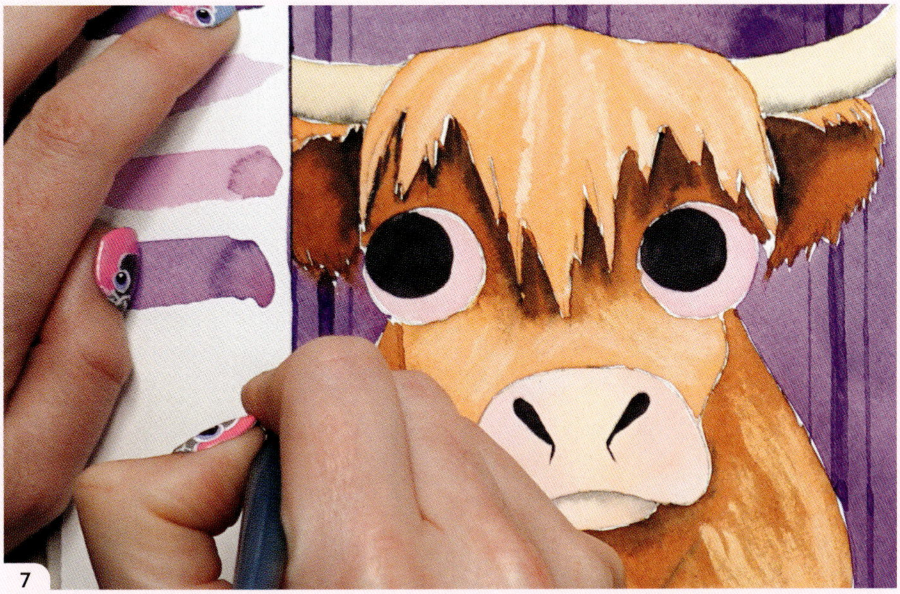

7

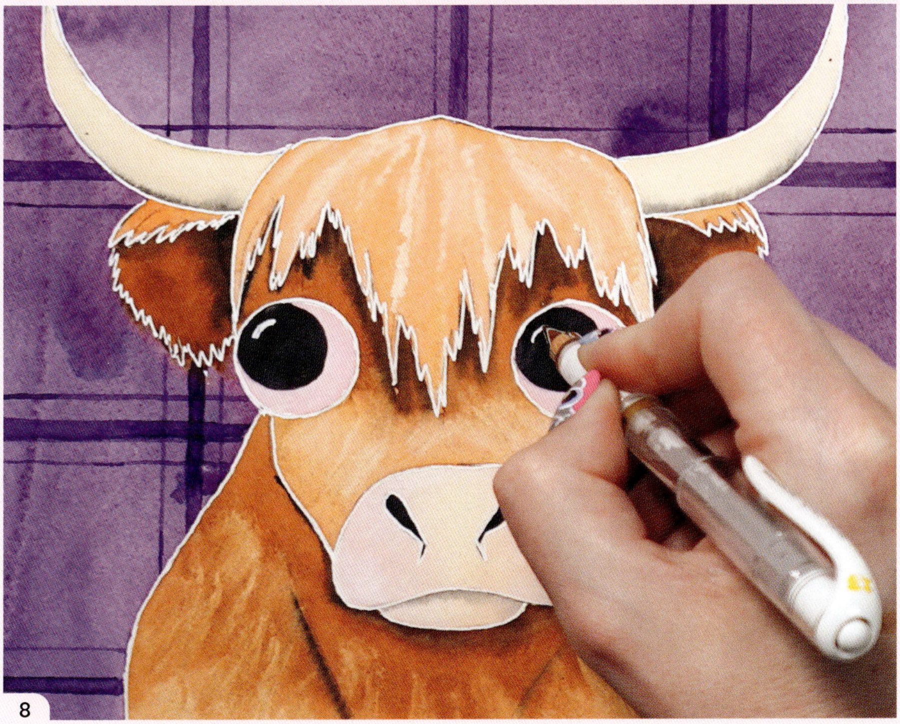

8

Step 7

Mix up a couple purple colors and fill in the background.

To create a fun plaid pattern, simply paint some straight lines. I always have a scrap piece of watercolor paper I use to test my paints, so I used that, but you can use a ruler. Darken the purple color a bit and fill your brush. Use a paper strip or ruler and allow your brush to glide along the edge. A word of caution: Be careful removing the tester strip and dab off any excess paint that gathers on the underside before moving it to a new position. You can dry the lines as you go so they don't smudge. You could do any line pattern you want; I decided to go for one thick line hugged on either side with a thin line. Let this dry or make it dry!

Step 8

Grab your white gel pen and outline the main shapes of the body—anywhere there is some scruffy hair, squiggle your pen! Don't forget those highlights to bring it to life.

Color Palette

Purple

Red

Pink

Black

Blue

Teal

Techniques

Adding Texture, page 28

Dropping In, page 27

Layering, page 29

Watercolor Washes, page 24

PRESTON THE PUFFER FISH

Puffer fish, or blowfish, are aptly named because they blow up like a balloon to scare predators or become too large to fit conveniently in the mouth of a predator. Their ability to change size isn't the only way they protect themselves—some have spines on their skin that contain a toxin that can kill other fish when ingested. This fish is special to me because it was the animal that started this series of paintings, which I called "Cute Little Animals" on social media. When I initially painted it, it was just a fun, silly painting, and viewers tried to guess what I was painting as I went. So this fish is quite literally the muse that allowed this book to come to life!

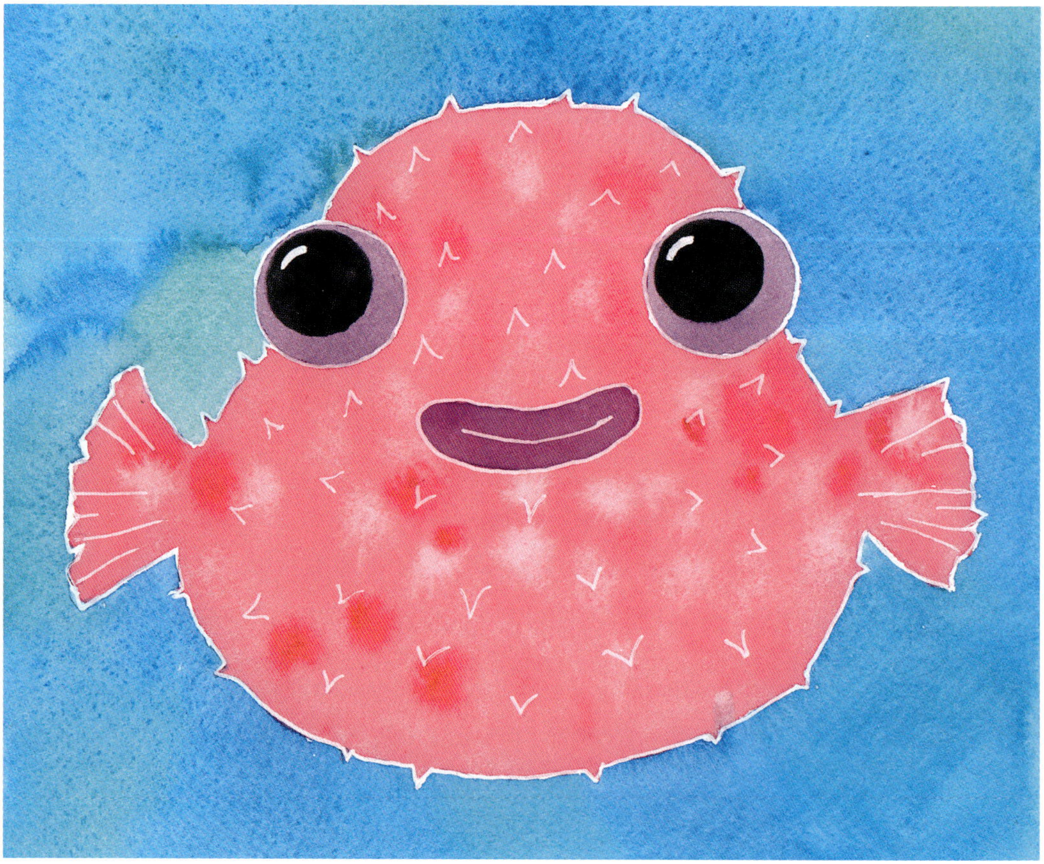

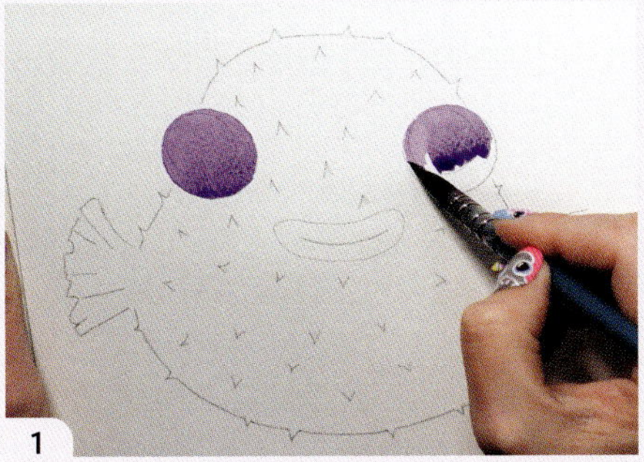
1

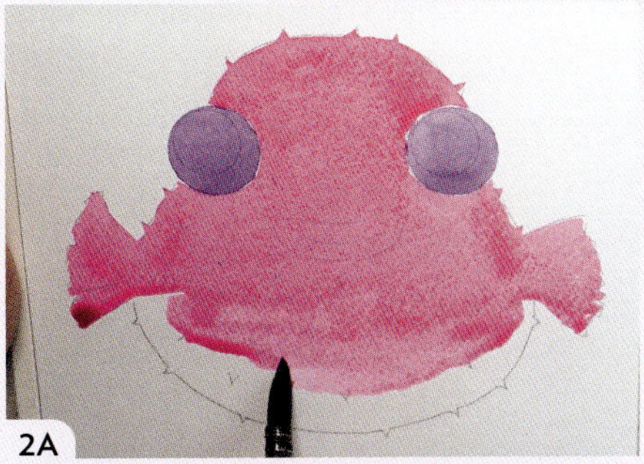
2A

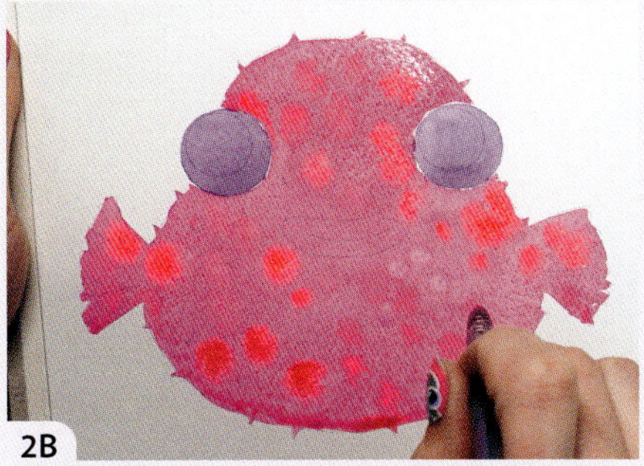
2B

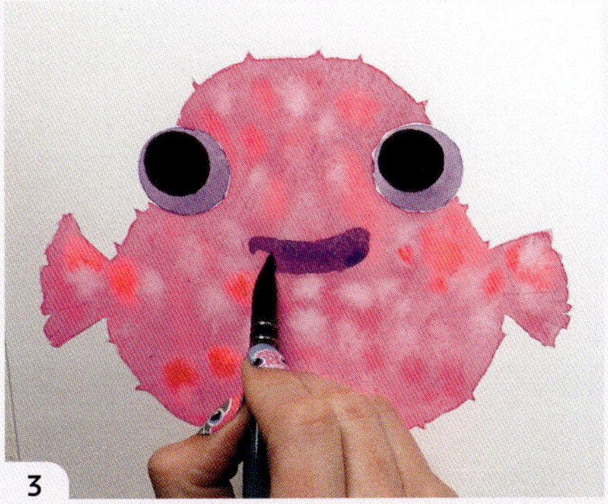
3

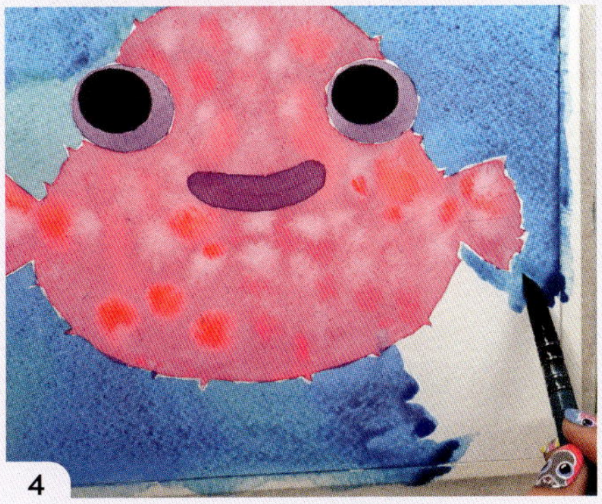
4

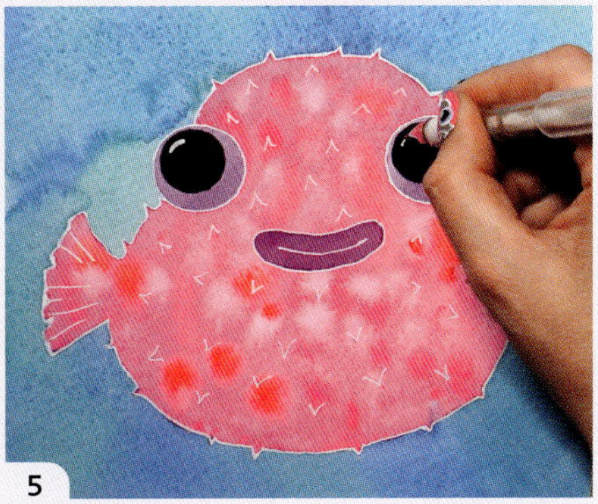
5

Step 1

Mix up a puddle of purple and paint in the larger eye circles. Let this dry or make it dry!

Step 2

Mix up a large puddle of pink. Fill your brush with pink and paint in the body and fins (2A). Do this with a generous amount of the water and color so it stays wet and at the satin or gloss stage for a bit.

While it's still wet, fill your brush with pink and red directly from your pans and drop in the more concentrated color. Then wash your brush and drop in a bit of clean water to make lighter-colored blooms (2B). Remember, blooms grow after they sit for a few seconds, so err on the side of less until you see how they start to develop. Let this dry or make it dry!

Step 3

Fill your brush with black and paint in the pupils.

Wash your brush, fill it with purple, and paint in the mouth.

Step 4

Mix up a couple blue colors and paint in the background using a messy wash. In order to work around this shape, I painted in both directions. So I would move to the right, leave a wet edge, then flip the page back to the left, leave a wet edge, and then rotate it back and forth until I was able to connect the two wet areas. Let this dry or make it dry!

Step 5

Grab your white gel pen and outline the body, fins, and eyes. Then add in the details like the spikes, mouth line, and highlights in the eyes!

Color Palette

Light Blue

Yellows

Brown

Black

Pink

Greens

Techniques

Dropping In, page 27

Layering, page 29

Watercolor Washes, page 24

GERTRUDE THE GUINEA PIG

Did you know that when guinea pigs are happy, they do something lovingly called "popcorning," which entails jumping up and twisting a bit, just like a piece of popping corn? This cutie is super fun to paint, and in this painting, I didn't mix a single color—I used them straight out of the pans, no preparation! The primary technique in this project—dropping in—works great for painting multicolored fur like this guinea pig, or a calico cat!

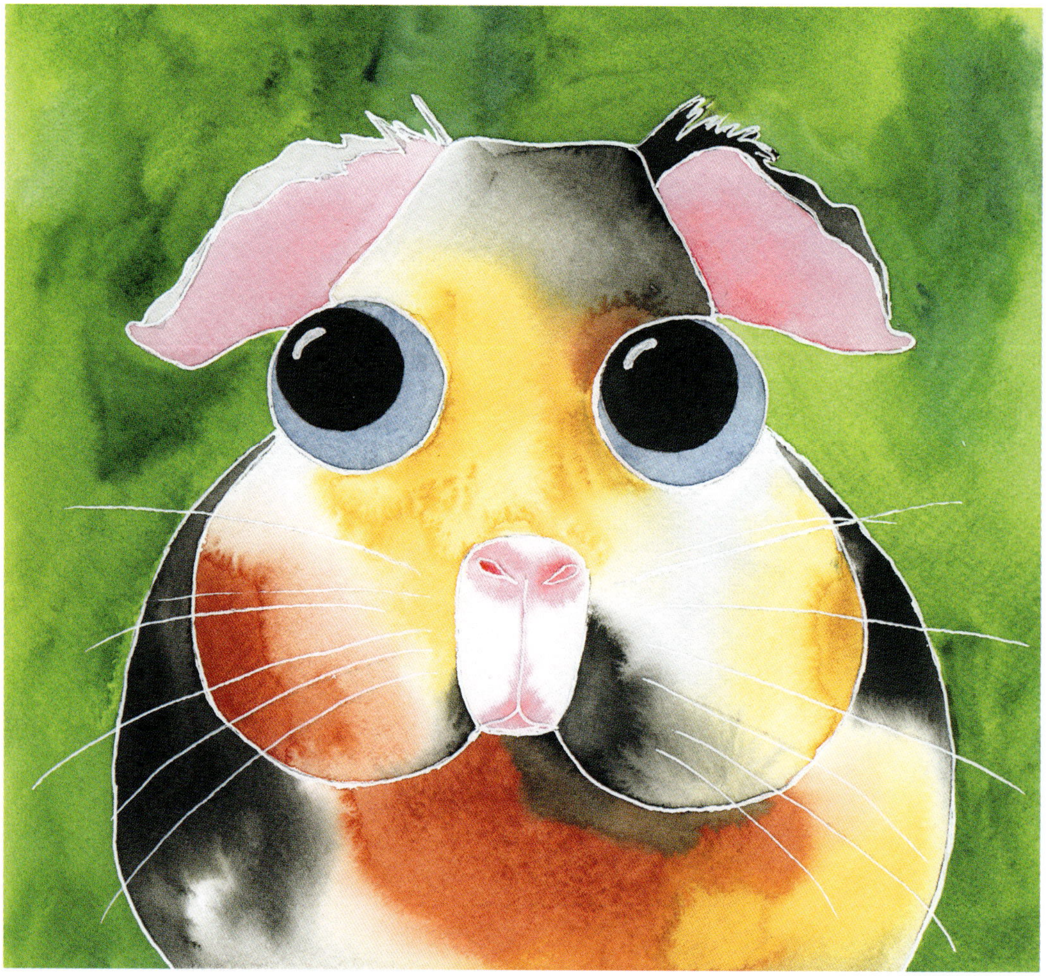

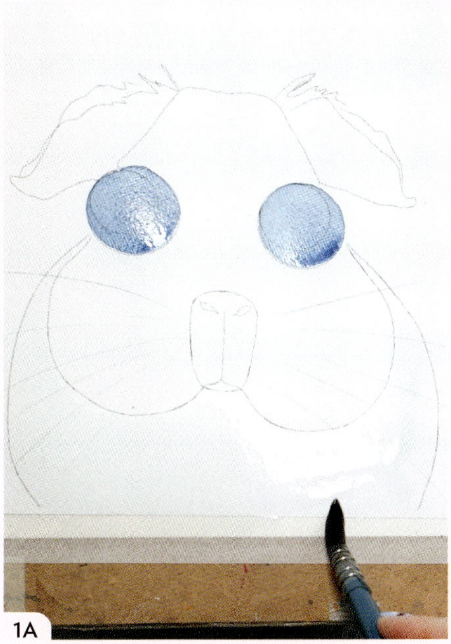

1A

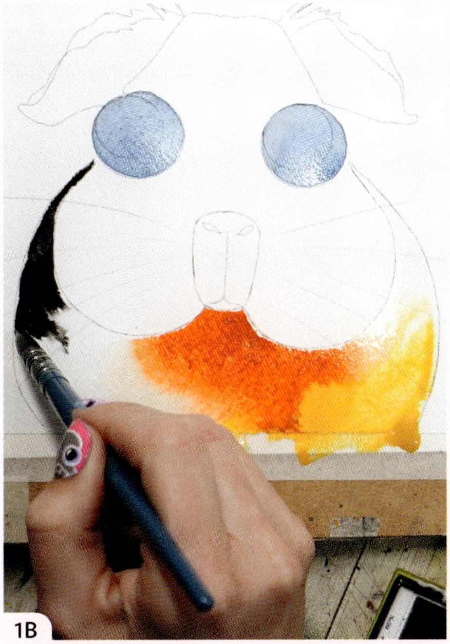

1B

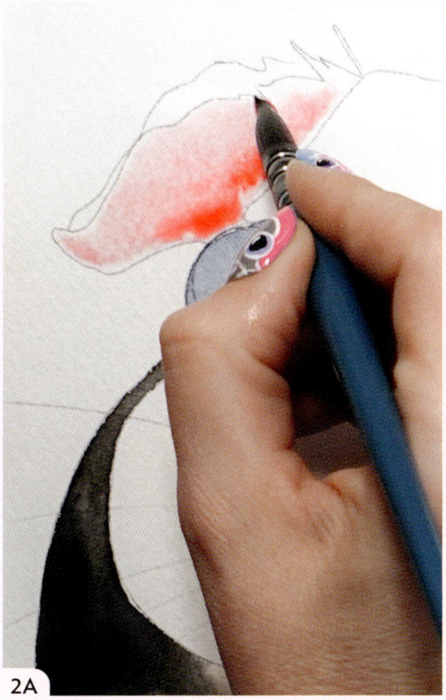

2A

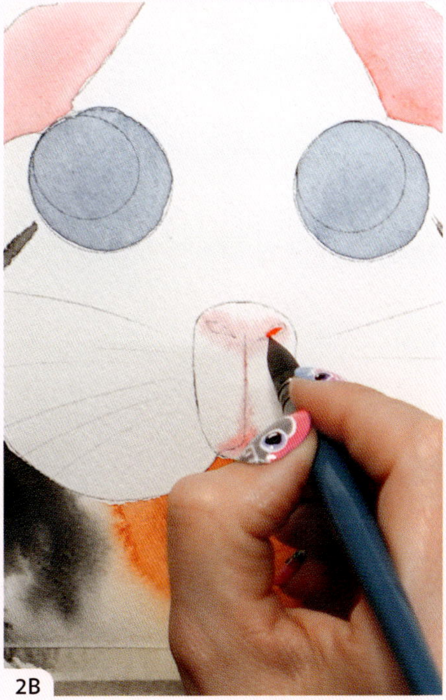

2B

Step 1

Choose a light blue color and paint in the main eye circles. Wash your brush, fill it with clean water, and paint in the body of the guinea pig until it's at the satin or gloss stage (1A). Then grab multiple colors and drop them randomly into the pre-wet body. I chose to drop in some yellow, brown, and black in a few spots (1B). Let this dry or make it dry!

Step 2

I worked directly from the pans in this tutorial, and my set did not have a pink, so I made a pink on the page. To do this, wash your brush and fill it with clean water. Then paint clean water into the inner ear—the water on the page will dilute the color you place here. Then dip your brush into your red or pink and make a stripe in the wet area, smoothing it into the water. The red paint will turn pink as it gets desaturated by the water (2A). Repeat on the other ear.

Wet the nose and then load just the tip of your brush with your red or pink and lightly drop it along the nostrils, as well as the mouth lines (2B). Let this dry or make it dry!

Step 3

Wet the face of the guinea pig until it's at a gloss wetness and then, using the same colors as the body, randomly drop some of those colors onto the face (3A).

Once your colors are deposited, pull some of the color near the ears to the top of the ears. For mine, I matched the black spot near the right ear and the gray near the left ear (3B). Let this dry or make it dry!

Step 4

Fill your brush with black and paint in the pupils of the eyes.

For this background, instead of having large quantities of my colors pre-mixed, I made sure my brush was full of lots of water and then generously tapped onto my pans of color and painted a messy wash on the background by switching between two greens in the palette and one yellow. Let this dry or make it dry!

Step 5

Grab your white gel pen and outline the shapes of the face and body. On the ears, I added a little extra scribble to suggest fur. Then add in the details like whiskers (rotating the page as needed to make the long, wispy lines)—and of course, don't forget the highlights in the eyes!

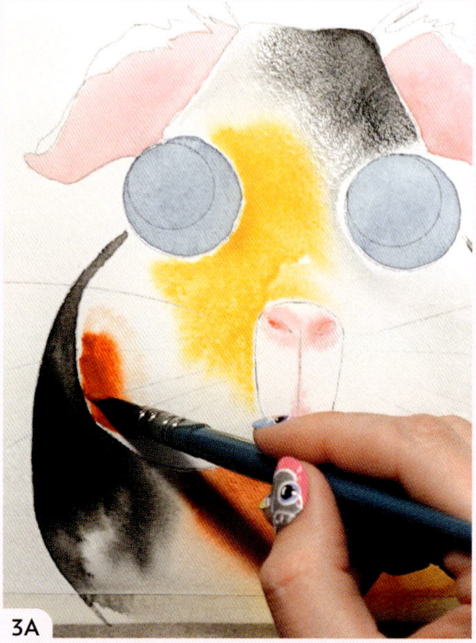

3A

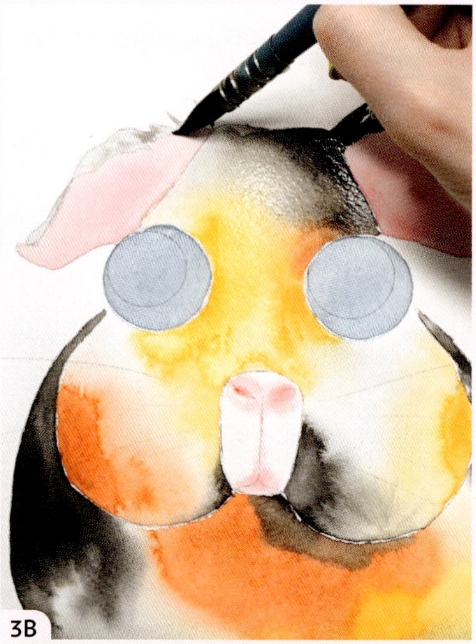

3B

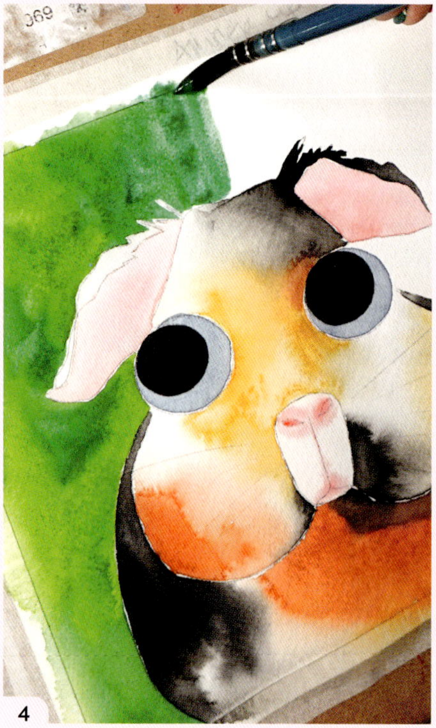

4

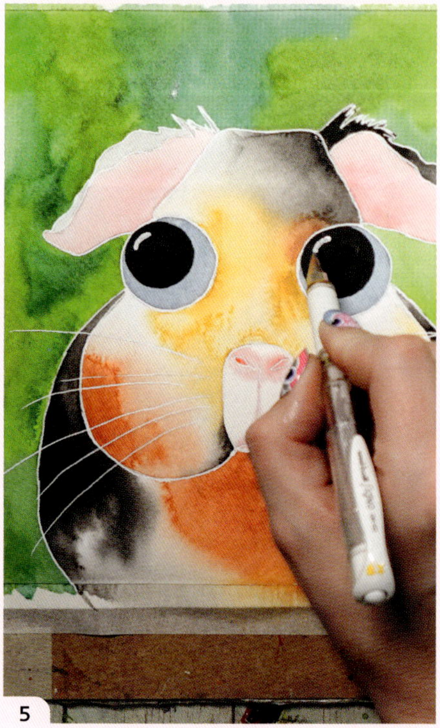

5

OWEN THE OTTER

Otters are seriously adorable, and I relate to them because they love rocks! Otters have been observed using rocks as tools to do things like open shellfish. I don't use rocks much to open things, but I often keep rocks I like in my pockets. Otters often have a favorite rock or two they keep with them. In this painting, the little heart is a loose interpretation of the rock this otter holds close to their heart!

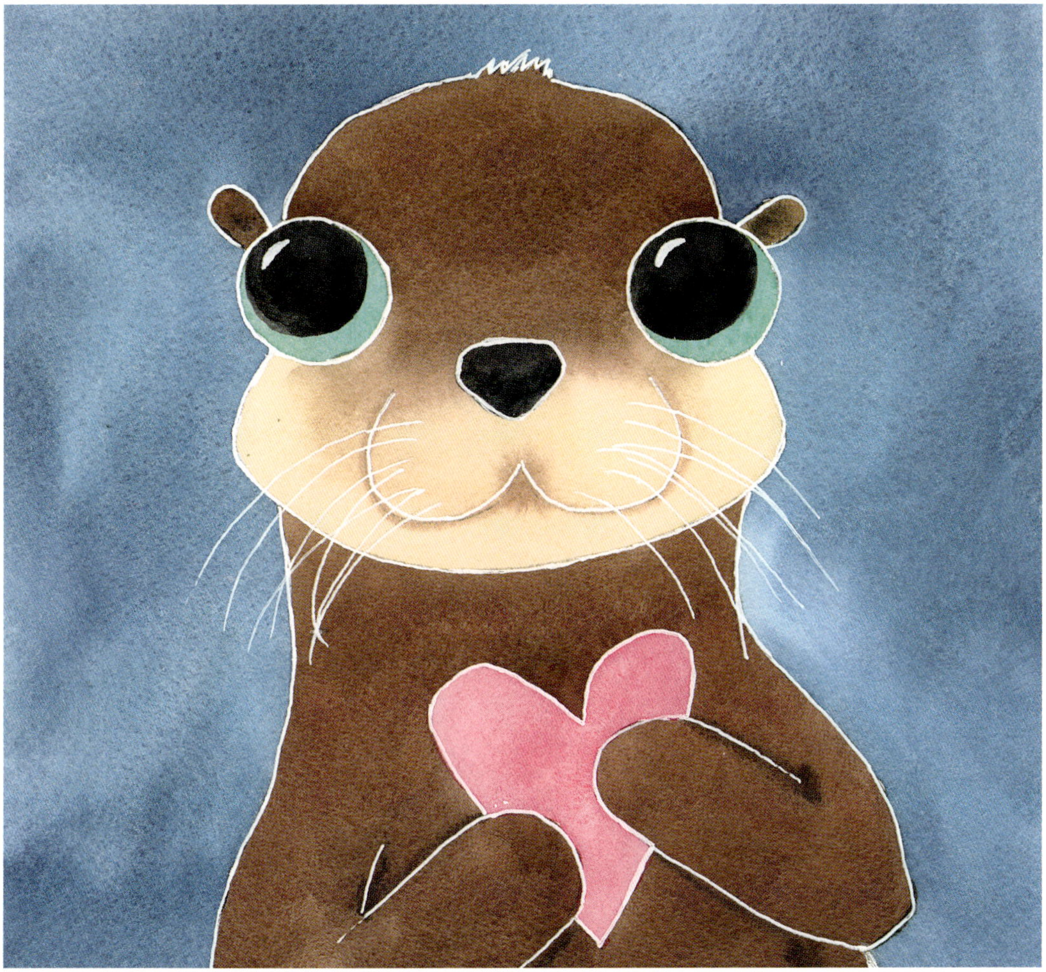

Color Palette

Light Green
Light Brown
Dark Brown
Black
Pink
Blues

Techniques

Adding Shadows, page 27
Dropping In, page 27
Lifting, page 26
Watercolor Washes, page 24

Step 1

Mix up a light green color and paint in the main circles of the eyes. Let this dry or make it dry! Then mix up two large puddles, one a very light brown and one a dark brown color.

Step 2

Fill your brush with your dark brown color and paint in the head of the otter until you reach between the eyes (2A). Leave a drip line of that dark brown. Then wash your brush and refill it with your light brown color. Grab the edge of the drip line and pull it down with the lighter brown (2B). Refill your brush as needed with the light brown to paint in the rest of the face.

Let this soak in a bit until it's at the satin stage. Then refill your brush with the dark brown, tap it on a paper towel so that just a bit remains in the bristles, and drag your brush along the mouth lines to deposit some of the darker brown color (2C).

For the ears, fill your brush with the dark brown and paint them in. Then wash your brush, dip the tip into black, and then drop that into the ear while the brown is still wet, near where it attaches to the body (2D). Let this dry or make it dry!

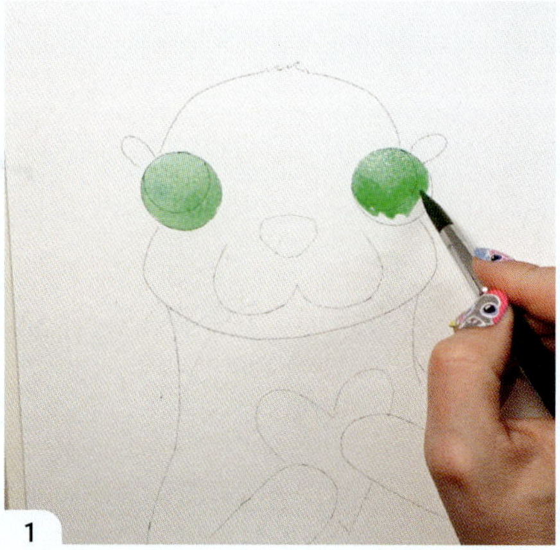
1

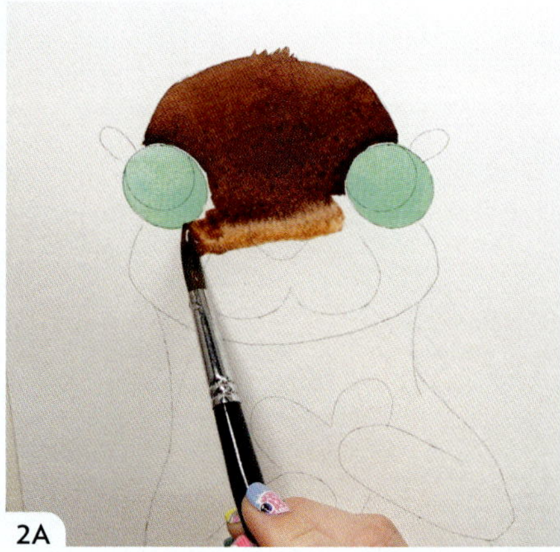
2A

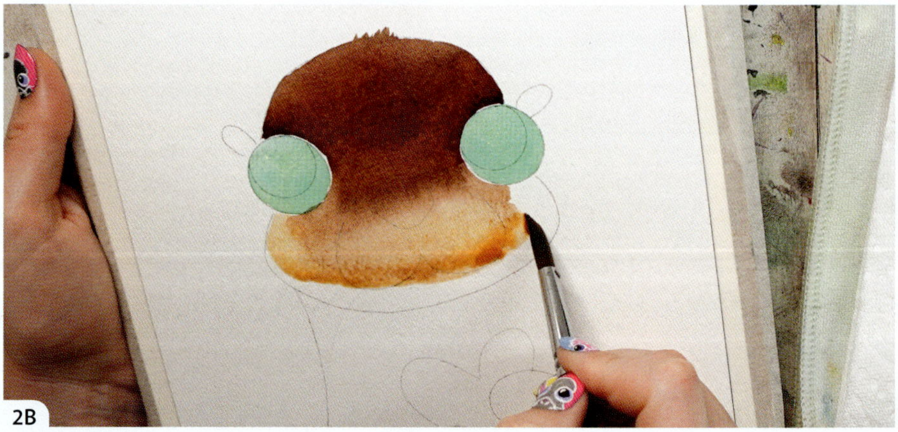
2B

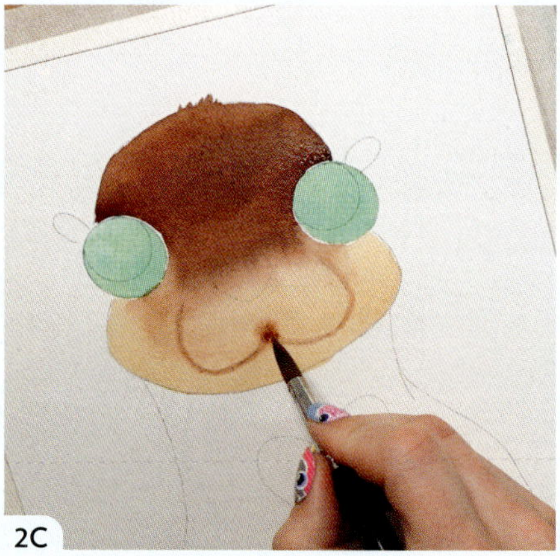
2C

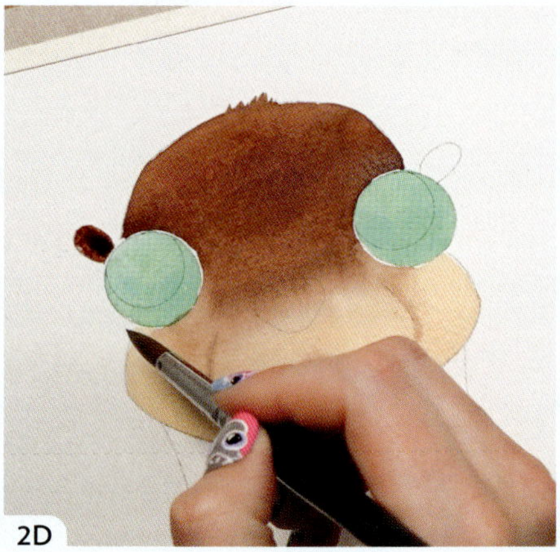
2D

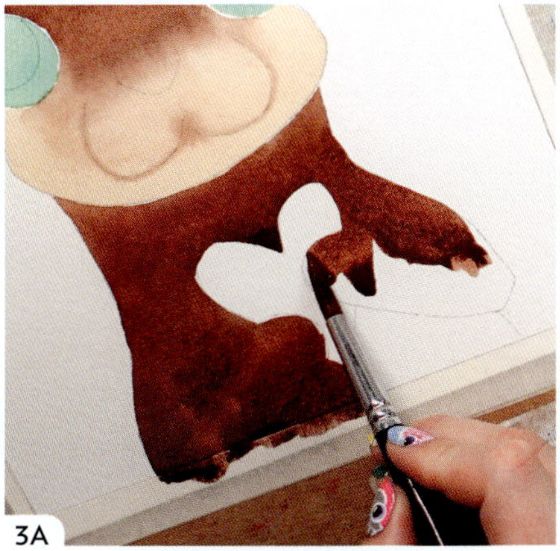
3A

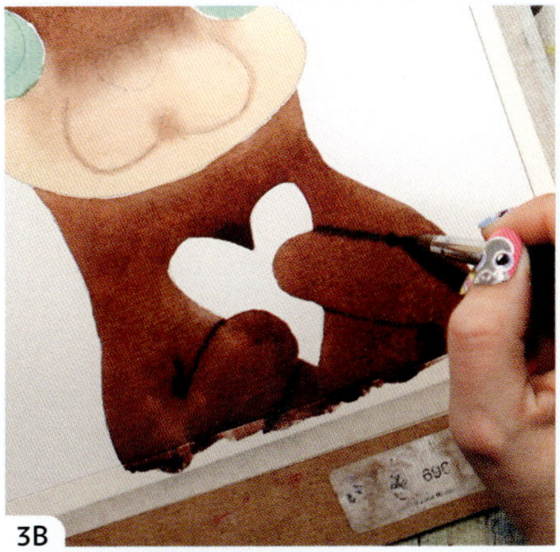
3B

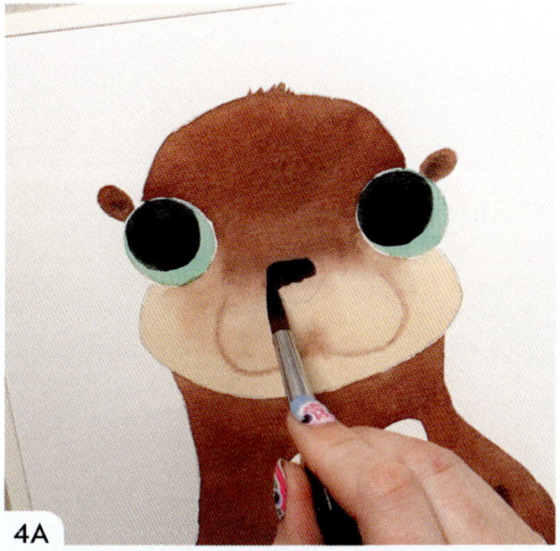
4A

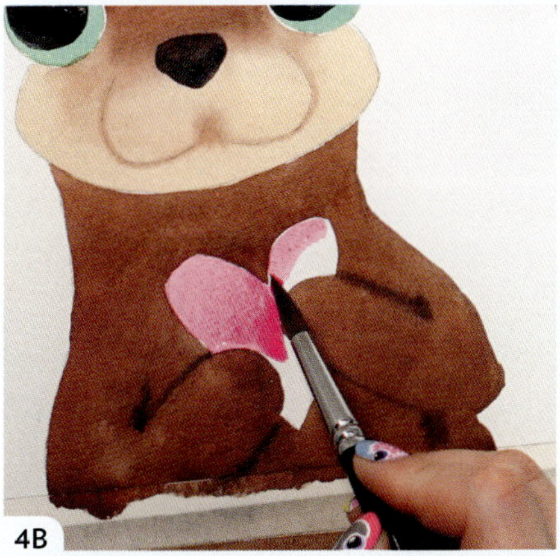
4B

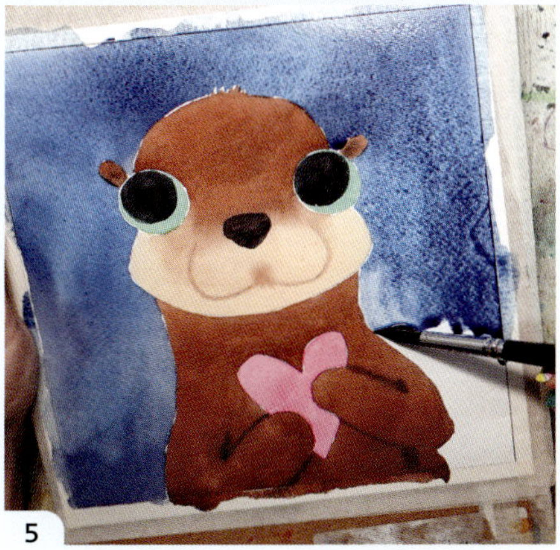
5

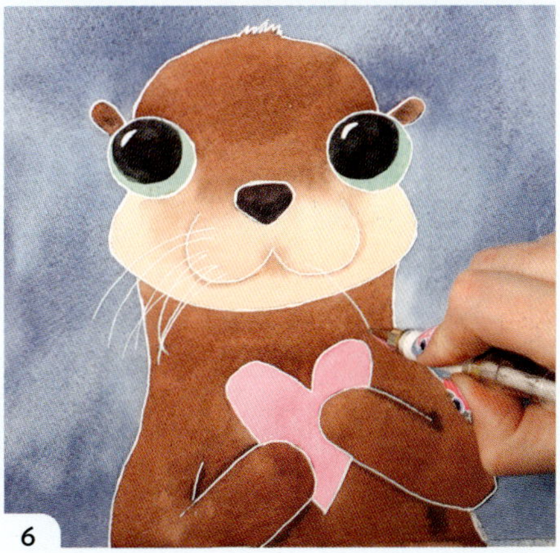
6

Step 3

Refill your brush with the dark brown and paint in the body and arms, avoiding painting inside the heart (3A).

While the body is still wet, wash your brush and dip the tip of your brush into black and then drag it around the lines for the arms to create a little shadow (3B). Let this dry or make it dry!

Step 4

Fill your brush with black paint and fill in the pupils of the eyes and the nose (4A).

Wash your brush, fill it with pink, and paint in the heart (4B). Let this dry or make it dry!

Step 5

Mix up a couple big puddles of blue colors and paint in the background. Remember, it can be easier to rotate your page as you paint this, and it's okay if it overlaps with the subject a little or a bit of white space is left. Let this dry or make it dry!

Step 6

Grab your white gel pen and outline all the major shapes of the otter. Then add in the finishing touches like highlights in the eyes and whiskers!

Color Palette

Pink

Yellow

Light Green

Dark Green

Brown

Black

Blue

Teal

Techniques

Dropping In, page 27

Watercolor Washes, page 24

Layering, page 29

SALVATORE THE SEA TURTLE

Sea turtles are truly majestic. I have had the opportunity to see them a few times while snorkeling, and each time is so amazing! Sea turtles live for a very long time—in the wild they live between fifty and seventy years!

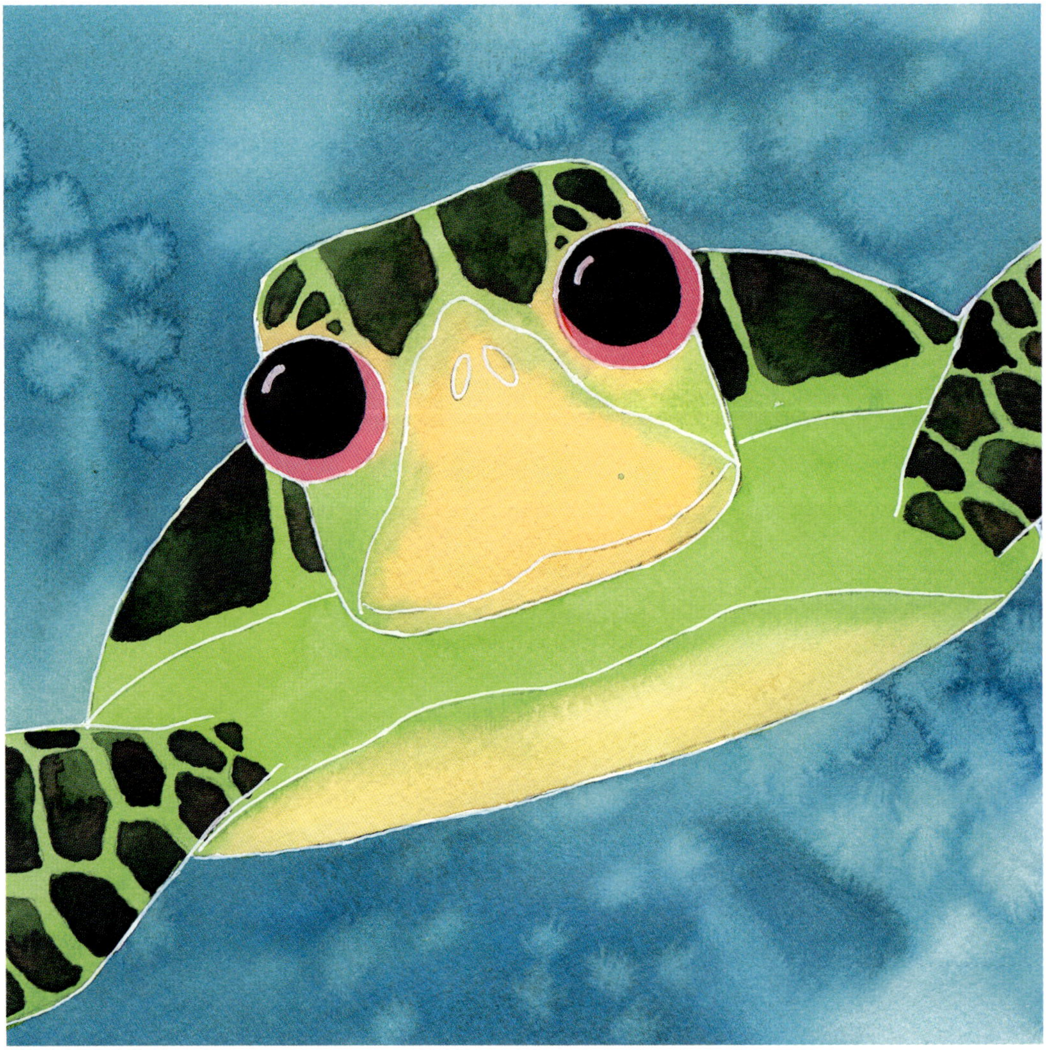

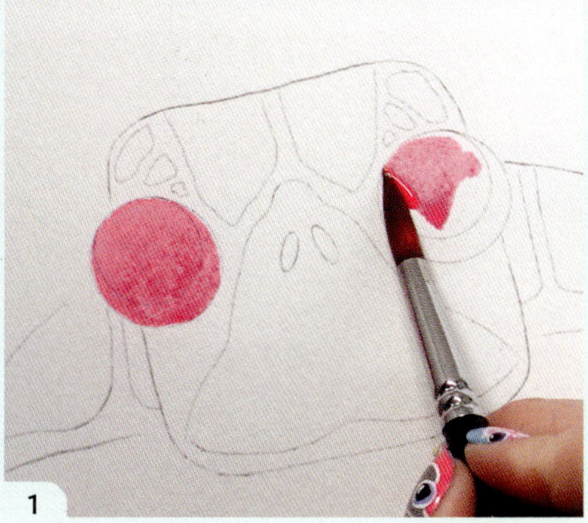

1

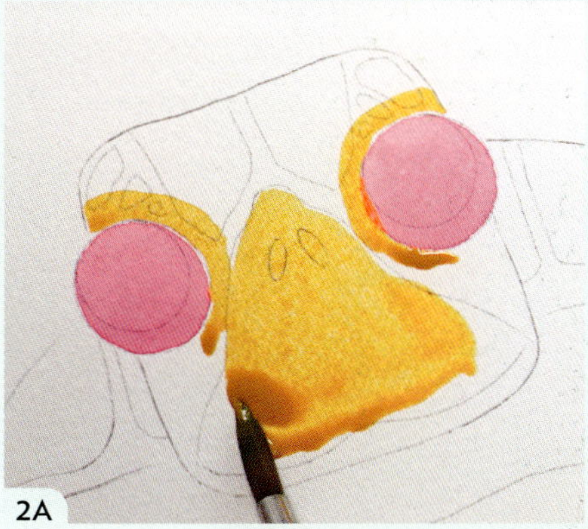

2A

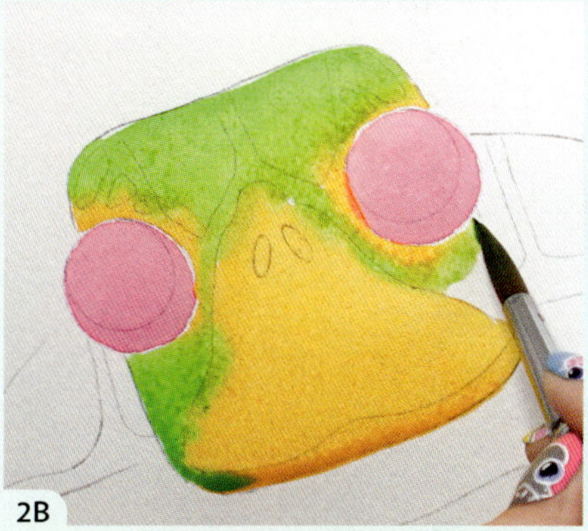

2B

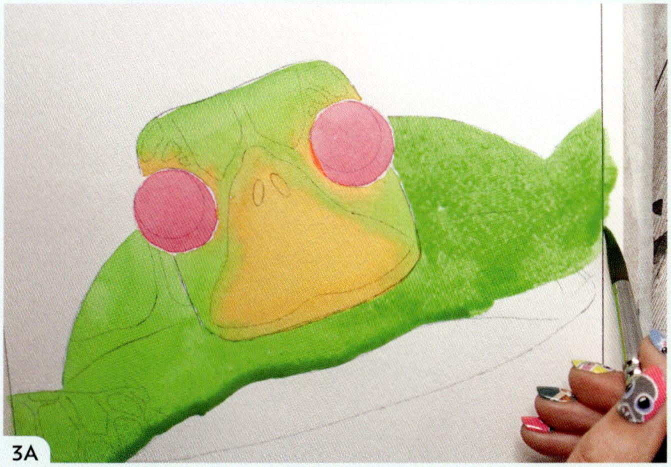

3A

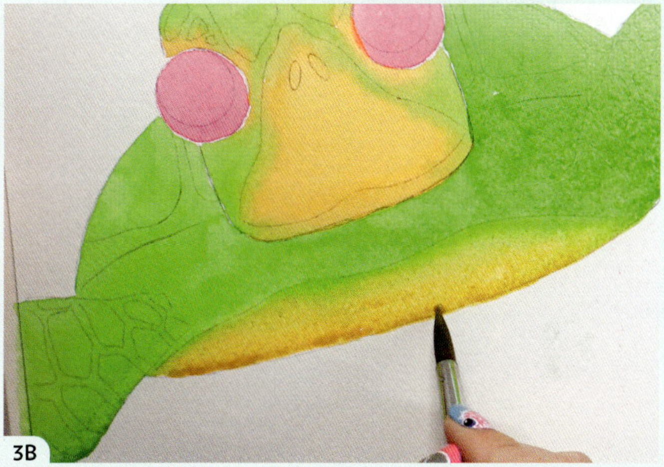

3B

Step 1

Mix up a puddle of pink, and then paint in the large eye circles. Let this dry or make it dry!

Step 2

Mix up big puddles of yellow and light green. Fill your brush with yellow and paint around each eye, as well as the nose and mouth (2A).

While it's still wet, wash your brush and fill it with the light green, and then paint in the remaining parts of the face, just touching the edges of the wet yellow color (2B). Let this dry or make it dry!

Step 3

Fill your brush with the light green color and paint in the main part of the shell, fins, and body, except for the bottom line. Along the bottom line, leave a drip line of green so it will make a gradient in the next part (3A).

Wash your brush and fill it with the yellow color. Drag your brush along the bottom drip line and fill in the belly area (3B). Let this dry or make it dry!

Step 4

Mix up a large puddle of dark green and a smaller puddle of brown.

Paint groups of the spots on the shell and then, while each group is still wet, drop a little brown into the wet green spot (4A). It won't look like it does much while it's still wet, but once it dries you will see the pattern has texture (4B)! Fill in the head, shell, and fins (4C). Let this dry or make it dry!

Step 5

Fill your brush with black and paint in the pupils of the eyes. Let this dry or make it dry!

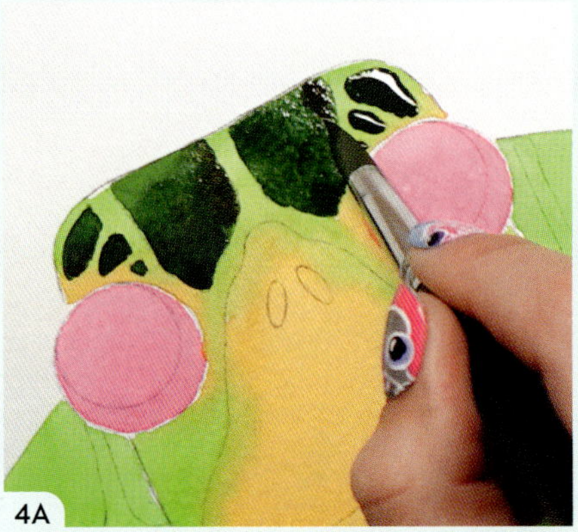

4A

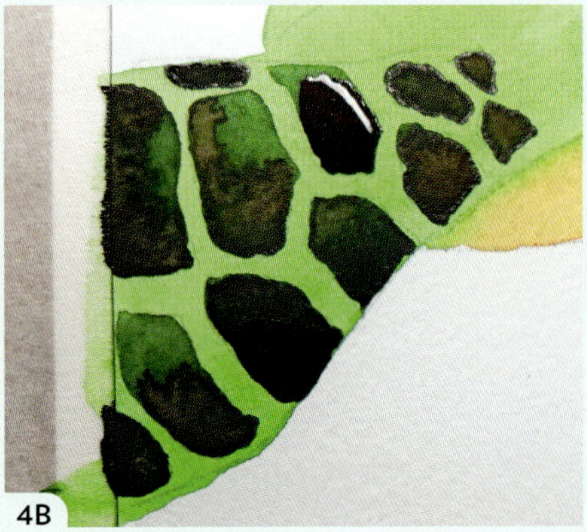

4B

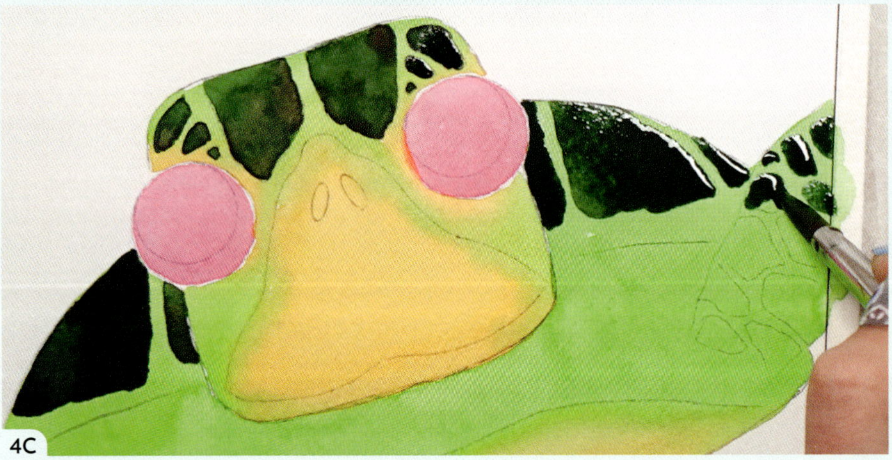

4C

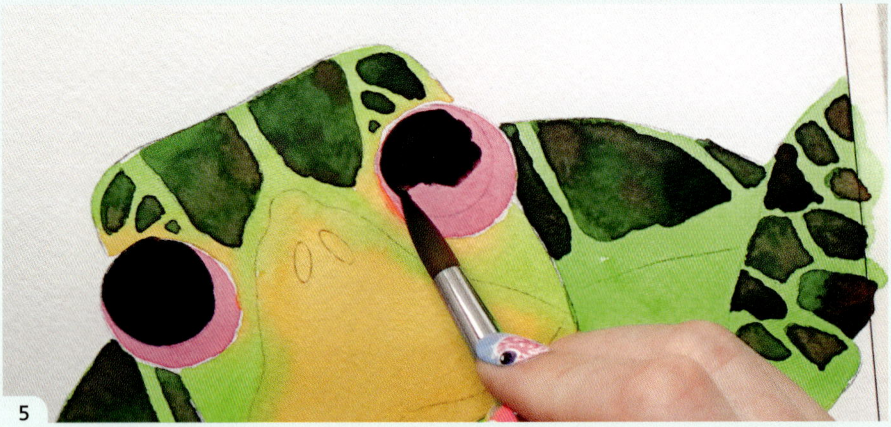

5

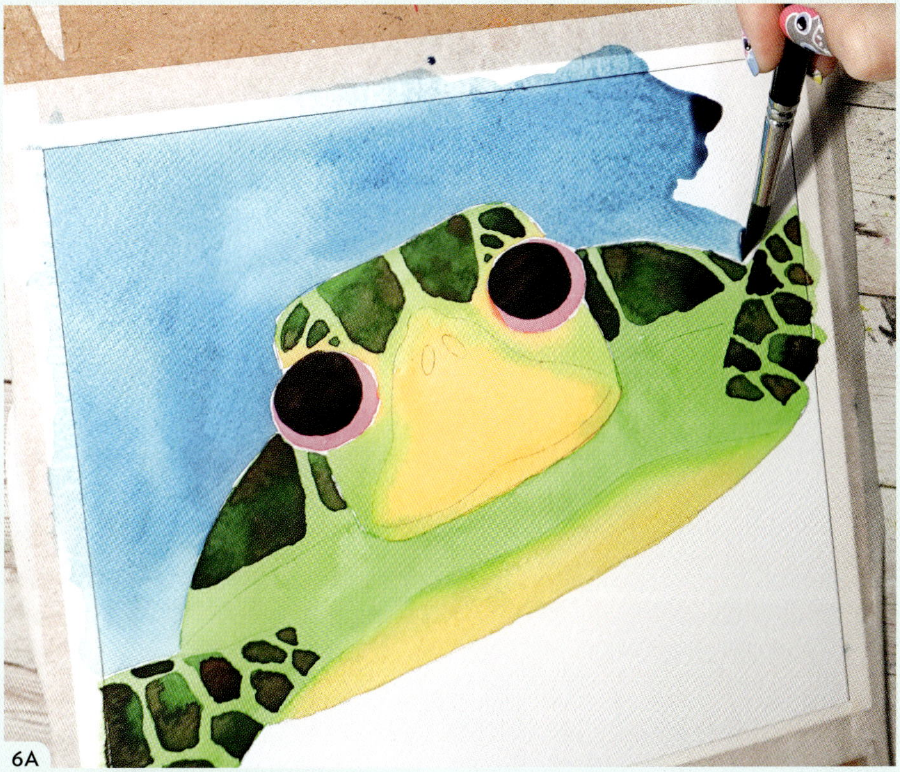

6A

Step 6

Mix up a couple puddles of blues and teals.

Using these colors, paint in the background. Each time I refill my brush, I dip into a different color as I work across the background (6A).

While the background is still wet, wash your brush, fill it with clean water, and then touch the tip of it to the background to deposit the water and create blooms (6B). This will give the background a bubbly texture. Let this dry or make it dry!

Step 7

Grab your white gel pen and outline the body shapes, as well as the nostrils, and add highlights to the eyes!

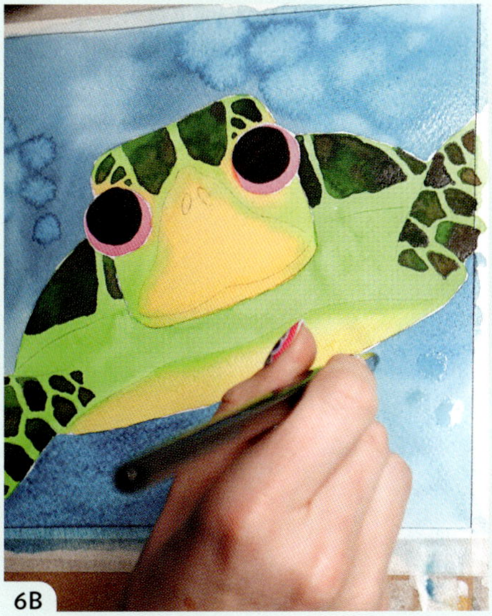

6B

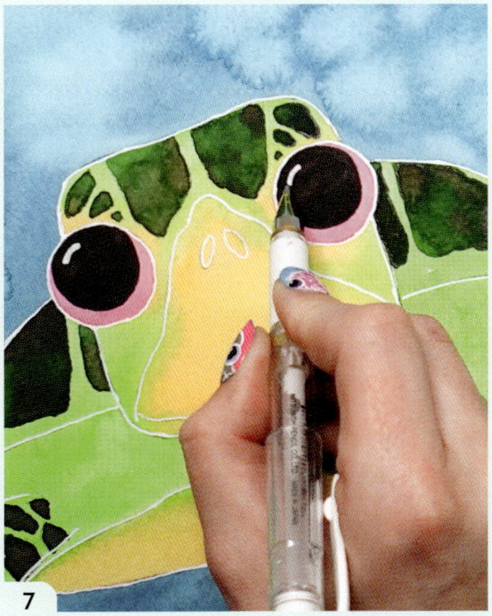

7

Color Palette

Purple

Black

Yellow

Orange

Techniques

Dropping In, page 27

Watercolor Washes, page 24

ZEUS THE ZEBRA

I love patterns, so of course I think zebras are absolutely stunning! Did you know that, like many patterned animals, zebra stripes are unique to each individual zebra? Scientists speculate this distinction could serve as a way for zebras to tell each other apart! Painting the stripes on this zebra does take a bit of patience, but the result is well worth it!

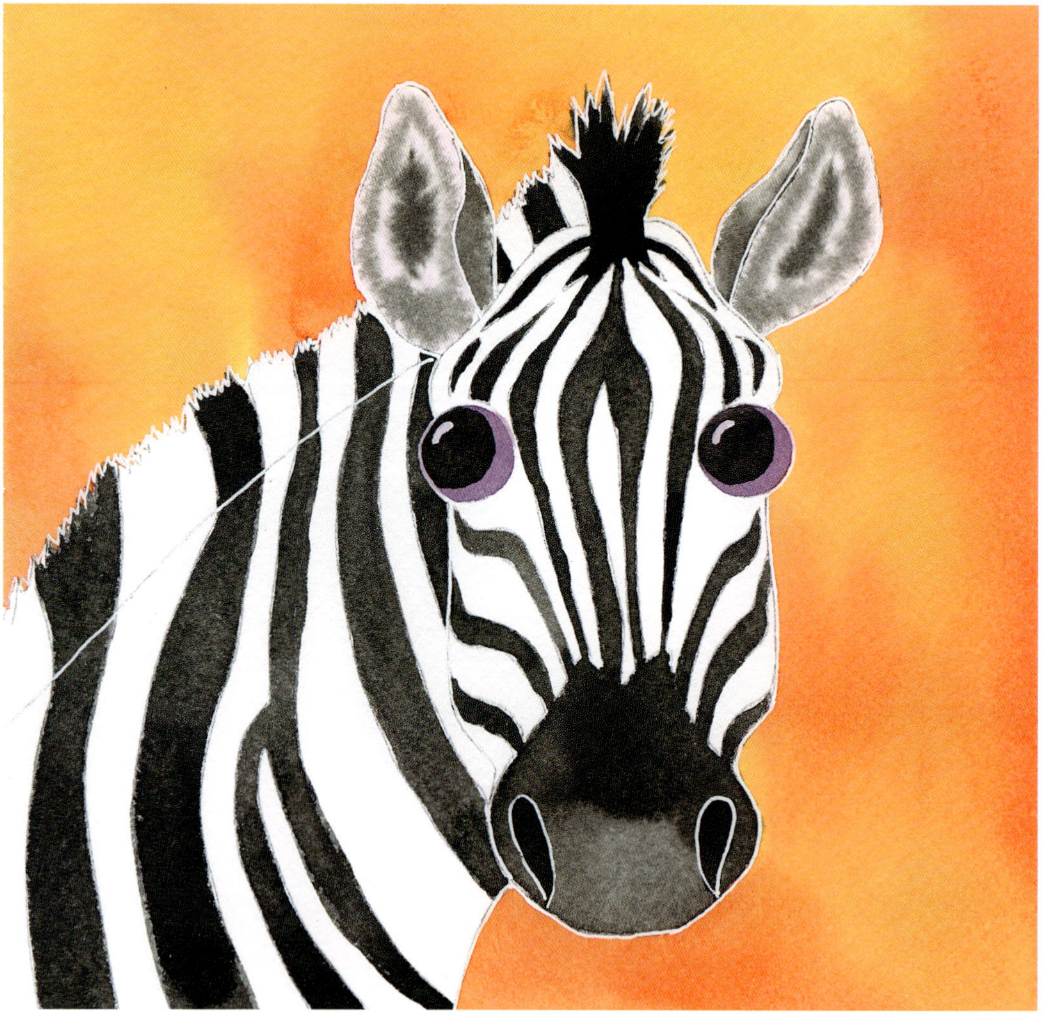

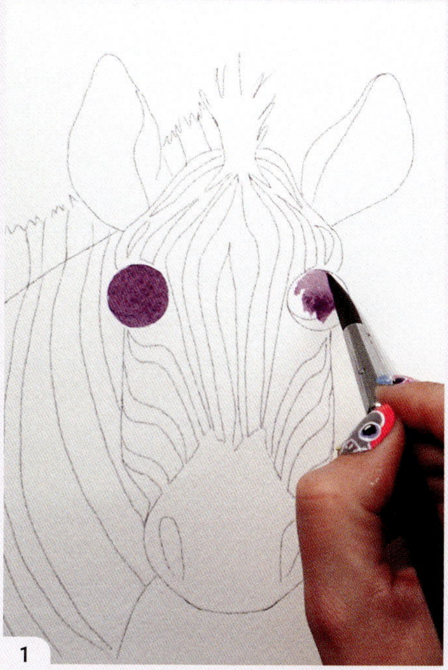

1

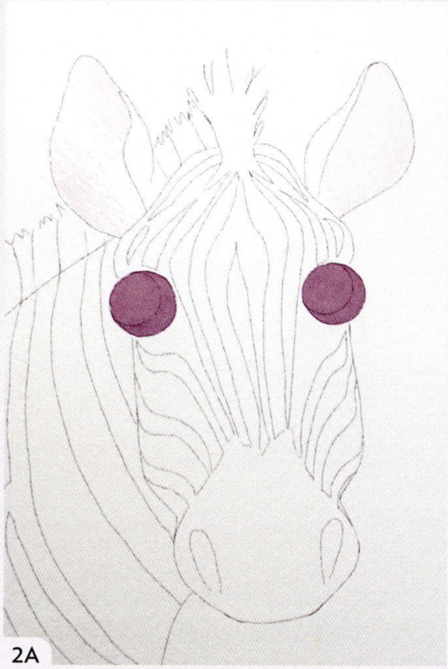

2A

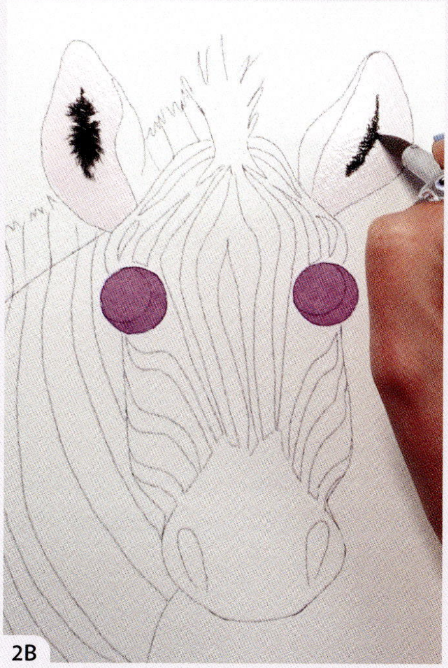

2B

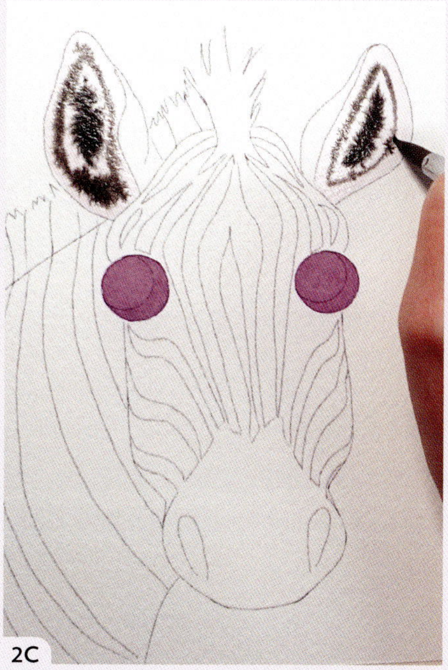

2C

Step 1

Mix up a puddle of purple and paint in the larger eye circles. Let this dry or make it dry!

Step 2

Mix up a large puddle of black—you'll need a lot of it, and it's not only easier to have it prepared but also creates more consistent color than constantly re-wetting your pan of watercolor.

Wash your brush and fill it with clean water. Paint clean water into the insides of the ears. Allow this to soak in until your paper is at about the satin stage of wetness (2A).

Dip the tip of your brush into black, and then in each ear, drag your brush in a line down the middle (2B). Then paint a diamond shape around the inside of the ear (2C).

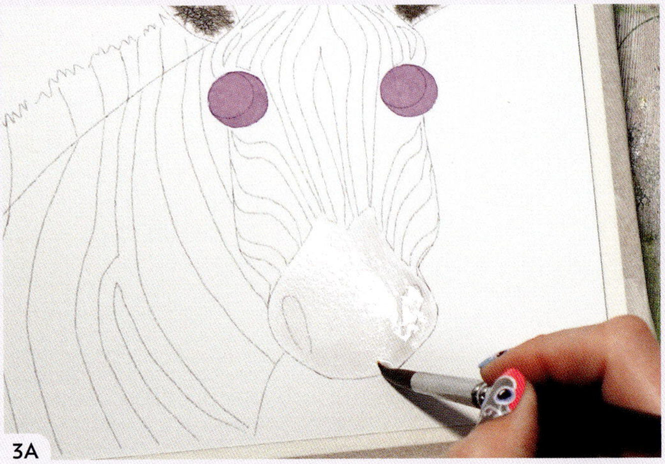
3A

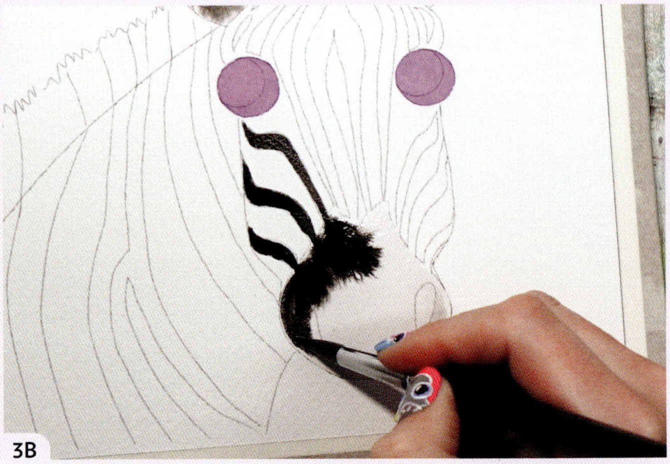
3B

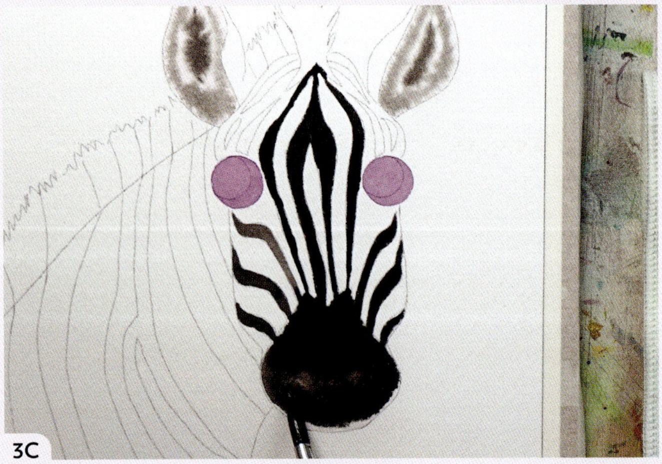
3C

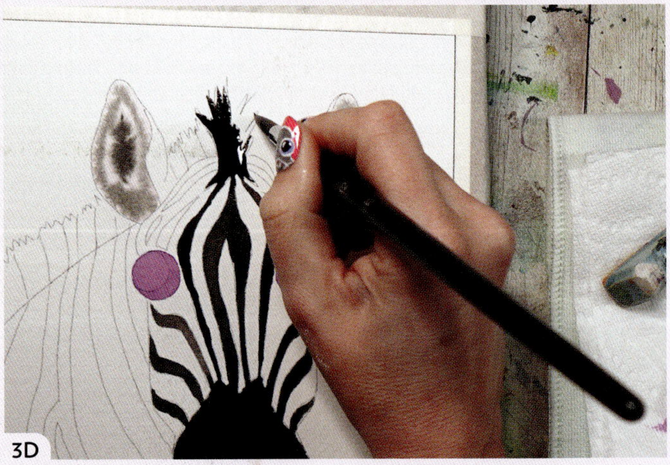
3D

Step 3

Wash your brush and then wet the nose of the zebra with water (3A)—keep this wet as you paint in the stripes that connect to it so that they will more seamlessly blend together.

Start to paint in the stripes that connect to the nose, depositing black into the wet paper as you fill them in (3B).

Once you've painted in all the stripes that connect to the nose, smooth the black down into the wet area to give it a more even appearance (3C).

Fill in the remaining stripes on the face, as well as the front tuft of the mane (3D). Let this dry or make it dry!

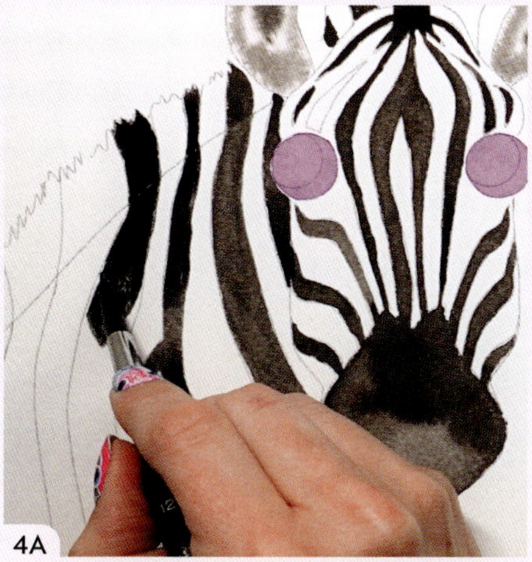

4A

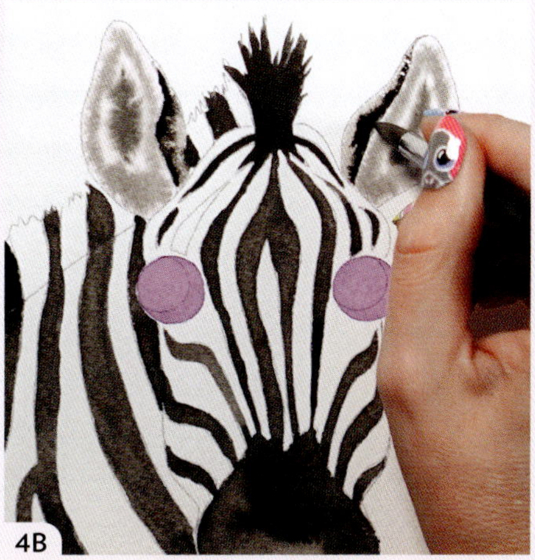

4B

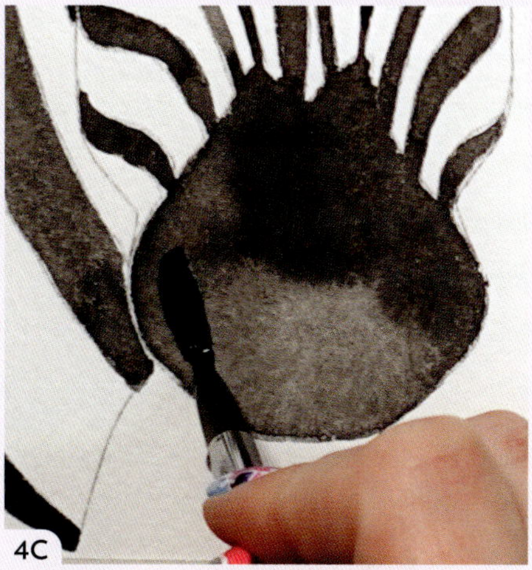

4C

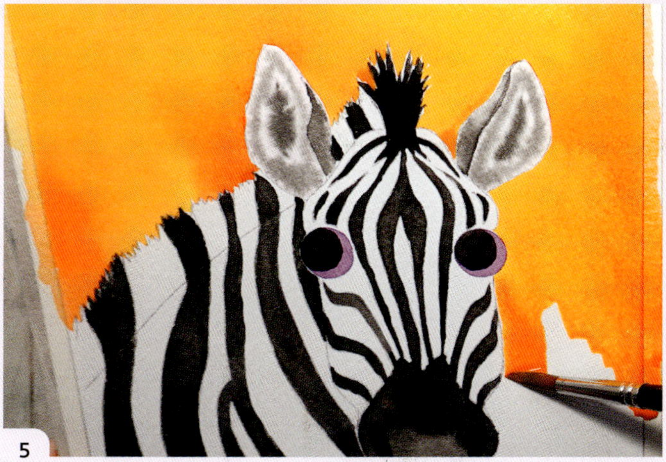

5

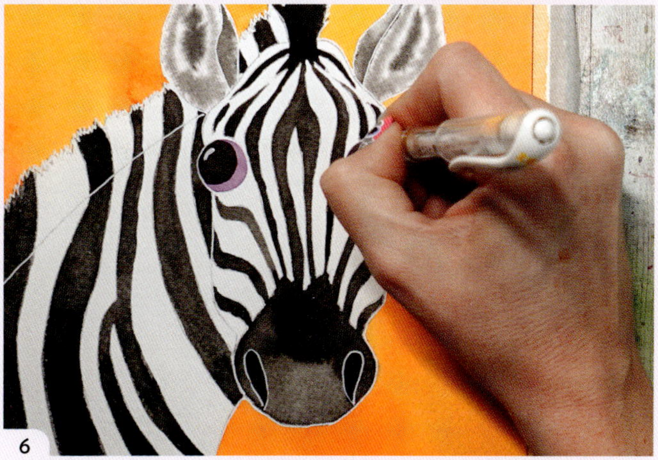

6

Step 4

Fill in the stripes on the neck of the zebra, making sure to leave white space between the stripes (4A).

Wash your brush and fill it with water, and wet the tops of the ears facing the mane with water. Then dip the tip of your brush into black and drop it along the front side (4B).

Refill your brush with black and paint in the pupils and nostrils (4C). Let this dry or make it dry!

Step 5

You might want to refresh your water before adding in the background—mine was very gray by this point. Fresh water will help the background be brighter. Mix up an orange and a yellow and paint in the background using a messy wash. Let this dry or make it dry!

Step 6

Grab your white gel pen and outline the main shapes of the body and add highlights to the eyes!

ABOUT THE ARTIST

LACEY WALKER is the artist and creator behind Rebel Unicorn Crafts (www.rebelunicorncrafts.com) and her encouraging, low-pressure painting channels on Instagram, TikTok, and YouTube @RebelUnicornCrafts. She has an unstoppable need to create, whether watercolor painting, drawing, crafting, pottery, or silversmithing. She is always thinking of new things to make and experimenting with new mediums. Guided by her belief that art and creativity are crucial to the world and essential for achieving happiness, she loves to spread knowledge and creativity through her social media videos, classes, shop, and her first book *Learn to Watercolor*.

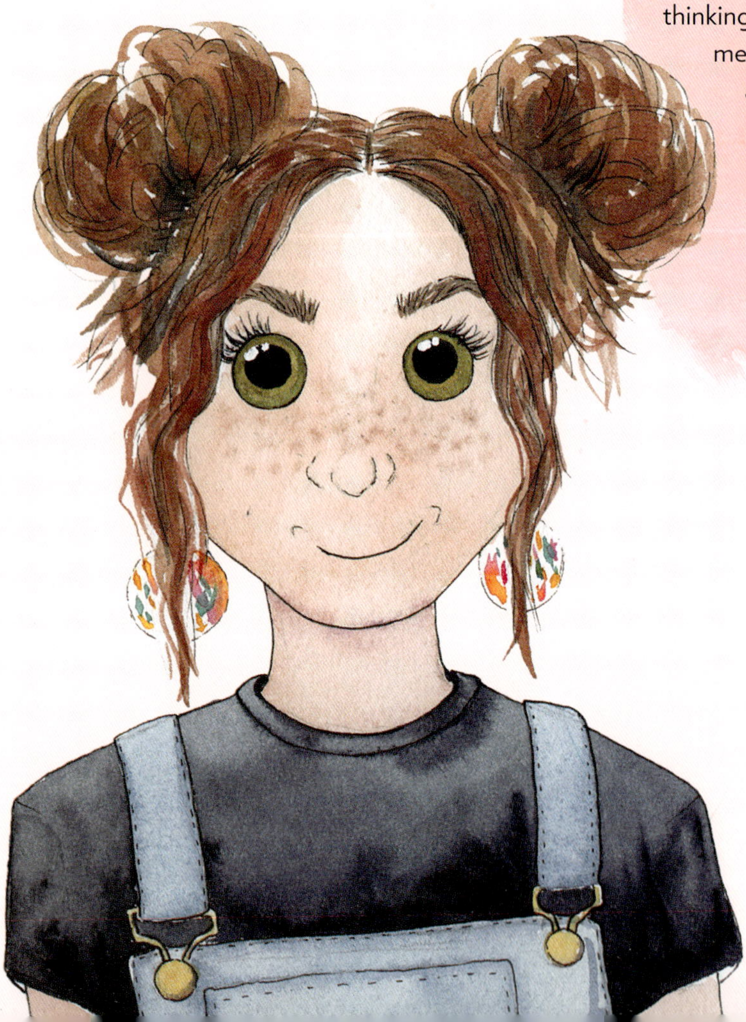